ADVANCE PRAISE FOR *ILLEGAL*

"What a vivid portrayal of the Arizona immigrant underground. *Illegal* is not afraid to show the bad decisions immigrants make along with their resilience and strength of spirit. This is the total picture, a heartbreaking one in a state that has chosen to demonize its Mexican residents."

—*Tony Ortega, editor-in-chief,*
Village Voice

"No one brings you into the illegal immigration underground quite like Terry Greene Sterling. Her gritty descriptions of border crossers, transvestites, and child molesters will linger in your thoughts. Her achingly beautiful accounts of everyday people and tragic situations really stick with you. From Sheriff Joe Arpaio's bravado to a locked-up mom's longing for her child, the stories in *Illegal* are strikingly vivid, and the author's reporting flawless. No one should even attempt to speak on the matter of illegal immigration in Arizona without reading *Illegal* first."

—*Ashlea Deahl, editor,*
PHOENIX Magazine,
and blogger of girlinapartyhat.com

"Arizona is ground zero in America's immigration battles and Terry Greene Sterling writes about the struggles of the people involved with authority, passion, and compassion. Her insights and observations are detailed with nuance and substance that can't be acquired by dropping in when the story is hot. This book and her blog, White Woman in the Barrio, reflect her ongoing commitment to telling stories about the people in addition to the policies that are front and center in the immigration wars. If you want to understand what is going on in Arizona now, *Illegal* is the book to read."

—*Rick Rodriguez,*
Carnegie and Southwest Borderlands Initiative professor,
Walter Cronkite School of Journalism, Arizona State University

DEC 2010

"With painstaking reporting, elegant writing, and a lifetime immersed in the culture, Terry Greene Sterling offers the most important lesson in the debate over illegal immigration: These are people we're talking about, not statistics. Read this book and borders melt, as the author reminds us again and again that each immigrant has a story to tell. Greene Sterling is here to give voice. A powerful, necessary book, it should be required reading for all."

—*Amy Silverman, managing editor,*
Phoenix New Times

ILLEGAL

Life and Death in
Arizona's Immigration War Zone

Terry Greene Sterling

LYONS PRESS
Guilford, Connecticut
An imprint of Globe Pequot Press

Lyons Press is an imprint of Globe Pequot Press.

Text design: Sheryl Kober
Layout artist: Kevin Mak
Project manager: Kristen Mellitt

Library of Congress Cataloging-in-Publication Data is available on file.

ISBN 978-1-59921-861-8

Printed in the United States of America

10 9 8 7 6 5 4 3 2 1

For Walter H. Sterling

CONTENTS

AUTHOR'S NOTE

I honestly don't know when I learned Spanish. All I can say is I don't remember a time when I didn't speak Spanish, so I must have learned Spanish and English at the same time. This wasn't unusual for children growing up in rural Arizona in the 1950s and 1960s. Like many Arizona ranch kids, I grew up knowing both sides of the border. My extended family raised cattle in Arizona and Sonora, Mexico, so speaking Spanish was just part of life. It wasn't until I entered journalism in 1983 that I became a rare bird—a Spanish-speaking Anglo reporter.

In the seventeen months it took to research and write this book, I conducted scores of interviews in Spanish. I automatically translated into English as I wrote in my notebooks during the interviews. Many of the quotes in the book are my direct translations. For clarity, I removed "uhs" and "ums" from quotes. I did not change their meaning, however.

All the people in this book are real people. I did not make up characters or create composite characters.

I did change the names of most undocumented immigrants and their family members to protect their identities. I did not change the names of undocumented immigrants who were public figures or were named in famous court cases. No scene in this book was fabricated. I witnessed most of the scenes myself. In other cases, scenes and quotes were harvested from court testimony, court records, or police records. Some scenes and quotes, especially those in narratives about life in Mexico, border crossings, and early days in Phoenix were based on extensive interviews with immigrants who had these experiences firsthand.

The chapter notes at the end of this book detail my sources.

I use the term *illegal immigration* to describe unauthorized immigration into the United States. I use *illegal alien*, *illegals*, and *illegal immigrant* only when quoting sources, reporting on documents, or describing scenes.

Although this book is titled *Illegal*, in the text I refer to border crossers without papers as *unauthorized* or *undocumented*.

Elie Wiesel, the Nobel Peace Prize winner and Auschwitz survivor, is credited with first saying what good people on both sides of the nation's divisive immigration debate inherently understand: "No human being is illegal."

PREFACE

Rodrigo, a Tehuacán transvestite, framed houses by day and seduced married men by night. Joaquín, a painter suffering from end-stage renal disease, deported himself to Mexico City in a desperate quest for a kidney transplant.

Like Rodrigo and Joaquín, most of the people you'll meet in these pages are unauthorized Mexican immigrants who lived in Phoenix during the seventeen months I researched this book. At this writing, some of these men and women still live in Phoenix. Others have vanished. This is not unusual.

The undocumented population is impossible to track, let alone count. What we do know for sure is that Mexicans make up the bulk of undocumented immigrants in the United States. The Department of Homeland Security *estimates* that of 10.8 million unauthorized immigrants in the United States, 6.7 million are Mexicans.

The geography is convenient for border crossers. Mexico and the United States share a two-thousand-mile border. Nevertheless, crossing into the United States is expensive and dangerous. The Mexicans you'll meet risked their lives to get to Phoenix for a number of reasons. Adventure. Ambition. Love. Survival.

Many had no choice but to come north. Most of the poorest Mexicans, the majority of America's undocumented immigrants, were pawns in games over which they had no control.

Like free trade.

The North American Free Trade Agreement (NAFTA) took effect in 1994. Its purpose was to stimulate North American economies by removing trade barriers between Canada, the United States, and Mexico.

It ended up causing a mass migration of Mexicans to the United States.

Proponents of NAFTA, including President Bill Clinton, had argued that the free-trade agreement would increase American jobs by beefing up exports to Mexico and Canada, but another convincing argument for some Americans was that NAFTA would keep the Mexicans home.

Former President Gerald Ford put it this way in 1993: "We want Mexicans to stay in Mexico so they can work in their home country. We don't want a huge flow of illegal immigrants into the United States from Mexico."

In fact, NAFTA had the opposite effect.

It supercharged illegal immigration into the United States. About half of today's total of unauthorized Mexican immigrants crossed the line *after* NAFTA took effect.

The reason: Some Mexicans couldn't afford to live in post-NAFTA Mexico. Experts blamed a slew of causes, including the failure of the Mexican government to install sufficient infrastructure to reach manufacturing goals and the failure of the Mexican economy to markedly improve, as NAFTA had promised. Others blamed the United States for subsidizing American corn farmers, who then sold their subsidized corn in Mexico. The result: Mexican corn farmers couldn't compete against American-subsidized corn. Some decided to grow vegetables and berries, but many others came to the United States.

Other global forces shattered NAFTA's promise of better jobs in Mexico. China blossomed as a cheap labor source, and factories that once would have gone to Mexico ended up in China. Ditto India. As a result, some special factories in Mexico designed to create products for export closed down. (The factories, often on the border, are called *maquiladoras*.) That left a lot of Mexican factory workers without jobs, and they decided to come to the United States, right along with the corn farmers.

After the United States opened up free trade with Mexico, its immigration quotas remained antiquated and inflexible. The temporary work visa program was a shambles, and work visas for uneducated Mexicans remained scarce. Further, the American government did not readily grant visas for family unification. If you're a Mexican, you might not live long enough to get to the United States if you stand in line and wait your turn. For example, in 2008, if unmarried adult children of Mexicans with green cards wished to obtain a visa to join their parents in the United States, the average wait time was estimated at 192 years. The other option: Hire a smuggler and risk your life crossing the border.

Beyond NAFTA and immigration quotas, other demographic forces drive illegal immigration.

Take, for instance, the inchoate bloodbath initiated in 2006 by Felipe Calderón, the Mexican president. Since Calderón declared war on the drug cartels, or, at least, some of the cartels, nineteen thousand men, women, and children have been slaughtered. Put yourself in the place of a Mexican citizen. You know people are kidnapped, tortured, and decapitated in your country every day. But you don't know who is on what side. You don't know if the guy in the ski mask stopping your car is a Mexican soldier working for a drug cartel or a lone assassin, a kidnapper, or an honest cop.

Mexicans are not pleased with this drug war.

The United States is the biggest consumer of Mexican marijuana and cocaine in the world, and drug trafficking has long been one of Mexico's few reliable sources of cash, right along with oil and remittances from Mexicans living in the United States. Drug cartels employ tens of thousands of Mexicans in legitimate and illegitimate business enterprises.

But even cartels can't put every Mexican on the payroll.

And you just can't get away from the fact that a rich country borders a poor country. A Mexican might earn four times as much in the United States for exactly the same work he did in Mexico.

Almost everyone agrees that immigration has slowed during America's recession, but experts also agree that tens of thousands still cross illegally into Arizona from Mexico.

This, despite billions spent to keep the Mexicans out.

To curb illegal immigration, the federal government began notching up border security in the late 1990s. After 9/11, a decade of fear-based politicking on possible terrorist threats on the border has spurred a frenzy of empire building in the newly formed Department of Homeland Security. President Barack Obama chose Arizona's governor, Janet Napolitano, to head DHS. Governor Napolitano's handling of local Mexicans sparked controversy, criticism, and distrust.

Napolitano's agency includes Customs and Border Protection, which polices the nation's border and was infused with $11.4 billion of taxpayer funds in fiscal 2010. Most of the money went into border barriers, technology, and manpower. The Border Patrol employed more than 19,000 agents in 2010, up from 5,878 agents in 1996.

Thanks to an earlier battening down of the Texas and California border, the Grand Canyon State is now the prime portal for illegal immigration into the United States. Today, immigrants braving Arizona's borderlands must navigate ever more treacherous trails slicing through cacti, slicing through Malpais rock, slicing through searing creosote flats, slicing through mountains littered with human bones, smugglers, kidnappers, Minutemen, and Border Patrol agents.

Their numbers may be reduced, but still, people keep crossing the line.

So, come with me.

Let's take the immigrant trails up from the border to Phoenix, ground zero for the nation's divisive immigration war, the hunting grounds of Sheriff Joe Arpaio.

The people in the shadows have long hidden from the sheriff.

But they won't hide from you.

They want you to know their stories.

CHAPTER I

By the Time They Get To Phoenix

Drugs and people are smuggled from Sonora to Phoenix.
Money and guns are smuggled from Phoenix to Sonora.
The people know they are the most expendable cargoes,
so they say their prayers.

Red high heels. A New York Yankees baseball cap. *Star Wars* figurines. Dirty diapers. Backpacks. Framed photographs. Gunnysacks. Tuna fish cans. Electrolyte solution bottles. Jackets. Hoodies. T-shirts. Hair ribbons. Human feces. Plastic water jugs. Pink thong panties.

In the years I've covered the Arizona-Mexico borderlands as a reporter for newspapers and magazines, I've come across hundreds of objects of immigrant trash strewn in the desert. The litter had always outraged and saddened me. On the one hand, it seemed disrespectful, contaminated pristine stretches of desert, and killed wildlife. On the other hand, I couldn't help but wonder about the untold story behind some migrant trash. Who abandoned that bright green hair clip beneath the acacia? Who speared those size-five Cherokee blue jeans on the angry spines of an ocotillo?

Each immigrant crossing illegally into Arizona drops an average of eight pounds of belongings during his or her journey, according to federal environmental officials. Even though illegal immigration has declined, tons of fresh trash are still strewn along Arizona's borderlands. Volunteers pick it up. Federal employees pick it up. Cowboys pick it up. Hikers pick it up. Although the trash is offensive, just about anyone who cleans up immigrant trash is moved by some of what the travelers leave behind.

Volunteers who leave water for migrants on the desert trails make shrines out of immigrant trash. I came across one such shrine near Arivaca, a tiny town that sits about twelve miles north of the border. Whoever made the shrine had arranged little stones (in the shape of a heart) around a pile of immigrant trash. A small figurine of the Virgin of Guadalupe, that beloved brown Mexican national goddess-Madonna, overlooked a choppy mound of photos, worn-out athletic shoes, T-shirts, baseball caps, plastic one-gallon water jugs, hooded sweatshirts, backpacks, blankets, and empty bottles of electrolyte solution. There was a cell phone in the shrine, a large black plastic garbage bag that had been fashioned into a makeshift raincoat, a yellow toy truck, an inhaler for an asthmatic, and a small sun-baked Spanish prayer pamphlet called *Oraciones de los Emigrantes*, which literally means *Prayers for Emigrants*.

The fragile booklet was tiny, about three inches square, designed to fit in a pocket of a jacket or a backpack. The sun-brittle pages con-

A shrine of immigrant trash in the Arizona desert near the border.
TERRY GREENE STERLING

tained prayers to patron saints of travel, prayers appealing for safe passage. But one prayer, in particular, caught my eye. I scrawled a rough translation in my notebook—*Dearest Infant Lord Jesus, who accompanied by your sainted parents Mary and Joseph, knew the bitterness of leaving your homeland for Egypt, we ask you on behalf of all the children who are homeless immigrants and refugees, these children who suffer as you once suffered, we ask that their parents find work, food and a home, and that they always be received with love, that outsiders they meet treat them as brothers, and that you please keep their bodies and souls safe.*

What would compel a border crosser to ditch the nearly weightless prayer booklet in this thorny desert? Had he or she died on the trail? Had the immigrant been robbed or raped by smugglers or border bandits who'd rifled through a backpack or a jacket, dumping the prayer booklet and everything else on the desert floor in a search for money or documents? Had the migrant lost the prayer book at night, when the smuggler led his group of men, women, and children through mesquites and oak trees and flesh-ripping acacia?

Assuming the person survived, would he or she end up in my city, Phoenix?

• • •

God help the owner of the tiny book of prayers if Phoenix was his or her final destination. The nation's fifth-largest city is also the nation's kidnapping capital, and virtually all the victims are undocumented Mexicans. Phoenix is a major transportation hub for human smugglers, drug smugglers, firearms smugglers, and money smugglers. We'll get to all that later.

You'd be hard-pressed to find an undocumented immigrant in the borderlands who hasn't heard of Maricopa County Sheriff Joe Arpaio, the self-described toughest sheriff in America, whose famed "crime suppression sweeps" have terrorized Latinos. Phoenix is Sheriff Joe's home base. His fans include neo-Nazi teens, middle-aged Minutemen, an aging Anglo conservative electorate that thinks

Mexicans will take over their country, and strong anti-immigrant activist groups.

Phoenix is Arizona's capital, the place where state legislators have enacted some of the harshest anti-undocumented-immigrant laws in the United States. Arizona laws deprive undocumented people of employment, health care, social services, public scholarships at universities, and driver's licenses. A 2010 law criminalizes migrants without papers and requires beat cops to enforce immigration laws.

All of this explains why Arizona in general and Phoenix in particular are at the epicenter of the nation's immigration debate. As the main portal for illegal immigration into the United States, Arizona began passing laws to control immigration in the face of the federal government's inaction over immigration reform. You can understand the initial frustration; millions crossed into Arizona after NAFTA was enacted. What you can't understand is why Arizona's laws became ever more punitive and racist as immigration declined.

Some immigrants couldn't take it in Arizona and moved to friendlier states. Others went back to Mexico. No one knows if the recession prompted them to leave or if Sheriff Joe ran them out. Whatever the case, the number of unauthorized immigrants in Arizona has recently decreased significantly, according to the Department of Homeland Security. In 2008, about 560,000 immigrants were thought to live in Arizona. In 2009, about 460,000 were estimated to live in the Grand Canyon State.

The majority of those still in Arizona are believed to reside in Phoenix.

Separated from their Anglo neighbors by language barriers, cultural differences, and the harshest anti-migrant laws in the nation, undocumented immigrants in Phoenix love, pray, play, sin, suffer, and survive in the shadows.

For migrants, Phoenix can be a living hell.

And yet, they risk their lives to get to Phoenix.

Dispatch from Nogales—about 160 miles from Phoenix

The Border Patrol calls it the "Tucson Sector." It slices across Arizona from the edge of Yuma County to the New Mexico state line. The Tucson Sector snakes along 262 miles of international border, and more unauthorized migrants enter through it than any other Border Patrol sector that lines the United States.

Prime smuggling corridors travel up from Sonora, a state in northwestern Mexico that borders Arizona, through the Tucson Sector. Mexican drug cartels control their smuggling byways and act like traffic cops. Cartels charge human smugglers, called *coyotes*, for the use of their corridors and tell them when they can move people through. Or else cartels diversify into human smuggling themselves. The human-smuggling industry brings in $2 billion to $3 billion per year. The drug trade brings in $30 billion to $35 billion per year. I got these figures from Terry Goddard, the Arizona attorney general in late 2009.

"It's like the Underground Railroad," Goddard said of the smuggling corridors, "and it's very efficient."

Which brings us to Nogales, the Tucson Sector's largest legal port of entry into the United States. It's also a major drug and human-smuggling center. About one out of five undocumented Mexican migrants enters through a legal port of entry, according to immigration scholar Wayne Cornelius, of the Center for Comparative Immigration Studies at the University of California, San Diego.

Migrants cross through the Nogales port of entry in a number of different ways. They might come hidden in secret compartments in vehicles or cross on foot using bogus or borrowed documents. Or they might travel underground. Nogales is a famous tunnel city—at least forty-seven subterraneous passageways between Nogales, Sonora, and Nogales, Arizona, have been discovered since 1995.

Once, Nogales had been an Arizona tourist destination.

For years, Arizonans took out-of-town guests to Nogales for border-crossing day trips. They'd park at the Burger King in Nogales, Arizona, and walk across the border to Nogales, Sonora. They'd go to

Elvira's or the Cave and pound down margaritas and Guaymas shrimp seasoned with fresh garlic and listen to *mariachis*. After lunch, they might order handmade cowboy boots, purchase Xanax at the *farmacias*, or wander the streets, bargaining for dirt-cheap Mexican curios. Then they'd cross back over to the Burger King and drive to Phoenix.

Now the twin Nogales communities are slashed apart by a border wall. In some places, the wall consists of a series of tall metal bars that bite into the sky. In other places, the wall is a slab of solid metal splashed with white graffiti. Right in front of the taxi stand on the Sonora side, for instance, someone scrawled FRONTERAS: CICATRICES EN LA TIERRA. (BORDERS: SCARS IN THE LAND.) Another sign says BOYCOTT THE UNITED STATES. Several crosses with names of immigrants who died during their treks into Arizona are painted on the wall as well.

Many Americans have stopped visiting Nogales, scared off by drug-war carnage. No border city in Mexico has been as brutalized by the drug wars as Juárez, Chihuahua, right across the Rio Grande from El Paso, Texas. In 2009 alone, 3,637 people were slaughtered in Chihuahua, and most of these killings happened in Juárez. Arizona's Mexican neighbor, Sonora, was peaceful by comparison. Only 294 people were assassinated in 2009. A lot of these killings took place in Nogales, and it wasn't unusual for local newspapers to print front-page photos of murder victims splayed on the street with blood pooling beneath their heads. This spooked American tourists. Even more Americans were scared away in 2009 by the swine flu. Others couldn't tolerate the long wait lines at ports of entry. Still others could no longer afford to travel in a recession.

These days, most visitors to Nogales are Mexican migrants seeking to cross into Arizona.

• • •

One winter day in 2009, I visited Nogales, Sonora. There were few American tourists on the street, and many stores and shops that once catered to Americans were shuttered. The only crowded place seemed to be the *Santuario de Guadalupe*, a shelter for migrants who are either

Alec looked at me through this Nogales fence. KATHY MCCRAINE

en route to Arizona or have just been kicked out of Arizona by the United States government. A group of weary migrants stood outside the *Santuario* building talking to *coyotes*. In the shadows, street thugs called *cholos* checked out the immigrants to see if they still owned anything worth stealing.

Right before dark, I stood in the parking lot of the Burger King in Nogales, Arizona. The few people milling around were migrants who'd successfully crossed the border and awaited rides from relatives or friends they'd summoned on cell phones.

From the Burger King, I walked a short distance to the Dennis DeConcini Port of Entry, where travelers were processed in and out of the United States. (In 2009, border officials destroyed a smuggling tunnel *right under* this particular port of entry.) A white bus with silver trim idled on the other side of the fence, returning Mexicans to Mexico. At first glance, the bus resembled the kind of motor coach that shuttled tourists to Monument Valley or the Grand Canyon. But this bus was not designed for tourists. It was designed to transport unauthorized migrants. The windows looked as if they were locked down so no one could escape. The interior was designed so that the passengers were separated from their armed guards. The black lettering on the side of the bus indicated that it belonged to the Wackenhut Corporation, a subsidiary of a global security conglomerate known as G4S. Wackenhut had recently signed a five-year, $250 million contract with the federal government to transport migrants to detention, court hearings, and the Mexican border.

On this evening in Nogales, a weary Mexican Consulate official stood in front of the bus, holding a clipboard. An armed guard, a man in his thirties dressed in a Wackenhut gray military uniform and tall black boots, waited at the foot of the bus steps. Several Department of Homeland Security officials chatted as they stood near the tall fence that separated me from the migrants, one world from another.

A second Wackenhut guard with tightly clipped white hair remained in the bus, ushering migrants down the stairs. One by one, the migrants descended, picked up their backpacks from the luggage compartment, and walked over to the Mexican official holding the clipboard.

A young migrant in a gray-and-black-striped long-sleeved shirt came over to me and looked right into my eyes.

"Your country doesn't want me," he said.

His name was Alec, and he lived and worked in Phoenix. At Christmastime, Alec told me through the fence, he returned to his family home in Mexico. After the holidays, he had reentered Arizona. He told me he came through a canyon and the mountains near Arivaca. He couldn't be specific about names, but from his description of the terrain, he likely crossed the border at Sycamore Canyon.

Sycamore Canyon fingers from Sonora through Arizona's oak-wooded hills. It's got steep cliffs, pools of water, endangered plants and animals, and lots of cover. Once it was a quiet, hidden spot, but now it's an immigrant highway in the Pajarito Wilderness northwest of Nogales. Conservationists have long feared that heavy migrant traffic will destroy wild places like Sycamore Canyon and the animals that live there.

This stretch of southern Arizona is famed for its biologically diverse mountain ranges, called "sky islands," that push up from oceans of semiarid grasslands and desert. Humans and animals have traveled on flat desert corridors in between the sky islands for hundreds of years. But ramped-up enforcement at the border has forced the travelers to abandon the natural corridors and navigate the isolated mountains themselves, through places like Sycamore Canyon.

Sycamore Canyon isn't a place you'd want to navigate at night, but if Alec took this route, he likely traveled in the moonlight. He would have made his way through tall grasses stiffened with white frost, over large boulders and loose rocks, and through ice-cold ponds of water. If he slept during the day, he must have taken cover beneath oak trees, on dirt that smelled of molding leaves. Many had gone before him. The trail was littered with signs of other migrants—a baseball cap, a backpack, and a tennis shoe bound with silver duct tape.

Alec told me he hoped that by traveling through the backcountry, he would elude the sophisticated sound and radar tracking systems, drones, helicopters, and SUVs that belonged to *La Migra*, which is what Mexicans call the Border Patrol.

He knew that even a well-prepared traveler, toting a backpack crammed with canned tuna, electrolytes, water, sunscreen, blister kits, extra socks, a GPS device, and a cell phone, might die. All it would take would be a moment of panic—like a dash for cover as a helicopter approached—for a man to unthinkingly dump his backpack in order to run faster. He might become separated from his group and be unable to find the tossed backpack and water. In such a condition, he could die of thirst or exposure.

Nothing so terrible happened to Alec. But after hiking for many hours, he was spotted by a helicopter and apprehended by the Border Patrol.

Alec and I couldn't have chatted through the fence for more than a few minutes, but something about us—a blue-eyed gray-haired American chattering away in Spanish, through bars, with a world-weary twentysomething Mexican—had attracted the attention of the guard in the bus.

The guard stared at us, stepped forward, lost his balance, and toppled down the bus steps.

Several uniformed officials rushed over to him. The guard pulled himself up, but he'd hurt his leg, and for just a second, he glared at me as though my conversation with Alec had caused his fall in the first place.

The Mexican official with the clipboard, perhaps sensing trouble, beckoned to Alec. I wasn't ready for our conversation to end. I needed a phone number, an address in Phoenix, contact information in Mexico, more of his story. I shouted: "Where are you from?"

Alec looked back over his shoulder.

"Cananea," he said.

Dispatch from Cananea—about 230 miles from Phoenix

My mother died in 2005, but I've still got her ashes in a wooden box on my dresser.

And my father's boxed ashes sit right next to hers. I know it sounds ghoulish, but let me explain. My mother had always wanted her ashes mixed with my father's and buried at the same time, in the same grave, in the family plot in Cananea, Sonora, Mexico. She wanted a Mass said. She wanted the family at the gravesite.

I keep promising myself I'll follow through with my mother's last wishes. I'll get the family down to Cananea, and we'll bury those ashes and we'll attend that Mass in the little church.

I'll do that just as soon as the human smugglers and *narcotraficantes* and kidnappers leave town.

Admittedly, I should have taken care of my funerary responsibilities in 2005, but I put it off. I had already orchestrated a formal Catholic funeral for my mother in Arizona, and I wasn't in any hurry to obtain international permissions, figure out burial permits, find grave diggers in Cananea, arrange a Mass, invite the family, host a lunch afterward.

I was lazy.

Then in May 2007, fifty or so masked gunmen roared into Cananea in SUVs and assassinated seven locals. Mexican state cops reportedly chased the gunmen into the mountains and killed sixteen of them. The official death toll was twenty-three, but Cananea residents aren't convinced that the death count is accurate. They saw bodies being loaded into trucks and whisked out of town.

A few months later, more masked men barreled into Cananea and slaughtered two more people.

Mexican law-enforcement authorities who met with me and requested anonymity (because they didn't want to put their lives in danger) blamed the Cananea violence on *Los Zetas*, ex-military thugs who served as assassins for a Mexican drug syndicate, the Gulf Cartel, and have reportedly diversified into drug smuggling themselves. According to the officials, *Los Zetas* swept into Cananea as part of the Gulf Cartel's ongoing war with the Sinaloa Cartel, which has been running drugs through Sonora and into Arizona for decades.

Sonorans call people who move drugs *burreros*, because they are like burros, or beasts of burden. For decades, the Sinaloa Cartel has smuggled pot into Arizona. In Sonora, transporting drugs is seen by many as just a way to earn a living. The fact that the Sinaloa Cartel has been doing business in Sonora for years may explain why Sonoran law-enforcement officials told me the Sinaloa Cartel was "peaceful."

The officials explained the Cananea shootings this way: The Gulf Cartel, squeezed by border and drug enforcement to the east, wanted some of the Sinaloa Cartel's excellent Sonora-Arizona smuggling corridors. Since Cananea is a staging area for moving people and drugs through those prime corridors, it became a site for the bloodbath. That's the official explanation.

But border violence defies official explanations. You can't be sure who works for whom.

When I recently drove the winding road from Naco to Cananea, for instance, I saw men in military uniforms at roadside checkpoints. They waved me on, but stopped cars and buses full of immigrants en route to the border. I couldn't be sure who the uniformed officials were. They might have been *Los Zetas*. They might have been officials who secretly worked for the Sinaloa Cartel. They might have been Mexican policemen or soldiers without secret attachments. Were they robbing the migrants, or were they on bona fide law-enforcement missions, checking for ne'er-do-wells and drug smugglers?

The point is, I couldn't know for sure.

It never seemed so sinister when my parents and I drove over this same road in the 1950s.

• • •

Cananea is a town of about thirty thousand people that sits forty or so miles south of the Arizona border. For decades, its main source of cash was a copper mine developed in the early twentieth century by a controversial Gilded Age copper baron named William Cornell Greene, my grandfather.

My grandfather died thirty-eight years before I was born. And since family legend has it that my grandmother hurled all his personal papers down a well in an effort to protect his privacy, I don't have many insights into his soul. I've looked for clues in history books, and all I can tell you is that historians either demonize him as a greedy American capitalist who exploited Mexicans or they extol him as a visionary businessman who had the moxie to develop a major copper mine and a town to go with it.

I like to think my grandparents were drawn to each other by the similarities of their waifish childhoods. My grandmother's father hailed from the American Midwest; her mother was a Mexican. My grandmother, Maria Benedict, was orphaned early and adopted by an Anglo family that looked down on her as a half-breed.

My grandfather came from a poor family. His own father died when he was young, so he supported himself from the time he was a kid. As a young man, he migrated from New York to the American West.

After his first wife died, he married my grandmother. He had staked copper claims in Sonora, and he'd persuaded New York millionaires to invest in his mining company. When he was on top of his game, he was reportedly worth $50 million. He and my grandmother split their time between a penthouse at the Waldorf Astoria and Cananea.

They could see the copper mine gnaw away at a mountain from the porch of their big house in Cananea. The mine was a major copper producer and employed hundreds of Mexicans and Americans. Only, the Americans got paid more for the same work. In 1906, the Mexican miners went on strike. Among other things, they wanted equal pay for equal work.

My grandfather called in the Arizona Rangers and other gunmen from Arizona to subdue the strikers. Several people were killed, most of them Mexicans.

Historians say that event helped bring on the Mexican Revolution of 1910.

My grandfather was so despised by many in Mexico that for years I kept my genealogy to myself. Honestly, I was ashamed by it.

I'm not ashamed anymore. I'm still troubled by the wage discrepancy, but proud that my grandfather built an entire town and had the vision to start an industry that paid Mexicans a steady wage for decades.

In any case, he didn't keep the copper mine long.

He lost it in a corporate takeover. Other companies ran the mine.

Until his death in 1911, my grandfather focused on his Sonora ranch. After he died, the family stayed in Cananea. When my grandmother was alive, several of her six adult children lived in Cananea, working in family businesses.

My parents lived stateside, on a family cattle ranch in northern Arizona. Coming from the isolated Arizona spread, I found 1950s-era Cananea a dizzyingly exciting place.

Crossing from Mexico into the United States and back again was as natural as breathing for us. The border region was its own fusion of Mexican and American culture. We'd cross at a tiny border town called Naco and drive an hour or so on a rutted dirt road through the grasslands. I'd be hot and carsick by the time we arrived at my grandmother's house, known as *La Casa Greene* or "The Big House" and everyone would make a big fuss over me. I loved Cananea.

Life for the Greene clan in Cananea was good when my grandmother was alive. But everything changed after her death. The Greene properties in Mexico were sold for very little for reasons that were never explained to me but had to do with the fact that we were Americans, and Americans couldn't own property in Mexico.

The living Greenes left Cananea.

The dead remained.

In Mexico, families tend graves. And some families have long been reluctant to return to bullet-riddled, economically depressed Cananea to clean up graves. Locals in Cananea proposed building a columbarium inside the church so that families wouldn't have to clean the gravesites each year in October, before the Day of the Dead, when families lay marigolds on the headstones of their ancestors.

My cousins and I considered the columbarium, but that would have entailed expensive and distasteful disinterment and cremation of our grandparents' remains. We mulled over what else to do with their bones and couldn't come up with a consensus. So as it stands, when we can't find anyone to clean up the graves, our dead grandparents lie beneath litter and waist-high weeds.

The Greene plot is big enough for a small house. A few drought-hardy juniper bushes poke up from the dirt, along with a peach tree that sprouted up on its own. The words *El Fundador de Cananea*, which means "The Founder of Cananea," are carved on my grandfather's giant marble tombstone. One of these days, perhaps, my parents will have a tombstone next to his.

Right now, I can't imagine burying my parents' ashes in such a depressing, violent place. Unemployment is rampant; the copper mine shut down after a long strike and a dip in copper prices. The hospital closed. Drinking water supplies are no longer reliable. In the winter of 2010, there was no gas for heaters. The church, schools, and all the quirky frontier-style office buildings are shabby and unpainted. My grandparents' house still stands; sometimes astronomers who work at a nearby observatory bunk there.

The main industry these days in Cananea is the smuggling of drugs and people, and such professions carry their own deadly risks.

Can you blame Alec for seeking honest employment in Phoenix?

Dispatch from Altar—about 200 miles from Phoenix

One winter morning, my friend John Ochoa guided his Dodge Ram down the main street of Sasabe, Arizona. It felt as though we were gliding through an abandoned Western movie set instead of a tiny border town. Only about twenty people lived in Sasabe, a cluster of adobe buildings lining a wide street that led to Mexico. The Hilltop Bar was closed. The ochre-yellow Sasabe Store, with its bilingual signs hawking ice, lottery tickets, firewood, and gasoline, hadn't yet opened for the day. Once the Sasabe Store had been a thriving enterprise; Mexicans bought Coca-Cola and cigarettes and hiking boots and canned tuna fish there. Now they had all but disappeared, fearful of being apprehended at the beginning of their long journey into Arizona.

Immigrants in Altar Plaza. KATHY MCCRAINE

John, my photographer, Kathy McCraine, and I were on our way to Altar, Sonora, the largest staging area for immigrants traveling north through the Arizona border.

Altar is a rough smuggling town. It sits about sixty miles south of the border, and few Americans ever go there. I didn't want to visit Altar alone. I'd begged John, who owns a Tucson construction business and a Sonora cattle ranch, to drive me to Altar.

John's Basque ancestors came to America in the eighteenth century to work in the Spanish silver mines. On this trip, John referred constantly to an old Spanish map, pointing out the routes Spanish explorers, and probably his ancestors, traveled from the Sea of Cortez into Sonora.

"This Sasabe Wash is an old migration corridor. The Spaniards used it. The Indians used it. So does everyone else," John said as we crossed over an angry dry gully that slashes through Sasabe, Sonora, on the other side of the line from Sasabe, Arizona.

The bumpy road wound past shrines to the Virgin of Guadalupe, past half-constructed block houses, past taco stands and tiny grocery stores, past the *Cafetería Disney* and the town plaza, past guest houses for immigrants and big houses for smugglers. Once a sleepy cattle-crossing town, Sasabe was now into the human-smuggling business.

Outside of Sasabe, the road dipped steeply and then vanished behind a bluff. John braked at the top of a hill, pulled out his binoculars, and glassed the area, looking for possible ambushes. We pulled our money and identification out of our wallets, just in case we had to hand over wallets to highway robbers.

There was no ambush awaiting us at the bottom of the hill, and we drove on. The country was Sonoran desert—tall saguaros with arms reaching every which way, chollas with needles that grabbed at the flesh, and clustered mesquite trees. We passed a jackrabbit, several hawks on fence posts, a cowboy with a white hat and a lariat on his saddle, a large truck with what was certainly a load of marijuana covered by a blue tarp.

We drove through picturesque towns built on the routes of Spanish missionaries and soldiers traveling up from the Gulf of California.

Sáric was my favorite, with buildings painted in different hues of yellow, and lemon trees and date palms.

At one point John thought a truck might be following us; we pulled off the road and parked behind a mesquite thicket until the truck roared past.

Then we got to Altar.

The Spaniards had settled it as a military outpost. Then it became a cattle ranching center. Commerce switched from beef to human smuggling when the Tucson Sector became the main gateway for illegal immigration. It's easy to see why Altar's economy changed. A major Mexican highway connects it to the rest of Mexico. Tour buses from the interior of Mexico deliver migrants to Altar. Passenger vans zoom through the creosote-bush flats, churning up contrails of dust as they shuttle migrants from Altar to the Arizona border.

Altar's population was hard for us to figure. Enrique Celaya, a human-rights activist who lives in Altar, told us the population of about eight thousand had swollen to sixteen thousand due to the immigrant trade. Before the recession, about two thousand to four thousand immigrants came to Altar each day, he said. Now, during bad times, about three hundred immigrants came into Altar each day. By his estimates, that would be twenty-one hundred potential border crossers each week.

Celaya believed that border enforcement was not a deterrent. Rather, he believed, illegal immigration expands and shrinks depending on the American economy. If the American economy is good, thousands of immigrants pass through Altar; if the American economy is bad, some of those immigrants stay home.

On the day we visited, it seemed as if every business in town was connected to illegal immigration. Dozens of entrepreneurs sold trail supplies—backpacks, water, sunscreen, boots, hats, food—from makeshift storefronts on the street. Shuttle vans were parked in practically every backyard. Homes were converted to hostels, where *coyotes* sometimes confined or kidnapped immigrants before amassing enough to make a profitable trip north. At the Hospedaje La Pasadita, which rented rooms for about $2 a day, a mural on the outside wall portrayed

Baboquivari Peak, a landmark on the immigrant trails stretching north into Arizona through Sasabe and the Altar Valley. The mural made the trail seem carefree and easy.

It's not.

Immigrants have several options when they cross into Arizona. The traditional path, the Altar Valley, a swath of high-desert grassland that extends almost to Tucson, is heavily patrolled, so many migrants choose to cross through the treacherous but more remote Tohono O'odham Indian reservation. Or they might travel farther west, risking their lives to cross the Barry M. Goldwater Range, hundreds of acres of desert that Air Force and Marine pilots use for target practice. Other migrants choose to travel through the mountains near Arivaca. Sometimes, they hike for four or five days before reaching a highway where they can be picked up and shuttled to Phoenix.

On all the Arizona trails stretching north from Altar, immigrants risk being assaulted, raped, robbed, kidnapped, and murdered. Even though volunteers from organizations like Humane Borders and No More Deaths leave water on migrant trails, many travelers die of thirst and heat. In the winter, a few die of the cold. Others die and are never found.

Once the walking is over, migrants are crammed like tinned fish in vans and trucks, and many head to Phoenix. En route, they sometimes die in high-speed chases between their *coyote* chauffeurs and law-enforcement authorities. A few have even drowned in irrigation canals as a result of those high-speed chases.

From 2000 to 2009, the Border Patrol reported finding nearly 1,200 bodies in the deadly Tucson Sector. Even though fewer migrants crossed over Arizona's southern border in 2009, a greater percentage of migrants died on the trails, according to the *Arizona Daily Star*, a Tucson newspaper that tracks the deaths.

The reason: Increased border enforcement squeezed border crossers into more treacherous terrain, where death comes easily and unexpectedly.

There's a disturbing mural near the church in Altar that warns migrants of the dangers ahead in Arizona. In the mural, the Virgin of

A mural in Altar depicts dangers to migrants in Arizona's desert. KATHY
MCCRAINE

Guadalupe prays over a band of half-dead migrants stranded in the sand near a cluster of human skulls and slithering, entwined snakes.

Immigrants see the mural, understand the dangers of the crossing. They get it. But they put their faith in the Virgin, human smugglers, and their own blind luck. They cross anyway. And if they don't make it, they return to Altar to prepare for another trip.

On the day we visited Altar, twenty-four-year-old Simon and twenty-two-year-old Socorro, from the southern state of Chiapas, rested in the shade. Several months before, they'd each paid a *coyote* $1,500 to get to Houston. One or two miles into Arizona, Mexican bandits assaulted and robbed them. Their backpacks were stolen, along with their water. They turned themselves in to the Border Patrol because they feared they would die of thirst. They came back to Altar and worked as day laborers. They tried to cross again, and got caught again. They spent the night in a Border Patrol facility, where they were given cheese and crackers and grape juice and blankets. Back in Altar again, they vowed to make it to Houston. And in ten years, Socorro said, he'd have a big house and a big truck. And maybe then his wife in Mexico wouldn't be so angry at him for leaving her alone with two kids.

That same afternoon, Rolando and his pregnant girlfriend, Abilena, sat in the plaza, looking worried. Rolando was twenty-three years old, a construction worker. He'd tried to cross a few months before, but the Border Patrol caught him. He returned to his home state of Oaxaca, in southern Mexico. Twenty-four-year-old Abilena couldn't bear for Rolando to travel to the United States without her. So the two had crossed the border three times, and had gotten caught three times. Once, they got as far as Interstate 10 before a Border Patrol dog sniffed them out in the bushes. They would try again that night, even though one blister traveled from the pad of Abilena's foot up between her toes.

Nearby, a man from Oaxaca, possibly a recruiter for a *coyote*, claimed he, too, was a poor immigrant. But he wasn't dressed like one. Unlike Rolando and Abilena, with their dirty clothes and baseball caps, he was freshly showered and wore a gold chain around his neck, clean clothes, spotless white athletic shoes.

A guy with spotless white athletic shoes would draw immediate suspicion at the one safe place in Altar for migrants who have failed in their journey north—the Centro Comunitario de Atención al Migrante y Necesitado, which sits a few blocks from the town square. The center's director, Enrique Celaya, studied for seven years to become a Catholic priest but instead got married, started a family, and felt called to direct the center, funded by Mexican and American nonprofits. One hundred percent of the clients are deported immigrants. "When they come through these doors," he told us, "they are depressed and sometimes suicidal. They had a dream they'd come to the United States, and they borrowed money from their family, sold their homes, and failed to cross the border. They were deceived by the smugglers. They don't have anything now. They are ashamed. Some become beggars. Others sell themselves to survive."

Enrique walked us through the immaculate kitchen and the safe, clean dorms. No human smugglers, drug dealers, drug addicts, or alcoholics were given a bed. Only people down on their luck could enter the center's doors. Once inside, they educated themselves, hoping their luck would change.

They could view a video on how to survive in the Arizona desert, what mountains to use as landmarks on the trail, how to fight heat and cold. In the center's little garden, they learned to identify plants of the Sonoran desert, and what to eat and what to avoid. They learned the meaning of the flying blue flags signaling water barrels set out by immigrant-sympathizing volunteers.

"Some think water barrels are a trap," Enrique told us, "but we tell them it's better to get trapped than to die."

The general thrust of the center was one of hope, an acknowledgment that even the most depressed migrant would somehow be blessed with the courage to turn his life around.

Enrique said good-bye after several migrants appeared at the center's door. We climbed back into John's truck and took one more spin around the plaza. It was late afternoon, and the plaza was filling up with migrants ready to cross the line. The men and women with the backpacks and sore feet would climb into the shuttle buses and drive to the Arizona border. Some had tried to cross before and had failed.

But they wouldn't give up.

Shortly after our Altar visit, Wayne Cornelius at the University of California, San Diego, came out with an astonishing finding: From 92 to 98 percent of migrants apprehended by the Border Patrol *actually make it* into the United States on subsequent tries.

The key, according to the study, is to find a good *coyote*—four out of five migrants now rely on human smugglers to guide them into the United States. These trail-savvy, GPS-and-cell-phone-equipped *coyotes* belong to sophisticated smuggling networks and have upped their fees substantially—average costs for a border crossing climbed from about $1,000 a head in 1998 to about $2,000 a head and more today.

Undocumented migrants who make it to their U.S. destinations after crossing the border tend not to return to Mexico, Cornelius reported in his study, because crossing back into the United States is too dangerous and too expensive.

And the longer they stay away from Mexico, the less likely they are to ever go home.

Dispatch from Arivaca—about 140 miles from Phoenix

The mesquite-flecked Altar Valley sprawls northward from Altar, Sonora, into Arizona. The land is soft and spongy and flat, good for hiking. It's high-desert grassland; during wet years it offers good forage for quail and antelope. Baboquivari Peak bites at the western sky; it is a time-honored landmark that points travelers to Phoenix and Tucson. For hundreds of years, humans and animals migrated north and south through the Altar Valley, between the sky islands.

Now a twelve-foot-high metal fence slices through the valley, preventing critical migration of large animals like antelope, mountain lions, jaguars, and ocelots. The precise biological fallout of the fence is unstudied in many areas, because biologists can't afford to hire bodyguards to protect them from smugglers as they conduct fieldwork.

About four-fifths of Arizona's border is now fenced in—the Department of Homeland Security has spent upward of $5 million a mile in some spots to secure the border with a tall line of metal posts filled with concrete. When Janet Napolitano, now the secretary of DHS, was governor of Arizona, she called in the National Guard to assist with border infrastructure. One key National Guard duty was building roads.

When I interviewed Napolitano for *Newsweek.com* in 2008, she was still Arizona's governor and voiced support for comprehensive immigration reform at the federal level. That meant to her a four-pronged approach of securing the borders, enforcing laws that prevent employers from hiring undocumented immigrants, providing guest worker visas for those immigrants who want to work in the United States, and enabling a "pathway to citizenship" for those undocumented immigrants who are already in the country.

Governor Napolitano signed an Arizona law that threatened to yank licenses of businesses that "knowingly" hired undocumented immigrants. That was just one prong of immigration reform, she told me, since the federal government failed to step up to the plate.

She didn't think the border wall would stop Mexicans from crossing, and once, on *Lou Dobbs Tonight*, she said, "The voters of my state understand that building a fence is not a solution. Indeed, what I'm fond of saying is, 'You show me a twelve-foot fence, and I will show you a thirteen-foot ladder.'"

Now Napolitano is in charge of building the very fence she derided.

While animals have a difficult time getting through in some spots, Napolitano is right; humans do use ladders. And ropes. Some fence posts now bear a patina from the sheer number of migrants who have shinnied down them. In some places, migrants climb mesquite trees on the Mexican side, get on top of the fence, and jump down. You can tell where they jumped by the hollows on the desert floor.

The fence does not deter immigrants from taking the well-established Altar Valley route to Tucson and Phoenix. What deters them from taking the Altar Valley route is the very geography that makes the valley such a great transportation corridor—its flatness.

The flatness enables sensors and cameras to detect human movement; the flatness allows Border Patrol vehicles to travel swiftly in pursuit of immigrants; the flatness makes it easy for bandits to rob and rape migrants on the trail.

On the other hand, the brutal sky islands offer cover. This explains why some immigrants, like Alec from Cananea, eschew the traditional Altar Valley route for the mountain trails near Arivaca, a tiny community of about 1,200 people.

Arivaca is an offbeat community. It's got a mercantile store with a gas pump, historic adobe buildings, a couple of bars, a couple of craft stores, a gem shop, a coffee shop, and cows that graze in the street. It has always been a smuggling paradise, first for bootleg whiskey and then for drugs, because it's hard to get to, sits twelve miles north of the border, and people who live there leave you alone.

The presence of immigrants in the hills around Arivaca may have lured Shawna Forde there. Like so many Minutemen, Shawna Forde came to the borderlands to fight illegal immigration, which many Minutemen consider a patriotic duty. It's also a lot of fun, if you happen to think like a Minuteman, to wear camouflage and tool around the border with video cameras, push-to-talk phones, GPS devices, and guns. Mostly, Minutemen alert the Border Patrol when they see Mexicans running through the mesquites. And sometimes, they get in shouting matches with immigrant-rights activists.

If any Arizona community could tolerate Minutemen, Arivaca would be it. That's not because Arivacans like Minutemen, it's because Arivacans tolerate practically *everyone*.

Different cultures have dominated Arivaca at different times— Indians, Spaniards, Mexicans, Americans. (I've even got roots in Arivaca—in 1871, my Anglo great-grandfather and my Mexican great-grandmother lived on the outskirts of town, camping by a mine set in hills the color of cinnamon.) The current residents of Arivaca include aging, destitute hippies who camp in ghost towns and gulches, retirees on pensions, ranchers, and a smattering of locals whose ancestors settled the place hundreds of years ago.

Albert Gaxiola, for instance.

When I talked to him in 2008, Albert Gaxiola was just another offbeat Arivacan.

Now he's an accused child murderer.

When we met, he was forty-one, a muscular guy with short black hair. He was dressed in jeans and a T-shirt, and he sat on a bale of hay in his family's feed store telling me about his Basque heritage and his grandmother who sold tacos from a stand on Arivaca's main street.

Like many Arivacans, he was concerned that DHS, and its sub-agency the Border Patrol, was infringing on the civil rights of locals. He and practically everyone else felt spied on by experimental "virtual fencing," motion and sound sensors and cameras stuck atop a ninety-eight-foot tower that overlooked Arivaca. (The tower was eventually taken down. It was part of a failed "virtual fence" project that cost taxpayers $1.1 billion before Napolitano scrapped it in 2010.)

Gaxiola had no sympathy for the Border Patrol, but he expressed seemingly heartfelt sympathy for the migrants who stumbled down Arivaca's main street.

"They've got an American Dream, just like everybody," he told me.

Then, sometime after we had our conversation, Shawna Forde came into his life and everything changed. Forde was forty-one years old and heralded from Everett, Washington. She belonged to the Minutemen American Defense, one of several Minutemen groups. Her sidekick was Jason Bush, thirty-four.

Forde had a half-baked plan to fund her surveillance of illegal immigration on the border by stealing from drug dealers, the police later said.

According to the Pima County Sheriff's Office, on the night of May 30, 2009, Forde, Bush, and Gaxiola allegedly dressed in camouflage and pretended to be cops looking for fugitives when they invaded the home of twenty-nine-year-old Arivaca pot dealer Raul Flores. They intended to rob Flores of his drug money, but instead they killed him, the police said.

They also allegedly murdered his nine-year-old daughter, Brisenia.

Although she was also shot, Flores's wife survived. She fingered Forde, Bush, and Gaxiola as the killers. Later, when police searched Gaxiola's home, they found guns and military paraphernalia. Gaxiola said the guns didn't belong to him; they belonged instead to the Minutemen who were staying at his house. He said he was in Tucson at the time of the murders. In fact, Gaxiola, Forde, and Bush all claimed they were innocent and had nothing to do with the murders.

A grand jury indicted each of the three with two counts of murder and a slew of other charges stemming from breaking into the Flores home. They all pleaded not guilty and faced trials in 2010.

I couldn't believe it when I saw Gaxiola's mug shot in the newspaper. How could he consort with Forde, who reportedly loathed migrants? Hadn't he told me migrants were just people pursuing the American Dream? What caused him to develop a relationship with a female Minuteman?

These questions puzzled Arivacans too. They'd viewed Gaxiola as a nice guy. The murders, and Gaxiola's alleged role, stunned them. How could this have happened in sleepy, live-and-let-live Arivaca?

The home-invasion killings were easily the ugliest known cases of violence on the Arizona border in 2009.

And they transformed Arivaca from a tolerant, quirky hideaway to just another place in the borderlands where anything can happen.

Dispatch from Douglas and Agua Prieta—about 210 miles from Phoenix

On the cusp of the twentieth century, the Phelps Dodge mining company built a smelter in the cattle-ranching flatlands of eastern Arizona. The town that sprang up around the smelter was called Douglas. Right across the border from Douglas, in Sonora, another little town called Agua Prieta sprouted up. For decades, revenues from mining, cattle ranching, and smuggling sustained the towns.

Now the smelter is closed and cattle ranches are vanishing. Empty storefronts line the streets of Douglas, which has a population of about 16,500. Agua Prieta, with more than one hundred thousand residents, struggles as the *maquiladora* industry loses jobs to China. Fortunately for smugglers, Agua Prieta and Douglas have ideal geography. Agua Prieta is the end point for the Janos Highway, a well-traveled road from the Mexican interior.

Douglas sits about an hour's drive from Interstate 10. The gullies and mountains north of Douglas offer sufficient cover for a rough hike to Highway 80, which connects to the freeway. For all of these reasons, the Agua Prieta-Douglas corridor remains a popular human- and drug-smuggling area.

The smuggling corridors wind through small ranches cobbled together with privately owned land and government-leased land. Through the years, I interviewed several Douglas-area ranchers who were members of the Malpai Borderlands Group, a band of ranchers who worked with environmental agencies and environmentalists to preserve the land. They wanted to save the brutal, big country they ranched, keep the land healthy and free of wildcat development. It's a mix of Sonoran and Chihuahuan desert lowlands peppered with varieties of thorny bushes and cactus and a sinister basaltic rock called Malpais (it means "bad country" in Spanish) that is mean enough to rip flesh. Jagged, oak-forested sky islands reach up from the thorny flatlands.

Robert Krentz was one of the ranchers in the Malpai group. When I met him in 2004, on his ranch near Douglas, he felt the United States government had turned its back on Americans living on the border. Border crossers and drug traffickers constantly vandalized his ranch, he told me. He showed me a long pipe that carried water from a spring on a hill to his cattle in the flatlands, and noted that when travelers cut the pipe to get water, his cattle went thirsty. Fences were cut, litter was everywhere, and traffickers deposited loads of drugs here and there.

Krentz was a big, stocky man, and you wouldn't want to cross him. His blue eyes grew fiercely angry when he spoke of the environmental devastation on his beloved family ranch. He always called the Border Patrol when he spotted migrants or drug traffickers, and sometimes the Border Patrol was slow to respond, which made him even more frustrated.

He and his dog were mysteriously shot on March 27, 2010, as they rode his Polaris ATV through a pasture. Krentz radioed two words to his brother *illegal alien* and *hurt*. (No one knew whether Krentz meant that a migrant was hurt or whether Krentz had been hurt by a migrant.) After he was shot, Krentz drove his ATV about one thousand feet before he lapsed into unconsciousness and died.

A state helicopter spotted his body late in the night. The dog was still alive, but suffering, and had to be put down. Trackers followed a set of footprints from the murder scene to Mexico, some twenty miles south.

Hours after the body had been discovered, his death was politicized. Anti-migrant activists blamed the unsolved murder on an unknown "illegal alien," and the death became a rallying cry for activists who wanted to militarize the border and send America's ten million or so "illegals" back to Mexico.

• • •

The Border Patrol's Douglas Station sits about a quarter-mile north of the border, on twenty-nine acres. The complex has its own water tank and a vast fenced yard that contains vehicles confiscated from smugglers, as well as rows of green and white Border Patrol Chevy Tahoes, ATVs, and trucks. The main buildings sprawl over fifty-three thousand square feet. There's a well-equipped gym. There are rows of offices connected by hallways that tout the local Border Patrol's good deeds—the Borstar emergency medical team that rescues migrants from the desert, the honor guard for Barack Obama's inauguration parade, the Christmas Angel program.

Undocumented migrants caught in the Douglas area are processed in Building C. They are interviewed. They are given juice and blankets. They are fingerprinted. They are asked to wait for hours while their fingerprints are sent to an FBI database. Analysis of the fingerprints determines who is "repatriated" to the border and who is shuttled to a federal holding facility for further court proceedings. Those who aren't returned to the Mexican border include undocumented migrants who've already been deported, or have been convicted of crimes, or are wanted for crimes, or will be accused of crimes ranging from murder to simply crossing the border illegally.

Migrants were crammed into the detention room.

In the glass-walled control room that looked down on the crowded migrant detention room, uniformed Border Patrol agents in office chairs surveyed computer screens displaying real-time data from radar sensors and cameras on the border. I couldn't distinguish whether the red dots on the screen represented migrants, animals, or vehicles, but the agents could. They communicated the exact whereabouts of border crossers to agents in the field. Given the masses of immigrants crossing Arizona's border, complaints about mistreatment at the hands of the Border Patrol are relatively rare. Once in a while you hear about a renegade agent shooting a migrant. Once in a while an agent gets caught smuggling drugs. Once in a while an agent roughs up an immigrant. Of course this should never happen. But honestly, I'm surprised it doesn't happen more often. It speaks well for Border Patrol agents; mostly they're average working-class guys who landed good federal jobs and found themselves enforcing a broken border policy.

The risk associated with their job is not that they'll resort to violence, but rather that the sheer numbers of migrants they apprehend will numb them to the fact that they're dealing with human beings.

• • •

On the same day I visited Building C, John Scanlon, the supervisory Border Patrol agent for the Douglas Station, drove me along a road the National Guard had built along the rust-red border fence.

Scanlon and others in the Border Patrol all say they know migrants will scale the fence with ropes and ladders. But the Border Patrol asserts that those multimillion-dollar fences slow down border crossers long enough for the Border Patrol to race down the new roads and, hopefully, catch them. Sometimes, migrants get so frustrated they throw stones. Mostly, they wait until the Border Patrol truck disappears down the road.

John Scanlon was closing in on forty. The father of three boys, he stood six feet tall and kept himself fit. He had blue eyes and a military haircut. He was born in Rhode Island and joined the Border Patrol in 1998 after graduating from Northeastern University. He never thought he'd fall in love with Arizona, but he did.

"This is where it all goes on," Scanlon told me. "Douglas has a very good smuggling infrastructure. It's a drug town. And illegal aliens don't have to walk far, like in the Altar Valley, to get to the highway."

We traveled along the fence line for a while, then veered into the desert. Immigrant trails wound around bushes and through gullies. At one spot, a pair of women's blue jeans was speared on a tall ocotillo. It was impossible to tell if the jeans marked a "rape tree"— a place where immigrants are sexually assaulted by *coyotes* or border bandits.

The jeans could have ended up on the tree as a practical joke, like running underwear up a flagpole. Undocumented migrants and immigrant-rights activists have long said both events—rapes and practical jokes—happen all too often in the borderlands. Scanlon, on the other hand, said he'd not heard of any migrant assaults in the Douglas area. No rapes. Nothing.

He stopped his truck on the side of Highway 80. The wind was peppered with grit and sand. Gray mountains in the distance gnashed at the clear blue sky. Immigrant trash was everywhere. A half-dead prickly pear cactus smothered a crunched plastic water bottle. An acacia lanced a black-and-white-checkered shirt.

Scanlon was an expert tracker. And he knew smugglers were expert trackers too. "If you wipe a trail clean by dragging a tire over it, you are likely to see fresh footprints the next day, unless the smuggler also wipes the trail clean," he told me. "All of us are trying to stay one step ahead of each other."

It was a chess game, then, between the Border Patrol and the smugglers.

Soon, Scanlon found the tracks of cowboy boots, tennis shoes, kids' sneakers. He theorized that the people who left the tracks had likely jumped the border fence, walked for several hours, then crawled under a barbed-wire fence to cross over to Highway 80, where they were picked up by a car.

At one point in our afternoon together, Scanlon told me that in the decade he had worked in the borderlands, he must have apprehended thousands of immigrants.

He was generous with his time, attentive, and guarded. He kept me away from any actual apprehensions and skirted political questions. At the end of our afternoon together, he gave me a beer mug decorated with Border Patrol insignia.

• • •

The Migrant Resource Center in Agua Prieta is the first place migrants go when they're returned to Mexico from the United States. Volunteers hand out food, clean clothes, hot coffee, and, most important, free telephone calls. On the day I visited in 2009, several volunteers were Americans. They helped migrants make phone calls to arrange to go back home. They helped migrants contact their families. They helped migrants in search of missing family members seek information from the Mexican Consulate.

I tried to talk to a woman in a blanket. She wouldn't look me in the eye and said she would not go outside because *coyotes* were milling about. *Los tengo miedo*, she said. "I'm afraid of them." I had this weird feeling she'd been sexually assaulted.

Felipe from Guanajuato was in tears—his wife and two daughters had been apprehended with him as they tried to cross the border, but they were separated in detention. Felipe had talked his wife into bringing the girls to the United States. Now he wondered if his family was alive. How could he have been so stupid? What had become of them? Felipe called the consulate, but the consulate knew nothing.

Jesús was a thirty-year-old carpenter. He was slender, with a round face and dark eyes. He sat on a couch reading *Los De Abajo*, a 1915 revolutionary novel about Mexico's abused underclass. Someone had left the book at the center, and Jesús was trying to distract himself. But he couldn't concentrate on the book.

"Don't you think it's weird," he asked me, "that you Americans don't want us in your country, yet you help us at these migrant centers? It doesn't make sense."

Jesús had lived in the United States for ten years. He was a professional carpenter but also picked apples in Washington State. He returned to Mexico City about two years ago, fell in love, married twenty-year-old Mariela, and fathered a daughter. He knew that if he came back to the United States, he might never see Mariela and his baby daughter again. So the two saved their own money, borrowed money from relatives, and paid a smuggler $5,000 to cross the child at the legal port of entry, in the arms of a Mexican with a visa who pretended to be the parent of the baby. The smuggler then delivered the child to Jesús's relatives.

The plan was for Jesús and Mariela to cross the desert, which was too risky for the baby, and meet up with their relatives and their daughter later.

That didn't happen.

Jesús and his wife actually made it across the Douglas borderlands, jumped in a truck along with several other migrants, and were almost to Phoenix when the truck got a flat tire.

They changed trucks and were on their way again when the Border Patrol picked them up. They were returned to Agua Prieta and tried crossing again. They were caught again.

This time, they were separated.

When I met Jesús, he didn't know what had happened to Mariela. He worried she'd been dropped at another town, like Nogales, and she had no money. Border towns were tough on pretty young women. He feared the worst.

The man from the consulate had no news of Mariela.

Practically all of the forty or so Mexicans who came into the aid station when I was there followed the same pattern. They made phone calls, ate, went outside to negotiate with smugglers, followed the smugglers down the street, and disappeared.

Felipe and Jesús ignored the smugglers. All they cared about was finding their families.

About an hour later, a Mexican Consulate official walked another group of migrants to the station.

Felipe's wife and two daughters were in that group. His wife seemed exhausted, but the children were in good spirits, as though they were on a grand adventure. A volunteer gave the little girls cocoa, cookies, and coloring books. Once Felipe was reunited with his family, he straightened up and his voice got loud and strong. He laughed and joked. Just a few minutes before, he'd been crying.

Jesús's young wife, Mariela, had been in the same group. Her jeans and shirt were dirty. Her long black hair needed washing. Her feet were blistered, and she limped. Jesús put his arms around his thin wife. She rested her head against his chest. Imagine what she was thinking: Her only child was in a foreign country; she couldn't get to her; she didn't know if she'd ever see her child again. Imagine what he was thinking: It had been a terrible mistake to send the baby across the line with the smuggler, but people did it all the time; this had all been his idea, and now he couldn't forgive himself for it.

For a long while, the two held on to each other. Jesús had tears in his eyes.

After a few minutes, they began to walk away. I stopped them, asked them what they would do next. Jesús said he'd cross again, find his daughter, bring her home to Mexico. Then he'd return to the United States, pick apples, and send money to Mariela.

Mariela would catch a bus home that evening.

I gave them my business card. Call me if you ever make it to Phoenix.

Arm in arm, they passed the *coyotes* with gold neck chains and an old lady selling sandwiches that smelled of onions and chili. They crossed the street, turned a corner, and disappeared.

I never heard from them again.

CHAPTER 2

Coyote Tales

Some migrants are imprisoned for smuggling
themselves into Phoenix. Others are kidnapped at
gunpoint, held for ransom, and shamed in dark closets.

In the winter of 2008, two men boarded an Estrella Blanca bus in Mexico City. The older man, Rosario, was short and lean, and his lined face hinted that his forty-one years on this earth had seen their share of disappointments. Rosario was getting too old to hold down a blue-collar job in Mexico City—men his age were shoved aside for younger, stronger workers—and so he decided to come to the United States. His traveling companion on this winter day was Selestino, who had attended school with Rosario's son. Selestino was in his twenties and still baby-faced, with soft vulnerable eyes, long lashes, and a head of thick, black curly hair.

The two men planned to cross into Arizona illegally and travel to Nebraska, where a female friend, let's call her Sally, lived and worked. Sally promised there were jobs in America's heartland. Neither Rosario nor Selestino had money to pay a *coyote*, but Sally would pay the smuggler once he delivered Rosario and Selestino to Nebraska.

Rosario and Selestino rode the bus all the way to northwestern Sonora, where they met a broker who promised his smuggling crew would deliver them to Nebraska for $1,800 apiece.

The broker took the men to a house, where they were each supplied with one gallon of water and enough food for a day. At the appropriate hour, Rosario and Selestino jumped in a taxi, which roared across a crust of brown desert until it reached a barbed-wire fence that separated the United States from Mexico.

No worries, the taxi driver said, just cross the fence and someone will meet you on the other side.

Rosario and Selestino crossed the fence, and just as the *taxista* said, two *coyotes* awaited them, along with several other immigrants who would also make the trek through the desert.

With one smuggler leading and the other taking up the back, nagging at stragglers to keep up, the group trudged through the rocky, spiny desert for five days. When people ran out of food, the smugglers reached into their backpacks and offered to sell snacks for exorbitant prices. The migrants refilled their plastic water jugs at mud puddles and cattle tanks.

On the fifth day, one *coyote* made a call on his cell phone. Soon a pickup appeared. The immigrants were ordered into the truck bed, where they crammed against each other like spoons, chests squeezing backs. The truck jounced along until a tire blew out. After the truck lurched to a stop, one *coyote* pointed a gun at the immigrants and told them not to run away.

They knew now that something was terribly wrong.

Once the tire was repaired, the *coyotes* loaded the immigrants back into the truck at gunpoint. After a few more miles, the truck parked near a van. A *coyote* herded them out of the truck and directed them into the van, then hid them beneath fabric used to cover speakers.

For hours, the immigrants listened to the hum of the tires and tried to understand what was happening to them.

• • •

On the same day Rosario and Selestino were herded at gunpoint from one vehicle to another, Marie and Phil were having a routine day in Peoria, Arizona, a suburb of Phoenix that is famous for its spring-training facilities for professional baseball teams.

Phil was a food tester—he inspected packaged foods, like cereals and cake mixes, to make sure they weren't tainted before they were shipped from warehouses to grocery stores. Marie stayed home on Mountain View Avenue and babysat her grandkids. Some days, Marie felt a little like a foreigner in a strange land.

She and Phil had moved to Arizona from Idaho several years before to be closer to their kids and grandkids. It was not an easy move. They were both in their early fifties, and loved the mountains and meadows and small-town atmosphere of the Boise area. Now they lived in a stucco-coated tract home in a cookie-cutter housing development in the middle of a sprawling suburb abutting a crime-ridden city that squatted in one of the driest, hottest places on Earth.

Still, they were near their children. And Marie treasured her family. She'd turned the scab of dust and grit the real estate agent had called a "backyard" into a happy garden with a robust green lawn encircled by bright yellow, scarlet, and pink flowers. Her grandkids loved this garden, with its shaded playground, the bouncy balls, and the wading pool. Inside the house, family pictures covered the walls, a Crock-Pot often bubbled on the shiny granite kitchen counter, and the immaculate fridge was stocked with the children's favorite foods. The house and the garden were warm and friendly, just like Marie.

If only her neighbors could be warm and friendly, maybe Marie wouldn't miss Idaho so much. But the man who rented the house next door kept to himself. The man's home was tidy, and curtains graced the windows, so Marie couldn't see inside. On occasion, the man watered the front yard or took out the garbage. He'd smile, wave at Marie, then scoot back into the house. Marie once peeked over her tall block wall at the man's backyard, but it was bleak, empty.

Just dirt.

• • •

Rosario and Selestino felt the van pull into a garage and inch to a stop. They didn't know, of course, that they had arrived at the house right next to Phil and Marie's home on Mountain View Avenue. After the garage door closed, Rosario and Selestino and the other immigrants were ordered out of the van, through a door, and into a house with little furniture. Six men, including the barbaric *coyotes*, now guarded the prisoners.

The immigrants were driven like cattle into an empty bedroom. Rosario saw right away that the windows had been boarded up with Sheetrock. The only light in the bedroom came from the closet. The room had no furniture. An air freshener was plugged into the wall. The immigrants were told to remove their shoes, socks, and belts, and to deposit their wallets and watches in a paper sack.

Next, the guards drew up a list of each immigrant's vital data— name, destination, and phone numbers of contacts in the United States and Mexico. One guard recorded the data in a spiral notebook.

Rosario and Selestino were told that the trip to Nebraska would no longer cost $1,800 each, notwithstanding the negotiations at the border. The fare had been raised to $3,500 apiece due to an unforeseen increase in expenses. The money would have to be paid before Rosario and Selestino were released. If the ransom wasn't paid, Rosario and Selestino were told, they would be killed and no one would know the difference.

Rosario and Selestino had been kidnapped for ransom.

So many undocumented immigrants were kidnapped in the Phoenix metro area from 2005 to 2010 that the city in 2009 earned the reputation of "Kidnapping Capital of the United States." The number of actual victims is not known. Thousands, for sure, if you believed cops when they said they only investigated a fraction of the actual cases. So many law-enforcement agencies sometimes competed, sometimes cooperated in the investigation of immigrant kidnappings. Local cops. County cops. State cops. Federal cops.

Sadly, there is little to distinguish the story of Rosario and Selestino from thousands of others.

One of the kidnappers of Rosario and Selestino was named Vic. He was stocky and planted his feet on the ground like a wrestler. He had small eyes, an unusually delicate straight nose, thick lips, a walrus mustache, and a scarred scalp. He waved a 9 mm semiautomatic pistol at the immigrants and told them he'd use it if he had to.

He did other things too. Terrifying things.

He forced Selestino into the closet and made Selestino disrobe.

Then, as Selestino stood nude in the closet, Vic said: *If you try to run away, I will kill you, and I will cut your corpse into small pieces and dispose of them. This would not be the first time I've done such a thing, and it will certainly not be the last.*

Rosario and Selestino and the others were held hostage in the empty bedroom in the little house on Mountain View Avenue for three days. They were allowed to speak only when the smugglers made cell phone calls seeking ransom from their friends and relatives. Twice a day, they were fed cheap food, like Top Ramen noodles.

The hostages lost any sense of whether it was day or night, since the windows were sealed with drywall. On the third day, though, agents from Immigration and Customs Enforcement, or ICE, surrounded the house and entered the door. Selestino and Rosario heard an explosion and hit the carpet.

Vic ditched his gun in the toilet and frantically took off his shoes and socks. He was just a humble immigrant, he told the feds in his Sinaloan Spanish; he was coming north to work so he could take care of his family and had been kidnapped by his *coyotes* after crossing the godforsaken Arizona desert.

• • •

Marie and Phil were sitting on their comfortable couch watching the flat-screen TV when they heard the commotion. Marie looked out her window and saw armed federal officers running across her garden, leaping over her fence, and storming into the yard of the next-door neighbor. When things quieted down, Phil and Marie peeked out their door and saw a gaggle of miserable, barefooted immigrants lined up against the garage wall of the house next door.

The next day, the house was empty. Phil and Marie took a look at the house for themselves. One bedroom stank of unwashed bodies, Top Ramen, and air freshener. Sheetrock blocked the windows, but curtains had been placed between the glass and the Sheetrock, so that a person looking at the house from the street, like Marie, would not know the windows had been boarded up.

Marie had no idea she'd been living next to a drop house.

Times like this, she wished she were back in Idaho.

• • •

Selestino and Rosario were taken to a federal detention facility and struck a deal with ICE. In exchange for their testimony, ICE would allow Rosario and Selestino to temporarily live and work legally in the United States. I don't know how long they were allowed to stay. I asked immigration officials whether Rosario and Selestino were returned to Mexico after their testimony, but they did not respond to my telephone and e-mail requests for information.

I first saw Rosario and Selestino when they testified in U.S. district court in Phoenix in the 2009 criminal trial of their kidnapper, Vic, the guy who took Selestino into the closet.

I was particularly stunned by the emotionality of Selestino's testimony. Months after the kidnapping, he wept on the witness stand as he detailed the humiliation of the closet. Even the court translator seemed a little taken aback by Selestino's fragility. I tried to make eye contact with Selestino when court officials escorted him in and out of the courtroom or shuttled him down the hallways, but he never looked up. He always hung his head.

Rosario corroborated everything Selestino said, although he didn't weep on the stand like Selestino. Rosario said he never wanted anyone to go through what he and Selestino had gone through.

Another witness, ICE agent Johnny Mabry, had participated in the bust. Mabry told jurors that agents retrieved the spiral notebook in which the kidnappers had scribbled the names, destinations, and key phone numbers of victims and their relatives. Such a book is called a "pollo book," Mabry explained. In Spanish, *pollo* means "chicken" and is a derogatory term smugglers use for migrants. Human smugglers are sometimes known as *polleros*, or chicken herders. I asked Mabry for an interview because I wanted to understand how ICE became involved in the bust, but he declined.

Despite his best efforts to convince the judge and jury that he was just an innocent immigrant from Sinaloa who'd been kidnapped himself, Vic was convicted of four kidnapping-related felonies and sentenced to twenty-two years in an American federal prison, after which he will be deported to Mexico. He was thirty-four years old when he was sentenced. That means he won't be out of prison until he's fifty-six.

Of the six kidnappers, only Vic had rejected a plea bargain, which meant he had been the only kidnapper to go to trial and face a jury. It was a tactical mistake on his part; of the six kidnappers, only Vic will spend more than five years behind bars.

Susan Bolton, the federal judge who sentenced Vic, noted that he had an "extensive criminal record" that involved several prior felony convictions pertaining to possession of guns and drugs in California. I looked at his court record, and it didn't seem as if he'd ever been in prison for those felonies—although he'd already been deported once. Had he evaded authorities?

I wanted to learn more from Vic, but he declined an interview through his attorney. The last thing he said to the judge before he shuffled out of the courtroom in his leg irons was that he planned to appeal his kidnapping conviction.

• • •

In 2009, more kidnappings for ransom took place in Phoenix than in any other city in the United States. Worse yet, only Mexico City trumped Phoenix in the number of kidnappings per city in *the world* in 2009. At this writing, data isn't in for 2010, but it looks as if Phoenix won't shed its reputation anytime soon. This isn't great PR for Phoenix, already battling an image as an anti-immigrant, anti-Hispanic city. It is all but impossible to figure out whether the recession, hate groups, or widespread media coverage of the city as the Kidnapping Capital of the United States caused Phoenix-area hotel occupancies to plummet in 2009.

Unsuspecting migrants are sometimes kidnapped on desert trails like this one in the Altar Valley. KATHY MCCRAINE

Phoenix is a kidnapping hub for lots of reasons. Keep in mind that most kidnapping victims are undocumented immigrants and a good many kidnappers are also undocumented immigrants.

After traipsing through the Tucson Sector, many undocumented immigrants are shuttled in vans, cars, and trucks to the Phoenix metro area by smugglers.

Phoenix is home to about 1.6 million souls. It is the fifth-largest city in the United States and sits in the heart of Maricopa County. The county itself has a population of about four million people, including the residents of Phoenix. Cookie-cutter suburbs encircle the city, sprawling out into Maricopa County, devouring cotton farms, citrus groves, and cattle ranches.

Mexicans owned and worked some of those historic farms and ranches. They have always been a part of Arizona, largely because Arizona was part of Mexico until 1848, when Mexico lost a war with the United States and signed the Treaty of Guadalupe Hidalgo. Phoenix grew into a predominantly white city, settled by Civil War veterans and Midwesterners who didn't like Mexicans. Unlike Tucson, Arizona's other major city, Phoenix has long displayed hostility toward Mexicans.

So, at first blush, it seems counterintuitive that Mexican *coyotes* would transport tens of thousands of migrants to Phoenix and make it a major human-smuggling hub. But when you look at a map, you'll see Phoenix links up nicely to interstate highways that take immigrants to their final destinations. And those sprawling suburbs with rock "lawns" and palm trees make good camouflage for drop houses, like the one in Peoria that was right next door to Phil and Marie's home.

All of this explains why Phoenix is the Kidnapping Capital of the United States.

There are two categories of immigrant kidnappings in Phoenix. Drop house kidnappings follow the Selestino and Rosario scheme—incoming migrants at the border are baited with low smuggling fares. Those low fares are ramped up by thousands of dollars once the migrants are held at gunpoint in a drop house. The new "fare" is actually the ransom.

The second type is the "home invasion" kidnapping, in which kidnappers abduct rich individuals, like drug dealers or human smugglers, or their family members. Ransoms in such cases might range from large quantities of drugs to millions of dollars.

There's no way to know for sure how many migrants are kidnapped in Phoenix. Untold numbers of crimes against undocumented immigrants are not reported because witnesses fear deportation if they come forward.

It's even harder to get numbers because law-enforcement agencies sometimes compete and sometimes form partnerships with each other.

I was blocked from interviewing the officers who could meaningfully answer questions about kidnappings. Tommy Thompson, a spokesman for the Phoenix Police Department, refused to grant me access to the Phoenix Home Invasion and Kidnapping Enforcement unit, known as HIKE. I requested interviews with HIKE several times, but Thompson told me that the police department did not consider any book author a journalist and would not grant me access.

I had a hard time cornering Thompson; he didn't always answer e-mails or phone calls, and after I finally booked an appointment with him he was so late I almost left the police station without seeing him. He wasn't apologetic about being late, but he did usher me into a small conference room in the Phoenix police headquarters. It was clear to me that Thompson faced a public-relations quandary. On the one hand, his job was to spin Phoenix as a safe city. On the other hand, he had to confirm that Phoenix was the Kidnapping Capital of the United States. (At the time, Police Chief Jack Harris was seeking federal stimulus funds by milking the Kidnapping Capital theme. It worked. The Phoenix police subsequently got $350,000 to battle the kidnapping problem.)

Thompson told me that from 2006 to 2008, Phoenix police investigated nearly one thousand kidnapping cases, and Thompson estimated these were only *a third* of the kidnappings that actually took place in the Phoenix area. Another 309 cases were investigated in 2009, the *Arizona Republic*, a Phoenix newspaper, recently reported.

If Thompson's assumption is correct; if only a third of kidnapping cases were investigated, it follows that from 2006 to 2009, about 2,600 kidnapping cases were not investigated.

No one knows for sure how many victims were involved. Authorities count cases of kidnappings, but they don't keep a running tally of the kidnapping victims, according to Thompson.

"There may be fifty victims in one case," he told me, "but when we go to court we may only list three or four victims because it gets redundant."

• • •

Phoenix Mayor Phil Gordon met with me on a summer day in 2009, in his office in downtown Phoenix. Gordon was once a teacher, which helps explain why part of his office is furnished with classroom chairs with retractable writing surfaces. I sat in a classroom chair. Gordon, a savvy politician with a thick head of black hair and smart eyes, faced me from behind his big desk.

We settled into a discussion of immigrant kidnappings, and Gordon told me Phoenix had an unfair rap as the Kidnapping Capital of the United States because other cities might not have been as fastidious when they counted cases. In other words, if all cities counted kidnappings in exactly the same way, Phoenix might not come out on top.

Even so, the mayor believed kidnappings were a sign that drug-cartel border violence was spilling into Phoenix. And that violence was a direct indicator that cartels were defending themselves against American law-enforcement authorities and President Felipe Calderón's war, he told me.

"We don't have beheadings of innocent people yet," he said. "But that's just a matter of time if we don't do something to stop the violence, because organized crime syndicates from Mexico are very violent. We do have spillover of border violence in Phoenix. And if we don't stop the violence and support President Calderón's war against cartels, it will be a question of when, not if, we'll get the worst kind of violence that plagues Mexico."

Like Thompson, the mayor was faced with confirming the kidnappings, a move that would likely bring federal funding to local law-enforcement authorities. And yet in the next breath, he felt compelled to spin Phoenix as a safe city.

He pointed out that the FBI had recently reported that overall violent crime had dropped in Phoenix for three years in a row.

"The truth is," Mayor Gordon told me, "unless you're being smuggled or having someone smuggled, Phoenix is a very safe city."

●   ●   ●

It's difficult to sort out who, exactly, is in charge of busting and prosecuting kidnappers in Phoenix. The Phoenix-area law enforcement community has long been fractured. In 2010, Maricopa County Attorney Andrew Thomas and Maricopa County "Sheriff Joe" Arpaio were political allies, facing off against the rest of the law-enforcement community. Generally speaking, if Sheriff Joe's deputies arrested undocumented immigrants for kidnapping, the prosecution went to Thomas's office. State laws, after all, do prohibit kidnapping.

But here's the catch: Federal laws also prohibit kidnapping.

The difference is that, while Sheriff Joe and Andrew Thomas arrested and prosecuted simple immigrants, other law-enforcement authorities focused on more hardened criminals, like Vic, who kidnapped Rosario and Selestino.

Federal and state law-enforcement officials in Phoenix also cracked down on weapon traffickers and money launderers.

As Calderón's war picked up, so did the shipment of assault weapons from Phoenix to Mexico. The same smugglers who brought drugs and people to Phoenix returned to Mexico with loads of assault rifles and cash.

"It's like a trucking company. You make money with loads both ways. When traffickers go north with drugs, they come back with guns, ammo, and money," William Newell, special agent in charge of the Phoenix division of the Bureau of Alcohol, Tobacco, Firearms, and Explosives, told me one day in 2009.

Newell, who is six feet eight inches tall, blond, and blue-eyed, grew up on a Honduras banana plantation and speaks excellent Spanish. Mexicans jokingly call him *El Chaparro*, which means "The Short Guy." Oddly enough, Joaquín Guzmán Loera, the head of the Sinaloa Cartel, carries a similar nickname, *El Chapo*, which means the same thing. It's likely that the two short guys don't see eye to eye when it comes to gun shipments from Phoenix. Newell's job is to keep the guns out of Mexico. *El Chapo* would likely want the opposite.

Since Calderón started his battle against cartels, Newell told me, there's been an "all-out war" between drug cartels and the Mexican government. He didn't see the drug war as many Mexicans saw it, as confusing, inchoate. Instead, he viewed the drug war as clear-cut, fought by distinctive sides with powerful, state-of-the-art weapons, such as high-caliber rifles that can penetrate armored vehicles. First, the Mexican Army used the weapons. Then, the cartels began to use them. The cartels get many of their weapons from Maricopa County, and that is why Arizona is second only to Texas as the source of American firearms traced to Mexico.

Phoenix is a gun city. It has a lot of gun shows, where you can buy assault rifles without paperwork from the "gun collections" of unlicensed vendors. It's all perfectly legal, as long as the purchaser is a U.S. citizen who is not a felon.

To get around that, weapons traffickers hire U.S. citizens with no criminal records as "straw purchasers" to buy the guns at gun shows or gun stores, Newell told me. The guns are then shipped south. The catch is that Newell's agents monitor the gun shows, arrest arms traffickers, and turn them over for prosecution to the office of U.S. Attorney Dennis Burke.

One reason that actual physical cash is moved south from Phoenix right along with guns has to do with Terry Goddard, who served as Arizona attorney general from 2003 to 2010. Goddard grew up in Arizona and has a close connection to Mexico. He understood that human-smuggling deals were one-time transactions and that payments to human-smuggling cartels were often made via wire transfers to Mexico. Also, he knew that local *coyotes* accepted some payments for *pollos* via wire transfers.

In 2010, the Arizona Attorney General's Office forged an agreement with Western Union Financial Services, which facilitates many money wire transfers to Mexico. Western Union agreed to let law-enforcement authorities from California, Arizona, Texas, and New Mexico monitor its wire transfers. The company also agreed to pay close to $100 million to cover legal costs for the four states, and future expenses associated with money-laundering investigations and enforcement. The company was not accused of any crime. It cooperated with prosecutors.

"Today's announcement reflects Western Union's commitment to promoting mutual solutions to these border issues," said David Schlapbach, an attorney for Western Union, when the settlement was announced.

The Western Union settlement meant that *coyotes* in Phoenix would have a harder time receiving and sending wired money payments. It also meant that actual cash would have to be moved back into Mexico, just like the guns. This, of course, made it more difficult for smugglers to do business.

Imagine if you were a drug cartel member.

Wouldn't you be annoyed at Goddard and Newell and Burke?

And wouldn't you be less worried by Thomas and Sheriff Joe, who often seemed to focus their energies on *pollos*?

• • •

Highway 85 stretches for thirty-seven miles through the borderlands southwest of Phoenix. The road connects Interstate 10 with Interstate 8 and is a prime human-smuggling corridor. It snakes through raw desert that climbs up to charcoal-black peaks, and at sunset saguaros are silhouetted against the orange sky. The flat landscape beneath

Increased border enforcement has pushed migrants and their kidnappers into more treacherous terrain, like this near Arivaca, Arizona. KATHY MCCRAINE

the peaks is a patchwork of cotton fields, raw desert, housing developments, 1960s-era farmhouses shaded by mulberry trees, and odd clusters of double-wides and farm equipment. There are two kinds of *coyotes* here—the wild canines that lap water from the irrigation ditches and eat roadkill, and the human *coyote*. The latter picks up migrants at the end of their long desert walks and drives them to Phoenix, camouflaging his cargo however he can.

Catching undocumented immigrants on Highway 85 is easy simply because so many are transported on this route, and Sheriff Joe Arpaio's deputies have long patrolled this roadway. This explains why, on the morning of June 23, 2006, just as the sun was rising, two Maricopa County sheriff's deputies pulled over a red Chevy truck.

Their reasons for stopping the truck had to do with a malfunctioning brake light, or at least that was what they wrote in their report.

The truck stopped. The deputies climbed out of their patrol car. The truck sped off. A chase ensued. Once, the truck pulled into oncoming traffic, just like in the movies. Finally, the truck slowed to a stop, and the driver and three others hightailed it into a nearby cornfield.

Several passengers in the bed of the truck peeked out. One of them was Juan Barragan-Sierra, a Mexican citizen. He was dirty and tired and admitted to deputies that he was in the country illegally. He said he'd paid a *coyote* $2,000 to take him to Everett, Washington. (The actual *coyote*, who'd run into the cornfield, was never apprehended.) Juan had already been deported once for entering the country illegally, but he said he reentered the United States because he needed to work.

There is nothing that distinguishes Juan's story from that of thousands of other undocumented migrants who are arrested in Arizona except for one thing: Juan was one of the first to be prosecuted under a newly enacted Arizona human-smuggling law that aimed to punish *coyotes* who knowingly transported undocumented immigrants through Arizona for profit.

Only, Juan wasn't a *coyote*.

Instead, he was a *coyote* client.

Maricopa County Attorney Andrew Thomas charged Juan with conspiring to smuggle himself into Arizona.

As Thomas saw it, Juan had struck a deal with a human smuggler and that amounted to a conspiracy to commit human smuggling. It was a unique interpretation of Arizona's new law, the only one of its kind in the nation.

Juan was convicted of conspiring to smuggle himself through Arizona and took his case all the way to the Arizona Court of Appeals, alleging that Thomas was trying to take over the federal government's job of controlling immigration. Juan lost his court challenge in 2008 and was deported.

A few months later, the victorious county attorney announced that his office had convicted one thousand people under the human-smuggling law. Of these, 868 were migrants convicted of conspiring to smuggle themselves.

Conspiring to smuggle yourself through Arizona is a Class 4 felony, and the sentence for first timers ranges from probation to three and three-quarters years in prison. Many migrants charged with conspiring to smuggle themselves through Arizona plea-bargain down to a lesser crime, spend only a few months in Sheriff Joe's jail system, and then are either sent home after their incarcerations or stay in Arizona, fighting their deportations in immigration court.

• • •

Andrew Thomas was elected Maricopa County Attorney in 2004 on the Republican ticket. He resigned in April 2010, after the rancher Krentz was murdered, in order to run for attorney general on a strong anti-illegal immigrant ticket.

He was born in 1966 and has a wife and four kids. He's got thick reddish-brown hair, inscrutable eyes, a baby face, and a slight build. He spent his boyhood in the Missouri Ozarks, graduated from the University of Missouri, and received a law degree from Harvard in 1991. He has written three books, including a biography of U.S. Supreme Court Justice Clarence Thomas.

Besides prosecuting undocumented immigrants for conspiring to smuggle themselves into Arizona, Thomas became a vigilant enforcer of the state Employer Sanctions Act, which he called the Legal Arizona Workers Act, after it became law in 2008.

The law requires all Arizona employers to run prospective employees' green cards and Social Security numbers through a Department of Homeland Security database called E-Verify. (The database is supposed to catch undocumented workers, but it is seriously flawed. A 2009 study by a DHS consultant found that 54 percent of undocumented workers were incorrectly categorized as legal workers.) The Employer Sanctions Act was widely promoted as a law designed to penalize businesses that knowingly hire undocumented workers by suspending and revoking their business licenses. But it also allows prosecutors to slap felony identity-theft charges on undocumented immigrants who use fake Social Security and green cards to obtain employment.

Sheriff Joe has used the law to raid thirty workplaces in Maricopa County, and undocumented workers, not the people who employ them, were targeted.

By early 2010, only one Arizona employer had been successfully prosecuted under the law. In 2008, Sheriff Joe's deputies raided a water park that allegedly hired undocumented immigrants. A year later, the Maricopa County Attorney's Office suspended for ten days the license of the water park operator, a company called Water World. On one hand, it was a silly settlement, since Water World no longer did business in Arizona. On the other hand, the parent company of Water World, Golfland Entertainment, agreed to use E-Verify in its operations across the nation.

The national perspective was played up by Thomas, who in a press release said: "We are especially pleased that the affiliate company of Water World will participate in E-Verify as a result of this agreement."

The Employer Sanctions Act had been sponsored in 2007 by Russell Pearce, Sheriff Joe's former chief deputy. In 2001, Pearce, a Republican from a conservative district in the Phoenix suburb of Mesa, successfully ran for the Arizona House of Representatives. He was elected to the Arizona Senate in 2008.

Pearce campaigned by calling his supporters "patriots" engaged in a battle to keep America, and of course Arizona, from being overrun by "illegals" who committed crimes and would break the country.

He sponsored and supported state laws that make life so miserable for undocumented immigrants that, at the very least, they'd think twice about living in Arizona.

In Arizona, undocumented immigrants cannot legally work, be released from jail on bond, sue American citizens for punitive damages, speak Spanish in state buildings (English is Arizona's official language), receive in-state college tuition breaks, drive, or seek state benefits. Arizona social workers face criminal misdemeanor charges if they fail to turn in any undocumented immigrant seeking any benefit from the state.

All of these conditions were enacted by legislation or proposition, and Pearce is linked to most of them.

Pearce's son, Sean, is a Minuteman. He's also a Maricopa County sheriff's deputy and was shot by an undocumented immigrant during a search-warrant raid in 2004. Once, I listened to Pearce preside over an Arizona Senate hearing in which Sean and several others from across the United States said they were brutalized by undocumented immigrants. Russell Pearce, pink-faced and balding, blinked back tears.

"You are a warrior," Russell Pearce told one speaker. "We need warriors. … We have a nation to take back."

In 2009, Pearce vowed at a press conference, he'd get a "trespassing bill" passed that might nail undocumented immigrants who set foot in Arizona with criminal trespassing. (People who drive undocumented immigrants in their cars, like family members with green cards, would also become criminals.) Members of the Arizona-based group United for a Sovereign America, long singled out by the Southern Poverty Law Center as a nativist extremist group, gathered round Pearce at the press conference. They applauded. Sheriff Joe and Andrew Thomas stood at Russell Pearce's side. In 2010, Pearce introduced his trespassing bill. Although the word "trespassing" was removed from the bill as it traveled through the Arizona Senate, the bill still criminalized each of the nearly one-half million undocumented immigrants for setting foot in Arizona. Because it could turn law-enforcement officers into immigration cops, police chiefs joined human rights activists to lobby against the Pearce bill. Arizona's law-enforcement agencies already faced crippling budget shortfalls that prevented them from expanding their staffs, and said they couldn't handle the added responsibility of arresting half a million people. It was a largely unfunded bill that would clog courts and jails, but Pearce pushed his bill hard.

The bill passed and was signed into law by Governor Jan Brewer in late April. The move kickstarted national protests, boycotts of Arizona, lawsuits, and earnest talks about reforming federal immigration laws so that the Arizona law would become moot.

• • •

Andrew Thomas occasionally issued reports on the Maricopa County Attorney's Office Web site that claimed undocumented immigrants committed crimes at higher rates than other groups in Maricopa County.

I wondered if his statistics were skewed by the prosecution of migrants like Juan Barragan-Sierra for committing felonies like conspiring to smuggle themselves into Arizona. Or by the luckless migrants slapped with identity-theft felonies after they'd been caught in Sheriff Joe's workplace raids.

I crunched the numbers of undocumented felons for 2008, the last year for which statistics were available on Thomas's Web site. Thomas's office successfully prosecuted 3,855 felonies involving undocumented immigrants.

From what I could tell, one-third of these felony convictions dealt with human smuggling, identity theft, and forgery—which likely were associated with the Employer Sanctions Act and human-smuggling laws. In other words, it's entirely possible a good percentage of the "felons" Thomas had prosecuted were dishwashers and hotel maids arrested for working with fake papers or for conspiring to smuggle themselves into Arizona.

I wasn't alone in wondering whether crime statistics about undocumented immigrants were skewed for political advantage.

In March 2010, the *American Conservative* magazine published an article by Ron Unz, who conducted an exhaustive study of national crime statistics and concluded that Mexican migrants didn't commit crimes at higher rates than other groups.

Unz wrote: "Conservatives have traditionally prided themselves on being realists, dealing with the world as it is rather than attempting to force it to conform to a pre-existing ideological framework. But just as many on the Right succumbed to a fantastical foreign policy that makes the world much more dangerous than it needs to be, some have also accepted the myth that Hispanic immigrants and their children have high crime rates. Such an argument may have considerable emotional appeal, but there is very little hard evidence behind it."

This was not the sentiment in Arizona, where anti-migrant furor ramped up following the mysterious murder of the Douglas rancher, Robert Krentz.

I wanted to sit down and talk with Andrew Thomas, get his views on the prosecution of migrants. I made several requests for an interview via e-mail messages and telephone calls, but Thomas's public relations assistant, Mike Scerbo, who schedules such interviews, did not respond to my requests.

The county attorney had made a series of political mistakes that began in 2007. That year, his office ordered the arrest of Mike Lacey and Jim Larkin, owners of the alternative weekly *Phoenix New Times* (where I was a staff writer from 1985 to 2000), for revealing the contents of a secret grand jury subpoena seeking detailed private information on the newspaper's online visitors.

Rather than complying with the subpoena, Lacey and Larkin had exposed it.

Thomas had hired an outside attorney to investigate *New Times* because the newspaper had published the home address of Sheriff Joe on its Web site as part of a larger story about the sheriff's financial holdings. It's not hard to find online addresses, and the county attorney's investigation of *New Times* appeared to be retaliation for the newspaper's stories that had questioned inmate deaths in Sheriff Joe's jails, among other things.

Thomas's office nevertheless ordered the arrests of Lacey and Larkin, both in their late fifties, who were handcuffed by sheriff's deputies and driven off to jail in unmarked sedans.

The public outcry from the American journalism community was swift and immediate: The subpoena was outrageous, and so were the arrests.

Thomas dropped the charges.

He then launched a legal battle against his funders, the Maricopa County Board of Supervisors, and several Maricopa County judges, alleging corruption. Sheriff Joe's office had conducted many of the investigations in these cases. Later, he dropped the charges, but the county infighting cost taxpayers at least $3 million.

By 2010, Thomas and Sheriff Joe faced serious political problems. Many voters viewed the legal dogfights as punitive measures taken against political foes. Nevertheless, when Robert Krentz was murdered, Thomas seized on the anti-migrant sentiment in Arizona and invoked the rancher's name when he resigned to run for attorney general, on a platform of immigration enforcement.

CHAPTER 3

Arrested

Lucy and Marco treasured their life in Phoenix
right up to the moment Sheriff Joe's deputies
zip-tied their wrists and led them into hell.

Lucy stood with her slender legs slightly apart, silently praying for strength and dignity as the female guard ran her hands up and down Lucy's clothed body. Lucy believed that the guard—let's call her Guard X—inappropriately touched her during these obligatory pat downs in the Maricopa County jail.

"Don't look at me, I'm just doing my job," Guard X said.

"I not looking," Lucy said.

She dared not complain about Guard X because she was an undocumented immigrant serving a ninety-day sentence in the Maricopa County jail. She feared that if she reported the guard she would be sent back to Mexico City. If this were to happen, she would be separated from her only child, nine-year-old Angie, an American citizen who was living with relatives after Lucy and her husband were arrested by Sheriff Joe Arpaio's deputies during a raid of a Phoenix car wash.

In order to meet Angie in the jail visitation room, Lucy underwent body cavity checks that the jail administrators deemed necessary for security. When the guards asked her to lean over, spread her cheeks, and cough, she complied. She knew several Latina inmates who had been so humiliated by the cavity checks that they chose not to visit with their own children.

During her brief visits with Angie in the jail visitation room, Lucy's manacled wrists were fastened to a ring attached to a table. Lucy joked about it, let her daughter know she was fine. She'd be out of jail soon, she told Angie. Then they'd go to the park with the merry-go-round. They'd eat hot dogs and Popsicles.

"Remember," Lucy told Angie every time she saw the child, "your father and I were arrested only because we were working in a car wash. We are not criminals."

Time in Sheriff Joe's jail passed slowly. Inmates received two meals daily, and sometimes, in between meals, Lucy paced the perimeter of the dormitory. Once, she circled the room one hundred times.

Other times, she made roses out of toilet paper. She learned to pluck her eyebrows with thread she pulled out of the hems of her black-and-white-striped chinos. She befriended other inmates who were prosecuted by the Maricopa County Attorney's Office for forgery and identity theft because they'd been found to have fake work papers during workplace raids. There was the college student from Colombia who was serving time for working with false documents at a Phoenix McDonald's, and the hotel maid who was serving time for working under false documents at an elegant resort in the upscale suburb of Scottsdale.

The hotel maid had been a *matachine* dancer, and Lucy became fascinated with her descriptions of the ritualized dances in honor of the Virgin of Guadalupe. Lucy herself prayed to the *Virgencita* every night in jail and asked her to watch over Angie. Lucy also took strength from weekly Mass for inmates, but at the same time she dreaded the Mass. Pat downs were obligatory for inmates returning to the jail from outside visits, like church, and sometimes, Guard X was on duty.

• • •

Lucy told me about Guard X in the fall of 2009, several weeks after she'd been released from jail. That afternoon, she sat on a dark leather couch in the small central Phoenix mobile home she shared with her husband, Marco, and Angie. Spanish-speaking reporters detailed breaking news on the Fort Hood massacre on the wide-screen TV.

In the kitchen, a *Support Our Troops* magnet decorated the refrigerator. Next to the kitchen, a small, round, glass-topped table was set with shiny cutlery, light-green place mats, glasses, and linen napkins folded like open fans. It was all for show. The family didn't eat there.

The family couldn't afford food. Angie ate two meals at school, then dinner with her parents at an aunt's house.

Four caged lovebirds squawked near Angie's loft bed, near the refrigerator. Dolls, stuffed animals, a toy tea set, and a Hannah Montana piano were arranged in a play area below the loft bed. The only light in the trailer came from the small, twinkling string of Christmas lights around the Virgin of Guadalupe statue and the glow from the TV. A plate commemorating Barack Obama's election sat on the entertainment center, next to an American flag and two wood carvings of dancers that Marco had purchased at IKEA, one of his favorite stores.

Angie played her toy piano. Marco watched TV. I scribbled notes as Lucy told me about well-meaning neighbors who had never been to jail offering advice on how to recover from incarceration. Suddenly, tears streamed down Lucy's cheeks.

"They don't know what I went through in the jail," Lucy said.

Marco took Angie outside for a walk. He didn't want his daughter to hear her mother talk about jail. His wife had changed since her incarceration. She could become uncharacteristically grumpy and withdrawn. And sometimes, late at night, she'd wake up in their bedroom and think she was still in jail and cry.

"The guards saw all my most intimate parts," she said. "This was so humiliating for me, I can't even describe how I felt. I couldn't believe I was there."

I clawed through my purse looking for a Kleenex. I wanted to comfort her, but I also wanted to hear her story. She seemed to sense this and reassured me that talking about "these humiliations" helped her heal.

"If I write about this," I said, "everyone will know about it."

"Write about it," Lucy said. "Shine a light on it. I am no longer willing to live a hidden life."

Lucy had been raised as a conservative Catholic in a conservative Catholic country. Her religion and her culture demanded feminine modesty. But there was no sensitivity to such modesty in Sheriff Joe's jails.

Beyond the pat downs and cavity checks, Lucy took showers and went to the bathroom in the presence of other women. The commodes were lined up side by side, without privacy, in an open room. Ten women at a time were herded into the stall-free showers. Lucy showered with a group of women she trusted, in order to protect herself from sexual assault.

I could understand how difficult it would be for a shy woman to undergo cavity checks and take public showers, but I wondered if Lucy's conservative Catholic cultural sensitivities had led her to believe Guard X had inappropriately touched her. Had she misinterpreted routine pat downs for something else? I asked Lucy about this several times, and she always answered that there was a marked difference in touches between other guards, who hastily patted her down, and Guard X, with her insinuating touches.

She didn't know the guard's name. She hadn't filed a complaint with the jail administration.

Without the guard's name or a formal complaint filed by Lucy, Sheriff Joe's spokeswoman Lisa Allen wrote me in an e-mail that "no comment can be offered" on the "female inmate who says she was inappropriately touched."

Lucy hadn't told her lawyer about the pat downs. She wanted me to know, though, because talking about the experience helped her work through the shame.

• • •

"We will go to Phoenix and live with your uncle," Marco told Lucy. It was a summer day in 1997. The two had just married in a Catholic church in their hometown—Mexico City. For sure, they would not leave their wedding album behind. He loved the portraits of his bride in her white wedding gown, with her large brown eyes and her long black hair gathered in a stylish updo. He cherished one picture, in particular, of the two of them looking at each other with tears of happiness in their eyes.

Marco had always been drawn to Lucy's vulnerability, trustfulness, and innocence. It made him want to protect and care for her. And he wasn't the only one. Lucy was the *consentida* among her seven siblings, the one child in the working-class family that everyone had wanted to take care of, and happily indulge, if it was at all possible.

He had been the *consentido* among his five siblings too. His academic awards (English and math were his favorite subjects) had decorated the walls on his family's rented home in Mexico City. His parents were poor; his mother cleaned houses, and his father was a baker. The family couldn't afford to send Marco to college, so as a teenager he followed his father into the bakery.

Lucy and Marco had met when they were still in school, through friends, and had fallen in love at seventeen. At that point, Marco worked in the bakery, and Lucy manufactured cotton swabs at a local factory. Later, she worked in a toothbrush factory. Between them, they earned the peso equivalent of about $200 monthly.

"I want to make real money," Marco told Lucy. "I want to give you everything you deserve."

She thought her husband was courageous. He wasn't afraid to talk to anyone. To Lucy, everything about Marco exuded confidence—his sure-footed gait, his English skills, his sense of style.

Marco and Lucy crossed into Arizona illegally a few months after they married, and soon they were in Phoenix at the home of Lucy's uncle. The quarters were temporary, and crowded. Lucy and Marco didn't have a bed, until they spied a mattress in a Dumpster. They retrieved it, scrubbed it, and slept on it until they could afford their own place, and their own bed.

Which didn't take long.

There were plenty of jobs for undocumented immigrants in Phoenix in the 1990s. But to get hired, migrants had to provide fake documents. This was in response to the 1986 Immigration Reform and Control Act, a federal law that forbade employers from knowingly hiring undocumented immigrants. (The Arizona Employer Sanctions Act was passed twenty-one years later, out of frustration with the federal government's failure to enforce its own law.)

Few Arizona migrants or their employers took the 1986 federal law seriously. In Phoenix, a newly arrived immigrant could pay a fellow on a street corner $50, and a day or so later someone would hand-deliver a fake Social Security card and a fake green card attesting to legal residency in the United States.

The document fabrication business was highly organized, strati-fied, and secretive; immigrants rarely knew who manufactured the fake green cards or who ran the operation. In that regard, the fake documents·racket was similar to the kidnapping, drug, and human-smuggling industries.

With new fake documents, immigrants like Lucy and Marco were snapped up as workers. Using their bogus Social Security numbers, immigrants paid income taxes, and pumped money into Social Security and Medicare. They knew, of course, that they would never enjoy the benefits of Social Security and Medicare, but they paid anyway.

As illegal immigration increased, the Social Security Administration's so-called Earnings Suspense File mushroomed. The file con-tained payments by workers whose names did not match their Social Security numbers; most of these unclaimed payments were probably made by undocumented immigrants, officials said. In 2007, the *New York Times* reported: "In the current decade, the [Earnings Suspense] file is growing, on average, by more than $50 billion a year, generating $6 billion to $7 billion in Social Security tax revenue and about $1.5 billion in Medicare taxes."

Since they'd never be able to collect Medicare or Social Security, undocumented immigrants were hardly welfare cheats. Instead, they were being cheated by a tax system that took their money and gave no benefits in return. Lucy and Marco, for instance, would contribute about $70,000 to the Social Security Administration in their twelve years in Arizona. They knew they'd never see any Social Security ben-efits. And they accepted this as a fact of life.

• • •

Two weeks after they first arrived in Phoenix, Marco found a job washing cars at Lindstrom Family Auto Wash on East Indian School Road. His weekly salary of about $250 a week eclipsed the $200 monthly that he and Lucy made together in Mexico City. Marco enjoyed the job because he hoped one day to become an auto mechanic and own a shop and supervise other mechanics. Driving the BMWs and Mercedes-Benzes and Hummers from the vacuum station to the wash line was thrilling. For just those few seconds, he pretended the cars were entirely his.

Besides his full-time gig at the car wash, Marco had other jobs—security guard, office cleaner. Lucy chopped vegetables for a restaurant, cleaned houses and offices, babysat. Eventually, she ended up working with her husband at the car wash. Between the two of them, they earned about $40,000 annually.

Marco studied English at a community college and got better and better at it. He embraced his new country and the people in it. "Ninety percent of Americans are good people with large hearts," he would tell Lucy. He was inquisitive, adventurous, and a natural traveler. He and Lucy visited museums, the zoo, the botanical gardens, the state fair. They celebrated the Fourth of July. "I love this country," Marco told Lucy.

Once, Marco and a group of adventurous guys from the car wash hiked Havasupai Canyon, a remote side canyon of the Grand Canyon known for its turquoise waterfalls. That was the only time he left his *consentida* behind, and only because she was pregnant and the hike would have been too dangerous for her.

In late 1999, Lucy gave birth by Cesarean section to Angie. The doctors set up a screen so Lucy couldn't see the surgeon make the pelvic incision. Marco, dressed in aqua-blue scrubs, stood up on his toes to peer over the screen and watch the doctors make the incision and pull the child out of the womb. Once the baby was born, Marco fastened a tiny gold ID bracelet on her wrist, so that nurses would not mistakenly give his child to the wrong parents. That hospital bill was paid for by a state program that distributes federal Medicaid funds. It was the only time Lucy would get free medical care.

Marco and Lucy shattered the stereotype of Mexican immigrants who refuse to assimilate. They both learned English, mixed with Anglos, and were enthusiastic consumers. They bought a $9,200 mobile home in a trailer court in the shadows of the freeway. Marco purchased and fixed up cars, then resold them. At the time of their arrest, even though neither could legally drive in Arizona, Lucy drove a red 1996 Mitsubishi Eclipse and Marco drove a maroon 2002 Honda Civic.

They vacationed in Las Vegas, Disneyland, and Colorado. They trolled garage sales, visited malls. They bought new furniture, new flat-screen TVs, and new clothes. They visited Starbucks and Applebee's and went to movies. They also bought land in Guanajuato, a state in Mexico, and slowly began constructing a house for Marco's mother. Marco had taken on the responsibility of caring for his mother; her marriage had failed, and she lived alone in a blighted, violent Mexico City neighborhood.

By then, Lucy's parents, brother, and sister Anita had moved to Phoenix.

Lucy's father washed dishes at a local hotel. One day he suffered a mild heart attack. He knew his family would have to pay his medical bills, so he refused to see a cardiologist for expensive follow-up studies. About a month after his heart attack, he returned from work exhausted. "Don't drive me to work if you're so tired," Lucy's mother said. He drove his wife to her office-cleaning job.

After she entered the office building, he died in his car.

The corpse stayed in cold storage in a morgue for eight days, until the Mexican consul referred Lucy and Marco to a funeral home that would embalm the body and ship it to Mexico City by air. Lucy's mother sold her furniture and her husband's clothes to help pay the bill, which totaled about $1,500. Other family members kicked in money, and the bill was paid. Lucy's mother accompanied her husband's remains to Mexico City, oversaw the burial, and grieved for two years. Then she crossed the Arizona desert for twelve hours on foot to be reunited with her two daughters in Arizona.

• • •

Lucy's sister, Anita, worked in a large Phoenix hotel as a housekeeper. For weeks, she had a secret crush on Jack, the hotel manager. It was hopeless, she knew, because he didn't speak Spanish and she didn't speak English, and besides, he was an important person who wouldn't look twice at a hotel maid. Then one day, Anita found a red rose on her laundry cart.

On their first date, Jack and Anita bought a Spanish-English dictionary.

Jack came from a middle-class family in Atlanta and had attended the University of Connecticut, where he majored in economics and political science. He once owned a furniture manufacturing business in Atlanta, and when he first moved to Phoenix, he manufactured Southwestern lodgepole furniture. When the Southwestern decor fad died down, his business dried up. He became a hotel manager. Until then, he had been fairly conservative and believed immigrants who had no papers entered the United States at their own risk. If they got caught, they deserved it.

Then he fell in love with Anita.

Anita's Mexican family viewed Jack as a celebrity for three reasons. First, he loved Anita. Second, he had an important job. And third, he was African American.

Jack had always been struck by the difference between his middle-class family in Atlanta and Anita's Mexican clan. In Jack's family, he and his two brothers were expected to be self-sufficient and advance their careers. In Anita's family, communal basic survival skills trumped career paths.

During the recession, absent access to social services like food stamps, welfare, and health care, Anita's family provided its own social services. In Anita's family, if a relative needed help, no one asked questions. The help was automatically given. In Jack's family, if a relative needed help, he or she was thoroughly questioned before help was offered.

One day, Jack told Anita: "In your family it's *Mi casa es su casa*. In my family it's *Mi casa es mi casa*."

After Jack and Anita married, Jack set out to get his wife legal residency. After all, he was an American citizen and they *were* married. Like most Americans, Jack figured that once an undocumented immigrant marries an American citizen, a green card would be a slam dunk.

He figured wrong.

Mexicans who enter the United States illegally, without visas, can't get green cards just because they marry American citizens.

Immigration law frowns on immigrants who enter the country illegally. Since most Mexicans in Arizona entered on foot, without visas, their chances of getting green cards were slim.

Anita's best shot, the lawyers said, was to lay low, never drive, and pray for immigration reform that would grant her a pathway to citizenship.

There was one other option, but the end results were usually disappointing: Jack, as a citizen and Anita's spouse, could petition the United States government to give Anita a visa, but she would have to return to Mexico for her interview. During the interview, she would be asked if she had entered the country illegally, and if she answered honestly, she would be barred from entering the United States for ten years.

She could petition the government to cancel the ten-year wait, but then she'd have to prove that her absence from the United States would cause an extreme hardship to Jack.

And this wasn't normal extreme hardship, like leaving Jack alone with two children to care for. This was life-or-death hardship, meaning that Jack or the kids would literally *die* without Anita.

Jack and Anita decided not to do anything, and pray for immigration reform. They lived together in a house that Jack owned, about fifteen miles from Lucy's trailer. Jack sold the house in 2008 and began to look for a new home.

"I want to live in a trailer near my sister," Anita told her husband in English, which she had learned in order to communicate with him.

"Why do you want to live in a trailer when I can buy you a nice house?" Jack asked Anita.

"Because she's my sister and I miss her," Anita answered.

Jack relented. He bought a mobile home in the same trailer court where Lucy and Marco lived, and invested the profits from the sale of his house into taxicabs. He left the hotel management gig to own and manage a cab company, and he became a part-time cabbie himself. By then, he and Anita had two children, and Anita wished Jack would spend more time with the family. After all, they had money for food and shelter. What else did they need?

"God will take care of us," she told her husband.

"God gives us the tools to take care of ourselves," Jack answered, "and by the time our kids are ready for college, tuition might cost $60,000 a year. I've got to work so they'll be able to go to school."

This was the excuse he gave Anita for leaving her and working so hard. But he knew that even if he didn't have to worry about college funds, he would still work hard. And he recognized that same trait in Marco, his brother-in-law.

The two men were close friends, and they both saw that an anti-immigrant sentiment had started to take hold in Phoenix. Sheriff Joe's workplace raids worried Jack. He warned Marco that he and Lucy shouldn't both work at the Lindstrom Family Auto Wash.

What if the sheriff raided the car wash and arrested them both?

Marco agreed it was a risk. But new laws made it exceedingly hard for undocumented people to get jobs in Phoenix. At least the car wash job was secure. After all, Marco was now the manager. He could watch over Lucy.

"God will take care of us," Marco said.

• • •

In July 2008, a former manager of the Lindstrom Family Auto Wash—let's call him Tom—was interviewed by a Maricopa County sheriff's detective. Tom had initiated contact with the sheriff's office and told the detective that many employees at the car wash were immigrants who were in the United States illegally and had presented what appeared to be fake work documents. He named Marco and Lucy, among others, as undocumented migrants. He described the color and location of filing cabinets where the alleged fake documents were stored. After interviewing Tom, the sheriff's detective filed an affidavit alleging that car wash employees were committing crimes stemming from "the illegal use of Social Security numbers not assigned to them by the Social Security Administration to gain employment."

For eleven months, the sheriff's detectives harvested employment data from state and federal agencies. They compared Social Security numbers and names of car wash employees to files at the Social Security Administration to see if names and numbers matched. The detectives also checked out the license plates of employees' vehicles parked at the car wash, to see who owned them and where the owners lived. They even cased out the trailer park where Marco and Lucy lived.

Marco and Lucy were unaware they were being investigated.

Almost a full year after a detective talked to Tom, on the morning of June 13, 2009, Marco and Lucy awakened early and dressed for work. Marco wore a blue Lindstrom Family Auto Wash T-shirt; baggy long shorts, and work boots. Lucy wore a purple car wash T-shirt, Capri-style pants, and tennis shoes. They woke up Angie in her loft bed. Around 7:15, Anita knocked on the door. She'd come to collect Angie, who would spend the day at her house. Anita had been fighting an unusual infestation of summer ants in her trailer and had scrubbed the ant trails with Clorox. Still, they kept coming. She told Marco and Lucy that the ants gave her a creepy feeling that something terrible was about to happen.

Anita dressed Angie in a flowered T-shirt, jeans, and sandals, and then took the little girl to her trailer. She fed Angie and her own two children and began gathering clothes to wash in the trailer park's laundry room. She turned on the wide-screen TV, so the kids wouldn't be bored.

Marco and Lucy, in the meantime, drove west on Indian School Road, past Filiberto's Mexican restaurant, and a shopping center with a bowling alley. They turned left into the parking lot beneath the familiar sign:

LINDSTROM FAMILY AUTO WASH
CAR WASH * BRUSHLESS * SHOESHINE * AUTO DETAILING

They parked the red Mitsubishi in the back lot and walked beneath the aqua-and-white-striped canvas canopies that shaded the car wash from the hot summer sun. Lucy was leader of the vacuum crew, so she made sure that the vacuum area was shipshape and that the vacuum trash canisters were empty. Marco checked all the other equipment and filled the large orange cooler full of water for the workers. One by one, other employees showed up, greeted each other in Spanish, and took their stations.

By 8:00 a.m., the car wash opened. Lucy and Marco worked steadily for an hour, until there was a lull. Lucy raced to the QT next door, bought two chocolate cream-filled doughnuts, a SoBe fruit drink for herself, and an iced coffee for her husband. When she returned to the car wash, vehicles were lined up again, so she put the snacks on a shelf and began vacuuming.

Then she saw the black SUVs and patrol cars parked on the perimeter of the car wash.

The sheriff!

She walked as casually as she could into the car wash building; down the hallway, past the gumball machine, the fish tank, the shoe-shine stand, and the tall rack lined with birthday cards decorated with smiling cats, frogs, and bulldogs.

She sneaked into the supply closet and called Anita. "The sheriff's deputies are outside," Lucy said, "but I am fine. They won't come into the building. I'm hiding in a closet."

Then the connection went dead.

"I'm going to do the laundry," Anita told the children. "I'll be just a few steps away, and I'll be right back. You kids watch TV for a while."

When she was out of earshot, Anita called Jack on her cell phone and begged him to rescue Lucy and Marco. Jack was driving his cab, and by the time he dropped off his customer, drove to the car wash, and saw the fleet of black sheriff's vehicles with blinking lights, the swarm of uniformed deputies and posse members, and the arriving television news crews clustered behind the police tape, Jack knew he could do nothing to help.

Marco felt powerless too. With his wrists cuffed by plastic zip ties, he couldn't protect his wife. Deputies discovered Lucy in the supply closet, confiscated her cell phone, and zip-tied her wrists too. Marco thought back to the conversation he'd had with Jack.

Why hadn't he listened? Why had he allowed Lucy to work with him at the auto wash?

Soon, Marco, Lucy, and twelve other "suspected illegal aliens" were grouped near the table and chairs where customers usually waited for their cars. Marco remembered advice he'd heard on Spanish-language radio stations and from immigrant-rights advocates who held neighborhood meetings in the wake of Sheriff Joe's raids.

"No matter what, don't sign anything. Ask for a lawyer immediately," Marco whispered to Lucy before the deputies led them past the TV news cameras and into the bus that took them to the jail.

• • •

This is how Angie learned her parents were arrested: She saw them on TV.

Univision, a Spanish-language TV station, broadcast live from the car wash, with shots of her parents in handcuffs. The little girl didn't know what would happen to her parents, or if she would ever see them again. As Angie cried in her grandmother's lap, a television news crew pounded on the trailer door and later interviewed the little girl, her grandmother, and her distraught aunt. When Angie made the news, an immigrant-rights activist videotaped her and turned her into a You-Tube sensation—the child who lost both parents in one of Sheriff Joe's raids. She'd become an overnight *cause célèbre*, but all she really wanted to do was be with her parents. She lost her appetite. She looked out the window. This was not unusual behavior for children who'd lost a parent in an immigration raid.

Uncle Jack told Angie to buck up, make her parents proud of her.

Angie learned to not show her fear. She became Phoenix's smallest immigrant-rights activist, largely because pro-migrant activists told her that she could help her parents this way. She was a pretty, self-assertive little girl with long curly hair and lively brown eyes. Everyone always said she favored her strong-minded father. So, at the request of immigrant-rights advocates, she marched in the streets of Phoenix with other children who'd lost relatives in raids. She gave press interviews, although such interviews made her nervous inside because she mistakenly felt that if she flubbed up, something bad might happen to her parents.

Sometimes, her aunt Anita would take her to her parents' trailer, and she'd go into Marco and Lucy's bedroom. She'd look at their bed with the lacy white spread, and the collection of Cabbage Patch dolls lined along the pillows, and the orange and blue flowers that her mother had pasted on the walls. It was a small room, cluttered with familiar things—crucifixes, dressers, floral arrangements, family photos, a TV.

But without her parents, the room seemed empty.

• • •

Marco and Lucy were both assigned public defenders and were given two choices. The first choice: They could fight the forgery and identity-theft charges in court and risk years in prison if they lost their cases. Or they could plea-bargain the serious felonies down to a lesser felony and serve three months in jail.

They each chose the path favored by most immigrants caught up in Arizona raids: They chose to plea-bargain their forgery and identity-theft felonies down to a lesser felony—"criminal imperson-ation"—and serve their ninety days in jail. The criminal imperson-ation raps would eventually devolve from felonies to misdemeanors under Arizona law.

Thanks to all the advice they'd heard in public forums and in Spanish-language media, they hadn't signed papers consenting to their deportations. This meant that, although they were formally deported, they had a right to contest their deportation orders at immi-gration court—officially known as the Executive Office for Immigra-tion Review.

They each hired an immigration lawyer and learned their com-bined cost of contesting deportation from start to finish would be $11,000.

In an incredible stroke of luck for undocumented immigrants in Maricopa County, the immigration court in Phoenix was over-whelmed with cases.

Waits for final hearings to contest deportation orders could be as long as three years.

They both knew that they didn't have much of a chance of contesting their deportation in immigration court and that they'd probably ultimately lose their cases.

But the key is, they were buying time.

They banked on immigration reform, with some sort of pathway to legalization, taking effect before those three years were up.

And Marco and Lucy were heartened by the fact that during those three years, while they awaited their hearings, they could work legally.

The reason: Federal immigration rules allowed immigrants who have pending hearings in immigration court to work legally. So the Social Security Administration would issue Social Security cards to Marco and Lucy. The only catch: It could take months of waiting and paperwork before those Social Security cards arrived.

During those months of waiting for the Social Security cards, Marco and Lucy could not work at all. They would have to rely entirely on the generosity of their large extended family.

• • •

Angie had gotten used to living with her Aunt Anita and Uncle Jack. Their mobile home was landscaped with pink vincas and roses. Two dried ears of corn decorated the outside entry, a Mexican symbol of good luck. The covered parking space adjacent to the trailer served as a play area for Angie and her cousins, and on holidays the parking space became an outdoor dining room. Inside, just like in her parents' house, there was a large shrine to the Virgin of Guadalupe in the living room. A smaller statue of Jesus as a toddler stood nearby. Angie's grandmother's Bible (with each gospel bookmarked by a piece of torn paper) lay on a table beneath the *Virgencita*. The place was cozy, even after Anita and Jack sold their living room furniture to help pay legal expenses for Marco and Lucy.

Anita had been distraught after her sister's arrest and didn't eat for a week, not even when Jack took her to Applebee's. She didn't think she deserved to eat and enjoy herself with her sister suffering in jail.

She threw herself into raising money for Marco and Lucy. Anita held two fund-raisers in a nearby park and netted about $700 from both events. That almost covered the $1,000 cost of phone calls from Marco and Lucy in the jail.

I met Anita at the second fund-raiser, held in September shortly before Marco and Lucy were sprung from jail. Anita wore a change belt, like a parking attendant at a rock concert. She sold a serving of Mexican custard for $1, gum and candy bars for $1, three *taquitos* or three *tostadas* for $3.50, pork rinds with lettuce for $2.50, and chips with salsa for fifty cents. She also sold $5 tickets to join a charity volleyball game. Marco had told Anita to go ahead and sell tickets to raffle off the beloved red Mitsubishi Eclipse. That effort failed; many immigrants said they'd buy tickets but never came forward with the cash. In the recession in Maricopa County, it was hard to part with even $1 for a game of chance.

A few days after Anita's fund-raiser, in mid-September 2009, Lucy and Marco were individually transferred from the jail to Immigration and Customs Enforcement detention centers, where they were processed by immigration authorities and released.

Jail had been difficult for Marco too. He and Lucy had been assigned to different buildings, and his greatest frustration was that he was unable to see or protect his wife. He wished there had been some way he could serve her sentence. While other inmates watched ESPN or played cards, Marco read his Bible. He kept turning to a passage in First Corinthians. It contains familiar phrases that you hear at weddings or funerals, like: *When I was a child, I talked like a child, I thought like a child, I reasoned like a child. When I became a man, I put my childish ways behind me.*

Marco decided that First Corinthians had a message for him: If he hated Sheriff Joe, he would be unable to love himself, his wife, his daughter, and God. So, in jail, he prayed for Sheriff Joe. He wanted to forgive him. Most of all, he wanted to forgive himself for asking Lucy to work with him at the car wash.

When they were home in their trailer again, they wept in each other's arms. They needed to heal, and they knew it, but they had no idea how difficult that healing would be.

• • •

When her parents returned to the mobile home park in Phoenix in the early fall of 2009, Angie transformed from a kid-trying-to-be-an-adult to a regular child again. She'd done as her Uncle Jack suggested; she'd bucked up in her parents' absence. Her efforts in that regard—all those tearful TV interviews and the marches—had been compiled on a CD by her extended family members so that her parents could review them when they got out of jail. But Marco and Lucy couldn't bear to put the CD in their laptop. They didn't want to see the trauma their daughter had endured.

That first night, Angie refused to return with her parents to their mobile home. She wanted everyone to sleep at her Aunt Anita and Uncle Jack's, where they would be safe. Angie feared that if she and her parents slept in their own trailer, Sheriff Joe's deputies would raid it and take her parents away again.

Angie turned ten in early November 2009. The family set long tables in the parking space adjacent to Anita and Jack's trailer and covered them with tablecloths. They strung streamers of pink crepe paper and cutouts of chocolate cupcakes on ribbons that ran across the roof of the parking space. They prepared Angie's favorite foods—spaghetti, pork chops, salsa, tortillas, and soda pop. Then they all sat down at the long table. Before everyone ate, Marco said grace. He thanked God for being reunited with his wife, and his child, and his family. He thanked God for being closer to his extended family than he'd ever been. And then he prayed for Sheriff Joe too.

The cake said **Happy Birthday, Angie!!!!** and was slathered with pink and red icing and decorated with butterflies and Oreo cookies. She blew out the candles as her large, warm, cohesive family sang *Las Mañanitas*, a traditional birthday song. Then Uncle Jack came up behind her and gently tipped her face into the cake.

Marco and Lucy, after their jail release, with Angie in their Phoenix mobile home. KATHY MCCRAINE

Angie laughed and squealed, Miss Icing Face, a happy ten-year-old kid again.

● ● ●

All through November, Marco and Lucy awaited their Social Security cards. They dared not work until the cards arrived. They believed they were being watched by authorities and knew that if they got caught working before the Social Security cards arrived, they might lose their opportunity to contest their deportation.

Jack paid their $380 monthly rental fee for their trailer space, helped with the $150 monthly electricity bill, paid for the cell phone, and made payments on their $5,000 credit card bill. A few churches had taken up collections for the family, and customers at the car wash, who'd known Marco for years, also pitched in. The church and car wash donations totaled about $1,000.

Marco was grateful for all the help, and accepted it, but it wore away at his sense of self-worth. He'd long prided himself on the way he had provided for his small family in Arizona, and for supporting his mother in Mexico as well. Now he could do neither.

Sometimes, Marco would be filled with hope. God would take care of him, he told himself, and soon he'd be back at work at the car wash and paying his bills. Other times, he became so despondent he wouldn't eat dinner at Jack and Anita's house, because he was embarrassed to eat food he hadn't paid for himself.

Marco and Lucy put a FOR SALE sign on their trailer and arranged the little lawn ornaments (a smiling scarecrow in a cart pulled by a comical donkey, a blond ceramic princess) on their postage stamp of a lawn. They loved their mobile home, but if they could sell it for $10,000, they would move into a small three-bedroom rental home in east Phoenix with Lucy's brother, Augustín, an unemployed undocumented landscaper, his wife, Dorotea, and their three kids.

But no one offered to buy the mobile home, and no one offered to buy Marco's cars either.

Desperate for cash, Marco, Lucy, Augustín, and Dorotea hatched the idea of having a massive garage sale every other week and decided they would sell everything they owned. I visited one garage sale, held on the lawn in front of the house where Augustín and Dorotea lived, just a few weeks before Christmas. Almost every item carried a memory—the lace tablecloth with the Last Supper imprint, the Frigidaire side-by-side, the hospital scrubs Marco wore on the day Angie was born, Angie's toys, desk, boots, the tiny TV Marco kept in his car for breaks from his watchman job, the life vest Angie wore on all those family outings to a nearby reservoir lake, the Halloween costumes, Winnie the Pooh towels, clothes.

"You get a big bag of clothes for $3. You pick the clothes out of the pile and stuff the bag full," Lucy told the Spanish speakers who stopped by.

An elderly Anglo woman picked up a ceramic kitchen sign that said DÍOS BENDIGA ESTE HOGAR (GOD BLESS THIS HOME). She puzzled over the foreign words, put it down, and focused on a large ceramic chicken that Lucy had used to store eggs. The woman bought it for $1.

At the end of the day, the two families had netted $190, thanks in large part to the sale of the $150 Frigidaire.

Two weeks later, the garage sale brought in $8.

The garage sale idea wasn't working, so the entire extended family made 360 tamales. They cooked pork and chicken in chile until the meat was fork tender; beat cornmeal dough, called *masa*, with lard until it was just the right texture. They softened dried corn husks in water and spooned *masa* on the moist, soft husks; added forkfuls of tender, spicy mea;, spread more *masa* on top of this; folded and tied each corn husk; then steamed the tamales in a tall, fat pot. They sold one dozen tamales for $10 and made $300. The same quantity and quality of tamales, made by undocumented immigrants in tamale shops, would have sold for $750 at upscale grocery stores in Phoenix.

Once, when Marco was in one of his darker moods, he told me: "Americans use us to make their money."

• • •

As I got to know Lucy better, I began to see her change. When I first met her, and observed her at family functions, she smiled at other people's jokes and lit up whenever Angie came near her. But when Angie wasn't near, or family members weren't talking to her directly, Lucy's eyes were sad and distant. I'd ask her what was on her mind, and she'd say she was happy to be home, far from Sheriff Joe's jail.

Then Lucy started dancing.

She remembered all those talks in jail with her friend the hotel maid. They'd spent hours talking about *matachines*. The troupe that the hotel maid belonged to was called *Matachines Estrella*, and it had been founded several years before by a heavyset laminator named Manuel, who'd been a *matachin* since childhood. Each October, Manuel assembled his troupe. In October 2009, Lucy appeared at his west Phoenix home with Angie, her sister-in-law, and two nieces. They had never danced as *matachines*, but they were eager learners.

They practiced at home every day and two nights a week in an alley behind Manuel's mother's house in west Phoenix. I accompanied them to one of these practices. First, Manuel hosed off the alley, to keep the dust down. Next, the dancers, dressed in sweatshirts, jeans, and tennis shoes, lined up against a block wall. Most of the dancers were women. Experienced dancers led, followed by the women and a few children. The adults carried gourd rattles or star-shaped tambourines decorated with green and red and silver Christmas tinsel.

I sat on a white plastic chair and waited.

Manuel's teenaged son, Matthew, the lead dancer, limbered up as Manuel strapped a large drum, the kind you see in rock bands, onto his waist. He'd cut the bottom out of the drum, to make it as loud as possible. The drumsticks were wooden dowels, and when Manuel beat on the drum, the lines of dancers began practicing ritualized steps. "High step, kick, tap one, tap two, tap three, now stomp, slide, heel-toe," Manuel's son yelled over the drumbeat to two lines of dancers behind him.

The *matachines* are a mix of indigenous and European tradition, just like the Virgin of Guadalupe and Mexico itself. The ritualized dances were brought to Mexico by the Spanish and Portuguese five centuries ago and adapted by Mexican Indians who'd been Christianized. Each region in Mexico has slightly different dances, music, and costumes. The dances tell stories. Frequently, they are stories of indigenous people and their European conquerors.

That historic subtext is not nearly as important to many dancers, including Lucy, who become *matachines* simply to honor their beloved brown *Virgencita*.

The feast day of the Virgin of Guadalupe is December 12, the day she appeared to the Indian Juan Diego in Tepeyac, Mexico. She had brown skin and spoke to him in his native Nahuatl and put magical roses in his cape. She became Mexico's completely emotionally available spiritual Super Mom. She will plead the case of even the most humble Mexican with all the male deities in her family.

A Mexican friend of mine once observed that working-class immigrants have such utter faith in the Virgin of Guadalupe that they see her image in tortillas and paint splatters on walls.

Lucy believed the *Virgencita* had kept her sane in jail and had protected Angie, and she wanted to dance in thanks. As I watched her practice in the Phoenix alley, I could see the dances had a transformative effect on her. She forgot the jail, Sheriff Joe, Guard X, and financial pressures.

By December, the forty-eight members of the *Matachines Estrella* dance troupe had perfected their moves and costumes. Manuel's family had roots in Durango, and the costumes reflected that geographical region. For headgear, dancers wore colorful bandannas emblazoned with an image of the Virgin of Guadalupe. They wore white, long-sleeved shirts with a likeness of the Virgin stamped on the backs and white, long pants. Over the pants they draped long, red skirts with side

Angie dances as a matachin. KATHY MCCRAINE

slits. Hundreds of tiny red, green, and silver rattles were sewn on the skirts, so that when the dancers moved, the skirts made music.

The troupe visited different immigrant neighborhoods as the feast day of the Virgin of Guadalupe neared, and danced after Rosary recitals. Once, they visited the trailer park where Angie, Lucy, and Marco lived. After dark, a procession of singing women carried a large statue of the Virgin of Guadalupe to a stand near the parking lot. The stand was decorated with roses and candles, and after the Virgin was placed on the stand, a group of about thirty people said Hail Marys in Spanish as the *Matachines Estrella* warmed up a few feet away.

When the Rosary ended, men, women, and children lined the parking lot, waiting for the dances to begin. You could hear the freeway traffic not far away, until Manuel pounded his drums and the *matachines* danced.

Lucy and Angie glowed with excitement and happiness, but it was a hard evening for Marco. The dances reminded him of his homeland, which got him to thinking about his mother and led him to worry that without his remittances his mother might not have enough to eat. It was one of those times when his frustration over not being able to feed his own family got the best of him, and he couldn't enjoy the spicy stew and traditional hot chocolate that his in-laws had prepared in honor of the *matachines*.

All during the holidays, Marco and Lucy sold tamales. It had been three long months since they'd been released from Sheriff Joe's jail, but they still didn't have their Social Security cards. They couldn't work. This meant they were still reliant on the support of their extended family. They faced extreme financial pressures. But this time, they were both upbeat.

Lucy had recently purchased a pregnancy test kit and had given herself the test. She was pregnant with her second child.

A few weeks later, she learned that she could live and work legally in the United States until at least July 2013, when she would appear in immigration court to fight her order of deportation.

· · ·

Marco received his Social Security card and work permit in February 2010, five months after he'd been released from jail. He could work legally in the United States until his immigration court hearing date in May 2012, almost a full year before Lucy's court date. He believed his court date had been scheduled earlier because he'd been assigned a judge with a less demanding docket.

The day after receiving his Social Security card and work permit, Marco was back on the job at Lindstrom Family Auto Wash. I brought my car in for a wash, just to see him on his first day at work. He didn't notice me as I watched him from the waiting room. He used both hands and red rags to shine a black BMW sedan. I'd never seen him so happy. He had his dignity again. He could feed his family. He could pay off his debts to Jack and Anita. He could pay his taxes using a legitimate Social Security number. He and Lucy could drive and travel. For two years, at least until his 2012 hearing in immigration court, Marco would no longer be forced to live in the shadows.

CHAPTER 4

America's Toughest Sheriff

First, Sheriff Joe Arpaio outfitted jail inmates
in pink underwear. Then he raided Latino neighborhoods.

One January afternoon in 2009, the Toughest Sheriff in America
stepped out of a black sedan parked near the front door of the Maricopa County Sheriff's Training Academy in Phoenix. The seventy-six-
year-old sheriff, who usually dresses in civvies, wore a pressed uniform
with metal collar pin. A large star-shaped badge was positioned just
above the left shirt pocket. This was a special day; Joe Arpaio would
soon be sworn in to his fifth term as sheriff of Maricopa County, the
epicenter of immigration controversy in America.

He'd gotten elected in part because his deputies and volunteer
posse members had been raiding Latino neighborhoods and workplaces, rounding up and jailing undocumented immigrants during
the election year. The immigrants were often turned over to Maricopa County Attorney Andrew Thomas for prosecution for such laws
as conspiring to smuggle themselves through Arizona. The sweeps
had resulted in outrage from pro-migrant activists, which Sheriff Joe
loved for two reasons. First, he delighted in conflict. Second, he loved
publicity.

Sheriff Joe knew the name of practically every reporter who had
covered him since he became sheriff in 1993, and he was an expert
manipulator of the media. "It doesn't matter if a story is good or bad,"
he once told me, "my poll ratings go up every time the press blasts
me." (The words *blast*, *Mickey Mouse*, and *garbage* surfaced often in my
interviews with Sheriff Joe.)

I stood in the January sunshine watching the sheriff joke with
aides who'd helped him win the 2008 election. His victory proved that
his round-up-the-Mexicans strategy had been politically astute. Once
again, Sheriff Joe was on top.

His wife of more than fifty years, Ava, had by then climbed out of the sedan and was standing by his side. She wore a black pantsuit, and her red fingernail polish matched her red lipstick. When Sheriff Joe laughed with his deputies, Ava smiled. When Sheriff Joe walked into the auditorium, Ava walked into the auditorium too. (In a rare Q and A with the *Arizona Republic* in 2009, Ava portrayed her husband as a romantic guy who never forgot Valentine's Day.)

I wasn't invited to this swearing-in event, but I attended it anyway, because as always I hoped to learn what made the sheriff tick. Was he all ambition and grandiosity? Was his ego so immense that it masked the pain he'd caused jail inmates and undocumented immigrants in order to advance himself?

Was he on some level a bully who'd been bullied himself?

There were plenty of empty seats in the room where Sheriff Joe's swearing-in ceremony would soon take place. Lisa Allen, a former television journalist and longtime Arpaio adviser and spokeswoman, began the ceremony by announcing that this time, a celeb would not swear in the sheriff. (Last term, John Walsh of *America's Most Wanted* had sworn in Sheriff Joe.) This time, she said, "we wanted to do something more substantive." So, she said, deputies had been dispatched to a citizenship ceremony at a hockey arena.

There they had found José Bello, a forty-five-year-old grocery store produce clerk from Mexico who had just become an American citizen. José had come to the United States twenty-five years before and had married a woman with a green card after knowing her for seventeen days. The Bellos' two adult children worked in Sheriff Joe's jails.

After Lisa Allen finished talking, José, a short man of medium build dressed in a gray suit, gave a short, nervous speech. (He spoke so softly I couldn't understand him.) Then he swore in the sheriff, reading from a paper. It took all of a minute or two.

Next, Sheriff Joe faced the reporters. Although he looked tall and fierce on television, in real life he was short and had a paunch. Square-shaped bifocals framed his shrewd, dark eyes. He said he supported José because José immigrated to America *legally*, just like his own parents, who had immigrated to America *legally* from Italy. When he emphasized "legally," he hesitated just for a split second and glowered, and this played well on TV, and he knew it. "I hope this sends a message: This is the greatest country in the world, and if you work hard you can do well here, especially if you do it *legally*."

This wasn't the first time Phoenix reporters had heard Sheriff Joe speak of his national and international fame, his parents who came *legally* from Italy, and his resolve to enforce immigration laws. "Does anyone have any questions?" Sheriff Joe asked. No one had any questions. "What's wrong with the news media?" Sheriff Joe asked, thin-lipped. One reporter asked gamely if the sheriff would go for Term Number Five. "This is Number Five," Sheriff Joe replied. "Can't you count?"

The reporters focused their attention on José Bello, who looked as if he'd rather be anywhere but in that auditorium, having just sworn in a sheriff who was reviled in the Latino community. But José's kids worked for the sheriff, and he didn't really have much of a choice. When the reporters asked why he'd swear in a guy who ordered sweeps of Latino neighborhoods, he looked even more miserable and said the sheriff was obligated to enforce the law.

• • •

The raids began in 2006 but picked up speed in 2008, almost a year before the sheriff was sworn in for the fifth time. Sheriff Joe called them "crime suppression operations," but everyone knew he was on the prowl for undocumented immigrants. His hunting grounds were Latino gathering places. Thrust out of jobs by the Employer Sanctions Act and a slowdown in the construction boom, highly skilled immigrants (like electricians and carpenters) now gathered on street corners seeking day labor. They hoped to move furniture or clean yards for a fraction of what they'd earned before the new law. This explains why Sheriff Joe's deputies raided the area around a Phoenix furniture store, where day laborers gathered. Next, they raided neighborhoods surrounding Macehualli, a day labor center for immigrants that had been approved by the city of Phoenix. After that raid, members of the hate group United for a Sovereign America (USA) picketed Macehualli and took down the license numbers of every car that picked up laborers there. They forwarded the license numbers to the sheriff's office.

And then, on April 3, 2008, Sheriff Joe's deputies raided Guadalupe, a Phoenix suburb. The raid lasted two days.

Guadalupe is home to about 5,500 people, and it sits just off Interstate 10, on the east side of Phoenix. Around 1900, Yaqui Indians from Sonora, Mexico, came to Arizona seeking refuge from persecution. They settled in the desert near Phoenix and named their settlement in honor of the *Virgencita*. The community has always welcomed a mix of Latinos and indigenous people, and until the raid, it was most famous for its Mexican-Indian Easter ceremonies, which included Catholic processions and Yaqui deer dances.

The little town has a missionlike Catholic church, a plaza, a marketplace, and pastel-tinted adobe houses with scarlet hollyhocks poking out of the front yards. Other sections of Guadalupe are blighted, gang-infested. For years, the Maricopa County Sheriff's Office had contracted with the town to provide law-enforcement services, but residents had long complained that the sheriff's office failed to adequately investigate crimes and took way too long to respond to their emergency calls. The sheriff's office maintained that it was shorthanded in Guadalupe.

But on the afternoon of April 3, 2008, the sheriff's office wasn't shorthanded in Guadalupe. I know. I was there. I had gone to Guadalupe to immerse myself in a raid, to learn from the people affected what it feels like when deputies sweep into town in dark SUVs with tinted windows, in unmarked cars, in marked cars, on motorcycles, in a helicopter, on horseback, and on foot.

I drove into Guadalupe in the midafternoon. The air smelled of motor exhaust and horses. Helicopter blades clacked overhead, and sirens went on and off. Otherwise, the town was creepily silent. Deputies stopped cars for infractions as minor as cracked windshields and broken taillights. I wondered how I'd feel about this raid if I had immigrated to the United States from a country like Mexico, where the police can be brutal.

I parked near the main drag, Avenida del Yaqui, and noticed police lights flashing in front of Guadalupe Market. Two sheriff's vehicles— an unmarked red four-wheel-drive truck with Sinaloa, Mexico, plates and a black sedan emblazoned with gold-tinted sheriff insignia—had stopped a car for a cracked windshield. The passenger of the car, a twenty-seven-year-old air-conditioning repairman named Matthew Gonzales, sat on the curb. He was offended, upset, and confused. He told me his cousin, the driver, had been arrested for driving with a suspended license. He and his cousin were both American citizens, he said, and his cousin should not have been hauled off to jail for a "freakin' misdemeanor.

"They treated us like criminals," he said.

"We didn't commit no crimes."

I offered him a bottle of water, but he didn't want it. He kept his eyes on the street, hoped that soon his brother would pick him up. Together, the two would drive downtown to Sheriff Joe's jail and bail out their misdemeanor-charged cousin.

Across the street, Andrew Sanchez, who was twenty-five years old, a Guadalupe resident, and a college student, ran from shop to restaurant to adobe home, knocking on closed doors. He clutched papers containing phone numbers of immigrant-rights activists who could offer help to anyone who might be arrested. I lost sight of him after he passed Cota's Garage, where a man tinkering with the bowels of an engine looked up from beneath the hood at me. "The sheriff deputies usually take their own sweet time answering our calls," he said. "Now look at this.

"This is something else."

He was right. This *was* something else. The sheriff's sweeps targeted Latinos by the very fact that they took place in Latino communities. I was becoming more and more uncomfortable.

At the Veda Frank Elementary School, a sign read ATTENDANCE IS THE FIRST STEP TO SUCCESS. Even so, seventy kids didn't show up for school on April 3, 2008. Their parents had seen the flashing lights and guns and deputies. They'd kept their children home. Now the school day had ended, and I saw a couple of sheriff's vehicles drive slowly past the school. Most of the kids had gone home, but a few hid inside the school. Teachers volunteered as chauffeurs, drove their pupils home, and made sure parents were inside, and not detained in the raid, before they drove off again.

Bernadette Kadel, the principal, met me in the school courtyard. "I guarantee you," she told me, "half of the student body will not be here tomorrow. Parents see sheriff cars and motorcycles parked by the school, and even if they are citizens, they won't think it's safe for their kids to be here. And testing starts next week. These kids are not in the right frame of mind to take tests. ... This whole experience is devastating to us."

Shortly before sunset, I walked a few blocks to the sheriff's command station. On the way, I passed two signs. One, in Spanish, warned that Sheriff Joe was raiding the town. Another said ARPAIO, STOP USING AND ABUSING US. The command station was set up in the parking lot of a dollar store, and as far as I could tell it was made up of a cluster of sheriff's vehicles—big buses, four-wheel drives, sedans. A crowd of journalists, along with about three hundred immigrant-rights advocates, attorneys, locals, and demonstrators, stood in front of a chain-link fence. This fence blocked the crowd from the command center. Uniformed men on horseback stood ready to break up the crowd should it get unruly. I couldn't tell who was a posse member and who was a deputy, but I figured the overweight oldsters guarding the perimeter of the command center had to be part of the sheriff's volunteer posse, which had three thousand members and was the largest posse in the United States.

Every now and then, a brown-skinned person in handcuffs was escorted from one vehicle to another in the command center. Alfredo Gutierrez, an immigrant-rights advocate who had once been a powerful and respected state senator, shouted into a bullhorn each time a handcuffed person stepped into view. "Insist on a lawyer. Don't sign anything." Later, he told me that he believed Arizona in the twenty-first century is to Latinos what Alabama and Mississippi were to African Americans in the 1960s.

As it grew darker, cars passed slowly by, blaring horns as a sign of solidarity for the immigrants. (Deputies arrested one horn honker for disturbing the peace.) In a corner, a group of Catholics finished up the Rosary, then sang *Ave María*. Every now and then the crowd would break into a chant: *¡Aquí estamos! ¡No nos vamos! ¡Y si nos echan, regresamos!* (We are here! … We aren't leaving! … And if they throw us out, we'll return!) A few locals sat in lawn chairs, observing the scene. Like practically everyone else, they were perplexed. How could this be happening in the United States of America?

I looked for the usual pro-sheriff demonstrators, mostly Anglo retirees, Minutemen, neo-Nazis, and bikers, many of whom were members of United for a Sovereign America. Sheriff Joe has always said he loathed racists and racism, but he didn't seem to discourage them from coming out to support him.

The Toughest Sheriff in America appeared just in time for the 10:00 p.m. news, live, from the sheriff's command center in Guadalupe. As Joe Arpaio talked to television reporters, Rebecca Jimenez, the mayor of Guadalupe, walked up to him, right in front of the cameras, and asked the sheriff to stop the raid.

He came back the next day in full force, but by then everyone knew the place was being raided. The Guadalupe raid lasted two days. The sheriff's office arrested forty-seven people in those two days. Only nine of the forty-seven were undocumented immigrants. Even though nine migrants isn't much compared to the estimated half-million undocumented people who lived in Arizona at the time, the psychological terror the raids caused was palpable and irreversible.

Migrants tend to be intense newshounds; they hunger for news in print, on the Internet, on TV, and on the radio. They monitor the news because it keeps them current on the laws in Arizona and the national politics of immigration reform, both of which determine their future. The televised Guadalupe raids unnerved many, especially those who had to drive long distances to get to work. Would the sheriff stop them for a cracked windshield? Commuters cut their wavy black hair and stopped wearing signature baseball caps when they drove. Still others stopped driving altogether, choosing taxis and buses for their transport. Local grocery stores that catered to Latinos shuttled wary housewives from home to the store, and back.

Sheriff Joe said his raids were perfectly legal. Everyone knew he had tremendous power in Maricopa County and ruled it like a kingdom. The county spanned 9,226 square miles and included Phoenix and twenty-three other cities and towns. Sheriff Joe had the statutory authority to enforce the law anyplace in the county, including towns and cities. This meant that even though most municipalities had their own police forces, Sheriff Joe could still perform a "crime suppression operation" anyplace he chose.

The sheriff had expanded his law enforcement authority in 2007, when he signed an agreement with Immigration and Customs Enforcement, called a 287(g) agreement. It's a clunky-sounding name, but what it boiled down to is that ICE-trained sheriff's deputies could enforce federal immigration law on the streets. The sheriff's 287(g) agreement with ICE also enabled deputies to check the immigration status of each and every one of the approximately ten thousand inmates in Maricopa County's vast jail system. The jail checks were political gold, because the sheriff could brag on his Web site about all the undocumented immigrants he'd turned over to ICE.

By March 2010, the sheriff's office itself had apprehended a total of 3,771 undocumented immigrants in Maricopa County.

Another 32,280 undocumented immigrants were flagged in Maricopa County jails under the ICE 287(g) agreement.

The sheriff liked to say things like: "I'm the only one enforcing immigration laws. I've turned over thirty-two thousand illegals over to ICE."

Few of his supporters understood that the sheriff didn't actually round up those 32,280 immigrants—*they were already in jail.* Most of them had been delivered to the jails by other police agencies.

In 2009, Janet Napolitano revoked Sheriff Joe's 287(g) powers to enforce immigration laws on the streets. However, she allowed him to keep the 287(g) agreement in the jails. Keeping the 287(g) agreement in the jails was political gold for Sheriff Joe. It ensured his head count of "illegals" turned over to ICE would remain high, which would cement his popularity with Minutemen and other anti-migrant groups, his core supporters.

Napolitano's denial of the 287(g) powers on the streets really didn't hurt Sheriff Joe. He vowed to continue his raids anyway, because he could catch immigrants under the state Employer Sanctions Act and the human-smuggling law.

Even though the number of immigrants Sheriff Joe rounded up in the raids was relatively small, the sweeps caused disproportionate psychological distress. Sheriff Joe told me that the fear factor was important, because immigrants wouldn't want to settle in Maricopa County. Or they'd pull up stakes and leave. I once told him that most of the undocumented people I'd talked to were terrified of him.

"I feel sorry for illegals," he answered.

"Why don't they come into my office and talk to me?"

Until anti-immigrant fervor took over Arizona, Sheriff Joe had been lionized by many in the Hispanic community in Phoenix.

"I was once the hero, the *hero*, of the Hispanic community," he told me, leaning forward a little. Years before, when one of his reserv-

Migrants in Sheriff Joe's Tent City in Phoenix. KATHY MCCRAINE

ists pulled a gun on a carload of people "who looked Mexican and illegal," he arrested the reservist. And once he arranged for a Mexican woman to fly from Phoenix to Puerto Vallarta to pick up her kids, who had been kidnapped by her murderer-husband. "She was illegal," he told me. "So people said, 'Sheriff, why do you allow illegals to come in the country?' and I said, 'Well I sent her there to rescue her kids, who were American citizens.' I was a *hero*. Now I'm the worst enemy of the Hispanic groups because I enforce immigration laws."

So what changed?

As illegal immigration picked up in the early 2000s, resentment of undocumented immigrants was particularly strong in Arizona, the gateway for most illegal immigration. Absent federal action, state legislators passed the strongest human-smuggling and workplace-enforcement laws in the nation.

I asked Sheriff Joe whether he began his controversial sweeps because they were politically expedient, and he said he was already popular, he could be governor if he wanted to, he didn't need the immigration headaches to be elected. He said he answered *only* to the people of Maricopa County. He didn't answer to Mickey Mouse activists and reporters. The people of Maricopa County wanted the "illegals" gone. His job was to enforce the law, and the Arizona Legislature had passed several laws that criminalized activities of undocumented immigrants. So he could and would continue his crime-suppression operations. He said he did not target Latinos. He said he did not racially profile. He said he was not racist. He said his raids were legal. Period.

• • •

Sheriff Joe ratcheted up the immigration raids even as his opposition strengthened in 2008. As newspapers, think tanks, and the federal government scrutinized him, his deputies raided more Latino neighborhoods, as well as workplaces, like the Lindstrom Family Auto Wash and Water World. They even raided the city of Mesa's library and city hall, in search of undocumented janitorial workers. (At the time Sheriff Joe was sparring with the Mesa police chief, who'd criticized the raids.) American citizens caught in the raids said that they'd been racially profiled, that they had been stopped simply because of their skin color.

Two reporters for the *East Valley Tribune*, a local suburban newspaper, pored over public records, including arrest documents and financial data, and reported that Sheriff Joe's transformation of his office into a de facto immigration agency came at great cost to the general public. According to the *Tribune*, Sheriff Joe funneled so much money and manpower into nabbing undocumented immigrants that his office failed to investigate serious crimes, like rapes of teenage girls in Latino neighborhoods. The *Tribune* reported that the deputies "regularly make traffic stops based only on their suspicion that illegal immigrants are inside vehicles. They figure out probable cause after deciding whom to pull over." The newspaper also claimed the sheriff's sweeps might have violated "federal regulations intended to prevent racial profiling."

The reporters won a 2008 Pulitzer Prize for the series, and when Sheriff Joe heard about it, he was on Comedy Central's *The Colbert Report* promoting his second book, *Joe's Law*. He told me he later called the reporters and congratulated them for their Pulitzer, but the entire series was "garbage."

"Let them blast me," he told me. "I ought to pay them for blasting me, since it makes me go up in the polls."

Sheriff Joe seemed to vacillate between loving bad press and hating bad press. Some days, he believed the leftist "local media" were out to get him. "When you arrest people who are illegal in the workplace, and two-thirds are committing a Class 4 felony, I am the bad guy. If we arrested forty-four redheads, I'd be the great guy. ... But the minute you mention *illegal*, it takes you to another area. I think that's sad."

Of course, a lot of those felony convictions were associated with state-immigration crimes like conspiring to smuggle oneself through Arizona or working with a fake ID.

The outrage among Latinos was palpable. Pro-migrant picketers stood daily on the sidewalk in front of the sheriff's office. Some carried signs that said, WE ARE NOT ILLEGALS. Others carried posters that depicted him as a Klansman. The picketers vowed to stand on the streets every day until Wells Fargo Bank, which owned the downtown Phoenix building where the sheriff's office was located, kicked the sheriff out. (In February 2010, Wells Fargo informed the sheriff it needed the space where his offices were located for an expansion of the bank. At this writing, the sheriff hasn't budged.)

• • •

In 2008, the conservative, Phoenix-based Goldwater Institute think tank issued a report that took Sheriff Joe to task for allowing a "huge backlog of outstanding warrants to accumulate" and for spending tax dollars on ineffective immigration enforcement that otherwise might be spent protecting the people of Maricopa County.

Even the local newspaper, the *Arizona Republic*, which in the early years of Sheriff Joe's reign had often written fawning stories about him, began to question him. The newspaper's editorial page was especially critical. What's fascinating about this is that the sheriff's son-in-law, Phil Boas, was editor of the *Republic*'s editorial pages. I've known him for many years, and have even written a few pieces for him. He's an ethical, top-notch journalist who excused himself from any editorial discussion of his controversial father-in-law, but as the negative editorials intensified, I wondered how the two dealt with it on a personal level. "Every time we have a family dinner, I hear about it," Boas told me. "But it's always with a gleam in his eye. We both understand that bad press goes with the turf." Boas believed Sheriff Joe was motivated by a "law and order thing," but he understood that immigrants were terrified of his father-in-law. Boas voiced great sympathy for undocumented immigrants and understood their need to come to the United States to provide for their families. "I hope I would do the same thing," he told me. Differences in opinion aside, he rated Sheriff Joe as a wonderful father-in-law.

I asked Sheriff Joe how he dealt with the potentially awkward family relationship, and he said, Boas "does his thing and I do mine. ... I don't talk to him every day. Once in a while we'll get together for the holidays. So, no, there's no problem at all. Great relationship."

Newspaper reports and think tanks and TV newscasts that showed handcuffed immigrants led away by deputies all served to galvanize Sheriff Joe's opponents, who took to the streets to protest his treatment of immigrants. On May 2, 2009, for instance, several thousand demonstrators marched about five miles to protest the treatment of undocumented immigrants in Maricopa County jails. (A few undocumented people had alleged physical abuse—a woman claimed jail guards had broken her arm, for instance, when she refused to be fingerprinted.) The march was led by religious leaders from different denominations and a troupe of indigenous dancers wearing peacock feather headdresses and shells tied to their ankles. A drummer pounded a beat for the dancers, and someone blew through a mournful conch shell. I heard the familiar Guadalupe raid chant, "*Y si nos echan, ¡regresamos!*" The marchers were of all ages and of all ethnic persuasions and from all walks of life. Some were undocumented and some were not. They carried signs saying, WE ARE HUMAN! and REPEAL 287(G). The march ended near one of the sheriff's jails, and a popular Spanish-language radio station had set up a stage there. A large piñata of Sheriff Joe's head was attached to the stage.

Phoenix police lined up to keep marchers from interacting with about a hundred supporters of Sheriff Joe standing on the sidewalk. Many of the pro-Joe crowd wore surgical masks and carried signs that said immigrants were diseased. One nineteen-year-old neo-Nazi stomped on a Mexican flag in an effort to provoke a fight with the marchers, but no one paid much attention to him.

"I am standing up for what I believe in," the young neo-Nazi told me, "and it feels good."

• • •

On the same day as the march, Sheriff Joe attended his own "Support Sheriff Joe Arpaio Rally" in Sun City, Arizona.

Sun City is a retirement enclave sitting on the west side of Maricopa County. It's got a lot of palm trees and tract homes with rock lawns, and if you're younger than fifty, you can't live in Sun City. Residents tend to be conservative, white, and Republican. Some are veterans of World War II and the Korean War, and they see the America they fought for vanishing. In my years as a Phoenix journalist, I've come to see Sun City as tense. People are afraid of falling prey to crime, afraid of going broke, afraid of losing America to brown people, and afraid of dying.

Sheriff Joe's rally was held outside a Sun City recreation center. At the time, swine flu had broken out in Mexico. This terrified a lot of his two hundred or so supporters who'd gathered to hear him speak. The supporters wanted those "illegals" out of Maricopa County, and fast, before they gave everyone in the county the deadly swine flu.

The sheriff's supporters wore sun hats and sat in lawn chairs. Some waved American flags. Some carried signs that said SUPPORT SHERIFF JOE ENFORCING THE LAW. Others carried signs that said WE SUPPORT THE SHERIFF AND 287(G). The sheriff, dressed in a black golf shirt and gray slacks, chatted with elderly women who hugged him. He shook hands with veterans. These were his people. He was in high spirits.

"Let me tell you my secret," he once told me. "I average two speeches a day, you know. I've been doing it for seventeen years. That's how I override all the [negative] media because the people get to see me and hear the *true story*. ... That's why my polls are always high."

At the Sun City rally, a woman named Jo, a sixty-one-year-old retiree wearing a white sun visor, a striped shirt, jeans, and white tennis shoes, carried a WHAT PART OF ILLEGAL DON'T YOU UNDERSTAND sign. She told me she'd worked at a school cafeteria and the illegal kids didn't have to get shots. "Can you imagine?" she asked. Nearby, a woman who declined to give her name confided she wouldn't even drive into Phoenix, what with all the illegals running around. She said: "I'll stay right here in my little compound."

I turned my attention back to the sheriff. He was shaking hands with Chris Simcox, a small man with an inscrutable expression on his face. Simcox once headed the Minuteman Civil Defense Corps, a group that patrolled the border looking for immigrants. (The group's Web site blamed "illegals" for all sorts of national ills. One posting said, in part: *Now we find out that 60% of the foreclosures causing the financial crisis are related to illegals getting mortgages.*)

Sheriff Joe climbed up a little hill and looked down at his supporters. He stepped up to the microphone. A gust of wind snapped a large American flag behind him. He said he answered only to the people of Arizona. He said his enemies didn't scare him. He said he'd never back down. He said he was the only lawman enforcing immigration laws to protect the people of Maricopa County. Then he let his guard down. After all, he was in Sun City.

"All those illegals sneaking in could have swine flu."

He waited for the applause to stop. "We have so many unemployed people; why are we giving so many jobs to *illegals*?" His officers recently arrested an "illegal" who earned $85,000 annually, he told the crowd. "An *illegal*," he said, incredulously.

In about ten minutes, he touched on every major fear Sun City residents harbored—loss of money, loss of health, and loss of America to "illegals." Then he spoke of the protest march that was taking place that very same day, and how "just for fun" he was going downtown to face the demonstrators. He suggested the Sun City folks go down there, too, and join forces with his supporters already on the sidewalk. He didn't seem to mind asking frail Sun City oldsters to join bikers and Minutemen and neo-Nazis.

"I need your moral support," he said. "If I don't have your support and go down in the polls, they will eat me up and spit me out."

A few ladies in the crowd sang "For He's a Jolly Good Fellow."

• • •

One day, I asked Sheriff Joe if he would draw a map of the route he took to the movies as a child in his hometown of Springfield, Massachusetts. I'd hoped to get him talking about his boyhood memories, since he rarely spoke about his childhood beyond the fact that his parents came to America from Italy *legally*. His two books, cowritten by Len Sherman, glorify his law enforcement career and anti-illegals escapades but say next to nothing about his boyhood.

Oddly, the sheriff would later say in a deposition that he'd never read at least one of his own books.

His books say that he was born in Springfield, Massachusetts, and that his mother died in childbirth.

On his seventy-seventh birthday, in 2009, on his @realsheriffjoe Twitter page, he tweeted: *My birthday is always a day of reflection for me as some of you may know, it is also the day that my mother passed.*

Several times, I'd asked how his mother's death affected him, and he would only say he never knew what it was like to have a mother, but he turned out just fine. His books hint of a waifish childhood.

Sheriff Joe's own memory seems foggy; once he told me he and his father lived with only one family. Another time he told me they lived with two families. In any case, his father had married a woman named Rose when Sheriff Joe was twelve. Soon, he had a stepbrother, Michael. I asked him to characterize his childhood, and he said, "Well, you know, it's tough. Stepmothers are sometimes tough." This is where the movies came in. As a kid, he walked alone to a little movie house, which he called The Gardens. He paid 25 cents to see a double feature. He remembers watching Flash Gordon, Batman, the Lone Ranger, and Gene Autry.

"I used to walk a mile," he told me.

He drew a circle to mark his house and a circle to mark The Gardens and connected them with a bold line, then shoved the pad and pencil across his desk to me.

"OK, this is my house, 21 Cedar Street, and uh, I walked down to The Gardens this way. It was pretty tough in the winter when the snow was over my head.

"I used to go to the cowboy movies, and I used to see the sheriff swear in private business people and say, 'Hey, go after the horse thieves,' and so they went after the horse thieves. They used to hang them before they got back to jail, but that's another issue. So I said, 'Wait a minute, I'm going to build up my posse.' I have the authority to swear in the whole county if I want to make them posse people. And I do have three thousand [posse members]."

He told me he never developed a single hobby, but he still goes to the movies, because "it takes you out of reality, it's enjoyable. I got DirecTV, it must cost me thousands. I got everything you can get on TV. I got the big screen TV, high definition, but still I like to go to the movie theater."

What kinds of movies did he prefer?

"All kinds of movies. Dog movies. Love stories. Actions. Bang, bang, bang."

I pushed for more details of his youth in Springfield, and he would only tell me that he played sports in high school and that he "wasn't the best student so I had to study very hard to get a C average [while] I worked at my father's grocery store delivering groceries."

Did anyone ever bully him?

"No."

He left Springfield when he was eighteen, joined the Army, became a cop in Washington, D.C., married Ava, became a cop in Las Vegas (he claims in his book he stopped Elvis on a speeding violation and took him down to the police station for laughs), and then moved on to a stellar (he says) career with the Drug Enforcement Administration. He and Ava were stationed in Turkey (he claims he helped solve the French Connection case) and Mexico, among other places, and he was the chief agent in several posts. He moved to Phoenix in 1978, replacing Phil Jordan as special agent in charge of DEA's local office. Jordan, who went on to other posts and eventually retired, told me in 2009 that as a DEA agent Joe Arpaio had "never worked on a big case" and was a "braggart" who was "paranoid about the whole world."

The future Sheriff Joe retired from DEA in 1982. Ava operated a travel agency, and the two bought real estate. For ten years he and Ava ran family businesses. In 1992, he was elected sheriff of Maricopa County. He told me he ran for sheriff because he was tired of working for his wife.

Shortly after taking office, he opened up "Tent City," a complex of Korean War surplus tents where sentenced inmates serve out their time. His early years were marked by one publicity stunt after another. After Tent City, the most famous publicity trick was outfitting inmates in pink underwear.

"Let me tell you a secret," Sheriff Joe once told me. "There isn't anything you can ask me that I can't give you a reasonable answer as to why I do something. I always have an official reason to ward off all the critics and lawsuits. Now I may have my own reasons too."

For instance, the official reason for making inmates wear pink underwear, he said, was to prevent theft. Inmates tended to steal underwear. But no one would steal *pink* underwear.

"You want my reason? Because they hate pink, that's why. At least in this county. They may like it in San Francisco, but they don't like it here."

We were sitting in his downtown Phoenix office. He wore a sports jacket and slacks, and his trademark gold tie clip shaped like a pistol.

Sheriff Joe Arpaio in his Phoenix office, several months before the grand jury probe. KATHY MCCRAINE

His office resembled a made-for-television stage, with a VACANCY sign pointing toward another sign that said: TENT CITY. The signs conveyed the idea that Tent City was comical, like the Pinkerton Detective Agency figurines he collected. A vanity license plate tacked on the Tent City stage read MY WAY. (The Sinatra song is his favorite tune; it's the ringtone on his cell phone, and he sings it publicly when asked.) He told me he was the most famous sheriff in the world, and that more than three thousand profiles had been written about him. Soon, he said, the *New Yorker* would run its profile of him, and a *GQ* writer was scheduled to interview him for still another profile.

The sweeps had made him more famous. Every major newspaper wrote about the raids, and Lou Dobbs, a CNN commentator, lionized him for his immigration raids.

"Well, you know, they call you KKK like they did me, that's an honor. It means we're doing something," Sheriff Joe told Dobbs in 2007.

Sheriff Joe even had his own reality show on the Fox Reality Channel for a while. It was called *Smile … You're Under Arrest*. In the show, actors punk'd Maricopa County residents with outstanding warrants after luring them on camera with fake giveaways. People with outstanding warrants don't usually elicit sympathy, but the actors were uncomfortably cruel and mocked the clueless people about to be arrested. In a spa giveaway sequence, for instance, a man about to be arrested agreed to wear a goofy black-and-white-striped spa robe. The actors covered the man's eyes with cucumber slices and painted his face like a clown, with mud. The cameras showed Sheriff Joe laughing in the control room.

"Let me tell you something and I'm not bragging," Sheriff Joe told me in 2009. "I'm so high profile I went from 98 percent to probably 99 percent on name identification. … You know, sometimes I understand how a movie star feels, or a celebrity. Actually you get tired sometimes of everybody coming up to you. And yet I like it because it drives me because the people appreciate what I'm doing. When they come up and say, 'Thank you, sheriff, we support you,' well, that keeps me going."

He was right. For years, Maricopa County folks had supported him. They supported him when he forced inmates to wear pink handcuffs to match the underwear, right along with those photogenic Laurel-and-Hardy-like baggy black-and-white-striped jail chinos. He'd initiated volunteer chain gangs, in which costumed inmates in leg chains dug pauper's graves and picked up litter. He'd gotten laughs from his supporters because he saved the taxpayers money by cutting inmates' meals down to two a day and by depriving inmates of coffee and condiments. He said the dogs in his animal-rescue operation cost more to feed than the inmates. People in Maricopa County loved that he ran austere jails for criminals. After all, criminals deserved it.

What few of Sheriff Joe's supporters understood was that only two thousand of the approximately ten thousand inmates in the jails were actually criminals.

The other eight thousand inmates in the sheriff's seven jails awaited court dates.

Once sentenced, serious criminals were sent to prison to serve their sentences. Minor criminals, including undocumented immigrants, served short sentences in the jails.

Many were housed in Tent City.

• • •

I visited Tent City twice in the summer months of 2009. I wanted to see the place for myself, although I knew my forays would not reveal whether undocumented immigrants were mistreated in the sheriff's jails. If bad things happened, they didn't happen in tents visited by journalists.

The tents and the immigrant-inmates were all part of Sheriff Joe's publicity machine. Both times I visited, the jail guards were media savvy. My visits to the so-called O Tents, where some undocumented immigrants were housed, seemed routine to the guards and the inmates. Everyone was used to visitors. Sheriff Joe told me four presidential candidates, including Bob Dole, the "Viagra guy," had visited the tents.

Anti-Arpaio demonstrators march in Phoenix. TERRY GREENE STERLING

"Why would they come here, next to the little old sheriff, when they're running for president, if the tents are that bad? If they're that bad, why would they come? I tried to get Hillary here last year. Oh no, she's not going to the tents."

On the days I visited, the temperature exceeded one hundred degrees, and some inmates had their heads wrapped in wet towels. I'd always thought that Tent City inmates had to survive in sweltering heat, but I learned that they could cool off in an air-cooled recreation-dining room. The cool room, the guards told me, was open throughout the day except for the few minutes when inmates were counted.

The rec room I walked through smelled of soap and disinfectant and was furnished with long tables with stainless steel tops. Phones and emergency medical equipment were attached to the wall. A television with a lock on it was tuned to Lou Dobbs.

Outside, two tall towers overlooked a razor-wired compound of about twenty neatly aligned green-brown tents. No jail guards manned the towers, but many a news photographer and videographer had climbed up to shoot pictures of the tents. Inmates slept on double bunks, fitted with sheets and blankets and flat pillows. Their bunks were placed in neat rows, and in the summer, unless it rained, the tent flaps were rolled up. No nudie magazines were allowed in Sheriff Joe's jails, so inmates cut out pictures of fully clothed women from approved magazines, like *Golf Digest*, and pinned these up on their bunks.

The immigrants wore plastic slippers, black-and-white chinos, and the world-famous pink underwear. Many inmates had been sentenced to short stints in the jail for their crimes, which ranged from making false documents to drunken driving. Thirty-nine-year-old Jorge told me he sold false ID documents to an undercover detective. A former mechanic, he'd lost his job when Arizona banned the hiring of undocumented immigrants and turned to forgery to take care of his wife and kids. He'd crossed from Mexico into the United States with a tourist visa years before. When the tourist visa expired, he stayed on. After serving three months for his crime, he and most other inmates would be deported to Mexico. He told me the bad food and pink underwear were minor nuisances compared to not knowing when or if he would ever see his wife again.

I sat on a bunk, and about a half-dozen men had gathered around me, hungry to tell their stories. Jaime, who was thirty-two, spoke nearly perfect English because he'd attended community colleges in the nine years since he left his native Michoacán and crossed into Arizona. He was a heavy equipment operator for a construction company, married to a U.S. citizen. Life was good, he told me, until the cops picked him up for DUI. Now he'd lost everything. After serving three months, he'd be sent back to Mexico. "I'll face years in prison if I try to come back," he told me. He could slap himself for his stupid mistake.

The stories were almost indistinguishable. The inmates had done stupid things, and had become petty criminals. Nevertheless, federal immigration laws were such that if they returned to the United States after being deported, they would become major criminals. They would face federal entry-after-deportation charges and, depending on their prior criminal records, could spend from one to twenty years in prison. Their greatest fears were not how they would survive in Mexico, but rather how they could exist without their families in Arizona.

No one complained of mistreatment, although a few said it was *poco caliente*—a little hot. No one liked the food, and everyone had lost weight. A few said they lived off the expensive snacks they bought in the canteen with money sent by their families.

• • •

Sheriff Joe seemed on edge during my last visit, in the late summer of 2009, to his office. His problems were mounting. He fretted that *GQ* was waffling about profiling him because its sister publication, the *New Yorker*, had just published his profile. He seemed disappointed. But he had more serious problems, and he knew it. Two men caught in the raids—an American citizen and a legal resident—had filed a racial-profiling suit against the sheriff. What's more, the jail health-care system was substandard, and accreditation had been denied. Inmates were suing over poor medical care. (He wouldn't talk to me about either lawsuit.) On top of all this, the U.S. Department of Labor was investigating back-pay claims of sheriff personnel.

The most serious threat to his career was a U.S. Department of Justice civil-rights investigation of the sheriff over racial-profiling allegations. Sheriff Joe deemed the investigation without merit, purely political. He'd decided he wasn't going to cooperate with the Justice Department's probe.

This wasn't his first trouble with the Justice Department. In 1997, Sheriff Joe agreed to a slew of improvements—more training of personnel, investigation of use of force on inmates, medical assessment of inmates assigned to Tent City—after experts hired by both the Justice Department and the county found some substandard conditions in the jails. He signed a second agreement with the Justice Department in 1999, promising to give inmates their prescriptions and other necessary medical care, and promising to investigate strange deaths and injuries of inmates that involved jail guards.

That settlement was worked out with then U.S. Attorney for the District of Arizona Janet Napolitano, the future governor of Arizona and director of the Department of Homeland Security. Napolitano's critics have long charged that the Democrat Napolitano opted not to sue Sheriff Joe and brokered the Justice Department settlement so that Sheriff Joe would endorse her for governor. She needed Republican votes, and got them, and won the election. I made several requests, via telephone calls and e-mails to Napolitano's Department of Homeland Security media office, over the span of several months, for an interview with Napolitano. The Department of Homeland Security would not arrange an interview. Interestingly, a spokesperson told me the department's legal division reviewed my request but concluded that book authors were not technically considered journalists.

Honestly, I've never been able to figure this *book-authors-aren't-journalists* excuse. Officials at every level of government had granted me interviews, with the exception of Janet Napolitano, Andrew Thomas, and the Phoenix Police kidnapping unit.

And Sheriff Joe spent hours with me.

• • •

In 2009, I asked Sheriff Joe if maybe he had made a political mistake going after undocumented immigrants.

"I don't do things for politics. I do it to serve the people. You want to say I do it for politics," he said.

I asked, was he in good health, what with all the conflict? Of course, he said. He ate too much spaghetti, but other than that he was fine. The conflict with *Phoenix New Times*, the *Arizona Republic*, the Justice Department, litigious inmates, and marching immigrant-rights supporters didn't hurt his health one bit. He pointed to his thinning, reddish-brown hair, which appeared to be slicked into place with some sort of hair product. "I don't dye my hair. If I'm fighting so much, why don't I have gray hair? Usually people who worry get gray hair, lose weight, look like they're ninety when they're seventy. Here I am seventy-seven years old and there is no one in this universe who will believe it when I say I'm seventy-seven. They say I'm sixty-five."

Was he was going to run for a sixth term, I asked. He said he already was running for a sixth term. (Elections wouldn't be held for three more years.) "I've already raised $300,000 in six months. ... Last time around, I raised $600,000, which is higher than any other county official, so why is it with all the controversy in the last six months I've raised over $300,000 without even trying? I'll be the only sheriff that has a million dollars the next time around. ... I'm getting checks from across the nation. That's a gauge."

An aide came into the office, told him an Irish television crew waited outside, ready to film him. They'd just been to Tent City, where they'd taken extensive footage. "Irish," Sheriff Joe mused. "I'm wasting my time with you, and I've got Irish TV outside."

• • •

Sheriff Joe's troubles mounted in 2010.

A federal grand jury in Phoenix was scrutinizing him and his office for abuses of power. This grand jury probe likely stemmed from allegedly retaliatory investigations by the sheriff's office of people or agencies Sheriff Joe believed to be his enemies: journalists, county supervisors, law-enforcement officials, judges. The *Arizona Republic* reported that Andrew Thomas, the former Maricopa County Attorney who'd stepped down to run for governor, was also being investigated by the same federal grand jury.

Sheriff Joe was also the subject of the ongoing Justice Department investigation over the alleged civil-rights abuses that took place during the raids. (Several racial-profiling lawsuits had been filed against the sheriff's office in local courts.)

I asked Lisa Allen, Sheriff Joe's spokeswoman, who would run the sheriff's office if the sheriff and his top advisers were indicted.

"Indictments, if they occur, are not convictions, but simply charges. The sheriff would continue to run the office," she wrote in an e-mail.

In March 2010, Allen told me Sheriff Joe had already raised $1 million for his next campaign.

Much of that money came from sympathetic out-of-state donors who had received Sheriff Joe's letters claiming he needed money because the left was attacking him from every front.

Sheriff Joe allied himself with the American Border Patrol, a Minuteman group based in Sierra Vista, Arizona. He endorsed J. D. Hayworth, who ran against John McCain in the 2010 Republican primary for the U.S. Senate. Hayworth's border advisor was Chris Simcox, a Phoenix-based Minuteman and Sheriff Joe supporter.

I'd often thought that Sarah Palin and Sheriff Joe shared a lot of traits—they were both sound-bite populists. They were both great on TV. They both appealed to Tea Party enthusiasts. They both had a national fan base but weren't as popular in their home states.

In early 2010, a local poll indicated that the sheriff's popularity in Maricopa County was collapsing. His 64 percent approval rating in 2007 had shrunk to 39 percent in 2009. The independent pollster, Earl de Berge, had been surveying Maricopa County for years. He knew his business.

According to de Berge, Maricopa County was split evenly among Republican, Democrat, and independent voters. The sheriff had lost support of the county's independents. Sheriff Joe rated especially low with Maricopa County's Democrats, young people, Latinos, rich people, and college graduates.

The pollster cited the grand jury investigation as one reason for the slumping voter approval. The other reason, according to de Berge, was Sheriff Joe's "hardnosed and sometimes perceived heavy-handed tactics toward illegal aliens."

CHAPTER 5

The Border Crosser

Rodrigo and his alter ego Erika came to Phoenix to
escape the "straight" men who loved and tormented them.

In the early spring of 2008, I was just another Anglo woman who had
hired a contractor to remodel her house, and Rodrigo was just another
Mexican worker in the framing crew. It's a scene that played itself out
over and over in pre-recession Arizona; at least 35 percent of the
state's construction workers were Latinos. An untold number of these
laborers were undocumented migrants like Rodrigo.

Rodrigo stood about five feet four inches tall, and weighed about
130 pounds. He wore a leather tool belt buckled low on his hips, and
some of the tools extended beyond his kneecaps. He worked quickly,
rarely stopping to rest. He ripped out walls, hauled construction trash
to the Dumpster, and framed new walls with fresh lumber with a
mean-looking nail gun. Like the two other guys on the framing crew,
Rodrigo was a Mexican immigrant. Unlike the other two guys on the
framing crew, Rodrigo plucked his eyebrows.

Those sculpted eyebrows fascinated me, and I wanted to hear
Rodrigo's story. I waited until he finished framing the house, then I
called him.

I met up with Rodrigo shortly before Christmas, long after the
framers had finished their work. Rodrigo lived in an apartment complex in a sprawling working-class neighborhood in Phoenix. It wasn't
a *barrio*, exactly. The stores in the nearby shopping center bore witness to the mixed ethnicity of the area—a Bosnian grocery store sat
near a meat market that also sold piñatas. An Anglo thrift store where
Rodrigo purchased his sturdy work clothes benefited Mormon charities. A hairstylist for Spanish speakers offered haircuts for $10. At the
neighboring dollar store, Latino immigrants could cash a check for a
1 percent fee, or pay a utility bill, or send a MoneyGram to Mexico,

or buy items ranging from cell phones to bananas to cigarettes. There was a QT gas station nearby, and also a Pure Fitness gym.

But lately, Rodrigo wasn't availing himself of any of these services. He had confined himself in his apartment, waiting for things to get better. The recession had hit Phoenix hard that Christmas season, and there wasn't much construction work. Migrants with no documents had additional worries—the state laws and Sheriff Joe.

"People don't go out anymore," Rodrigo said. "If they have work, they just go to work and return to their homes. If they don't have work, they stay behind closed doors."

For a gregarious fellow like Rodrigo, the isolation was almost too much to take.

Rodrigo bunked in a second-story apartment with a balcony that looked over a covered parking area littered with discarded cans and bottles. Rodrigo's apartment, on the other hand, was immaculate. He'd just vacuumed the tan carpet, and the air smelled faintly of carpet deodorizer. The kitchen was tiny, with a stove, a sink, and a refrigerator that contained only a quart of milk, a half-full box of strawberries, and a cabbage. A statuette of the Virgin of Guadalupe sat on the kitchen counter. Ceramic cowboy boots perched on the microwave. A poster of Jesus wearing a crown of thorns hung

Rodrigo in his Phoenix apartment.
KATHY MCCRAINE

on one kitchen wall, and a poster of a bare-shirted, buff male model hung on the other.

Vases of bright artificial flowers decorated the living room. A large mirror hung from one wall, opposite a picture of San Francisco's Golden Gate Bridge. A tall black floor lamp reached to the ceiling like a yearning Georgia O'Keeffe flower. An old TV was tuned to a Mexican talk show; the topic was marital infidelity. A little Christmas tree with red lights sat on a coffee table. There weren't any presents beneath the tree, just a plastic figurine of a beagle. This year, Rodrigo planned on spending Christmas Eve with his sister, then inviting some friends over for dinner on Christmas Day. He'd drink a few beers with his friends, and he'd make a chicken. They'd listen to *ranchero, cumbia,* and salsa music on the boom box, and that would be the extent of their Christmas.

There were two small black leather couches decorated with pink silk shawls in Rodrigo's living room. I sat on one couch. Rodrigo, dressed in a long-sleeved Aéropostale T-shirt, jeans, and black-and-white basketball shoes, sat on the other. He'd gelled his short black hair and wore a small, thin gold loop on each ear. He wasn't handsome, but he wasn't ugly either. His facial features all worked together— black eyes shaped a little like almonds, a broad wide nose, lips that frequently smiled, revealing strong, straight white teeth.

Since he spoke little English, I explained in Spanish that I wanted to interview him for a book and that I didn't pay for interviews. He smiled. "That's fine," he said. Then he folded his hands and looked down at his shoes and rocked back and forth slightly. "There's something I would like to tell you," he said, "but I am embarrassed and I don't know how to say it." He lifted his face a little and looked out the window. "One of the reasons I left Mexico is that I am, how can I say it ..."

"Gay?" I asked.

Sí.

• • •

Then Rodrigo told me his story.

He was born in 1976 in Tehuacán, a city in the Mexican state of Puebla. The city had ancient indigenous roots but was "founded" by the Spaniards in the sixteenth century. Among other things, the modern city is known for its colonial buildings, hot springs, jean factories, and bottled water.

Rodrigo's parents owned a *carnicería*, a meat market, which could not support their four sons and daughter. They lived in a small home and as Rodrigo's older brothers married, their wives moved in. Babies followed. The house seemed to grow more crowded each year.

Rodrigo always felt different from his siblings, and he believed his tiny, curly-haired mother favored him and confided in him in part because he *was* different. His father, on the other hand, was hypercritical of Rodrigo, and the slightest little thing, like a dust ball in a corner, might trigger an insult. "You're lazy," he'd say. "You're worthless," he'd say.

Rodrigo had a secret word for his father—*el enojón*, the grump.

Although his parents never mentioned it, they must have known their son was gay. Rodrigo felt ashamed about his attraction to boys in part because he was a Catholic, and Catholics were taught that homosexuality was a terrible sin. At school, when kids asked Rodrigo if he was a fag or a queer, he denied it. He tried to fit in with the other students by playing soccer and joking about girls. Secretly, though, he worried about himself.

When he was ten years old, Rodrigo had his first sexual experience—with a seventeen-year-old neighbor. He would never view this particular experience as child sex abuse, but rather as a pleasurable awakening and an orientation into a forbidden world he would never abandon.

Rodrigo had crossed his first border.

Like many working-class Mexican kids, Rodrigo stopped going to school after he completed ninth grade so he could help support the family. At the time, Tehuacán was in the midst of a blue-jean *maquiladora* boom; dozens of factories churned out blue jeans that would be shipped to the United States and other countries. Rodrigo found a job operating a sewing machine at a factory that manufactured blue jeans. He worked nine hours a day, six days a week and earned the peso equivalent of a couple of hundred dollars per month. The pay was terrible, but he loved his job, the clatter of the 200 or so sewing machines, the camaraderie among the 350 or so employees. After work, he and his friends would stroll on the plaza, and he quietly kept an eye out for the men who were most attracted to him—married men with families. He had a name for them—*mayates*.

By the time Rodrigo was nineteen, he'd had hundreds of sexual experiences. But he yearned for something new. He was still living at home, but he'd often go visit his friend Diana on weekends. At Diana's house, Rodrigo crossed yet another border.

He dressed up like a woman.

Rodrigo named his feminine alter ego "Erika." With her long black hair, thick eye makeup, fake breasts, revealing dresses, and platform heels, Erika became a part-time prostitute. She struck deals with local bar owners—she could recruit clients in the bars at will, as long as those clients bought lots and lots of booze. Erika had a vested interest in getting her johns to buy as much alcohol as possible—she wouldn't sit at their tables unless they paid her five pesos—less than a dollar for each beer she drank with them. She charged the peso equivalent of about $10 for oral sex. She charged double that for intercourse.

A lot of her clients were married men or guys with girlfriends.

It wasn't exactly easy being either Rodrigo or Erika in conservative Catholic Mexico. Rodrigo tried to hide his homosexuality, and Erika flaunted it. She was regularly taunted on the street with insults like: *maricón, pinche joto, puto joto*. (This amounts to calling someone a fag, a fucking queer, and a queer whore.) Some of Erika's transvestite friends had been beat up, raped. Erika had managed to escape violence, until the evening she was almost stoned to death.

She had volunteered to work as a bartender at a friend's transvestite booth at a local carnival. A particularly fierce gang of men began throwing stones at her. She escaped because she ran faster than her persecutors.

Rodrigo made up his mind to come to the United States. He was twenty-two years old. His motivation was twofold. He needed to make more money, and he was tired of prostituting himself. He was also tired of persecution. He'd heard gay people were accepted in America.

"I'm going to the United States," Rodrigo told his mother.

She was in the hospital at the time, recovering from minor surgery. Rodrigo had helped pay for this operation, just as he helped with all the family bills. He promised to send money and to return to Mexico to visit. She must have sensed his reasons for leaving.

One day in early March 1998, Rodrigo traveled by car from Tehuacán to Agua Prieta, that gritty town in Sonora that sat just across from Douglas, Arizona, in a prime human-smuggling corridor. Like most Mexican immigrants, Rodrigo already had a friend in the United States. In this case, his friend lived in Phoenix and promised to find Rodrigo lodging and work. All Rodrigo had to do was successfully cross the desert.

He called a phone number given to him by his Phoenix friend and waited on the streets of Agua Prieta. Soon, a car came and took him to a ranch on the Mexican side of the border. Here, several other Mexican men waited for the *coyote*. The ranch was a staging area for human smugglers. Sometimes, entire buses would empty out immigrants at the Mexican ranch, and the bus drivers ran a side business selling hiking boots and water.

At the time, tens of thousands of undocumented migrants successfully crossed into Arizona as part of one of the largest migrations in human history. The message most Mexican immigrants got when they crossed the border in 1998 was that they were wanted in the United States in a *wink-wink-get-yourself-across-the-border-and-we-will-give-you-work* sort of way. The Border Patrol was more of a hurdle than a real impediment.

Rodrigo, who'd already crossed two borders—into homosexuality and transvestitism—found his third border crossing much easier. He simply stepped from the Mexican rancher's land onto the United States. The rough country on the American side was full of cacti and rocks and gullies, but more than anything it was cold and windy. By the time the smuggler delivered Rodrigo to his friend, who waited in a car on Highway 80, Rodrigo was freezing. Rodrigo's friend paid the *coyote* $1,000, and the two drove to Phoenix.

Rodrigo already had a job waiting for him, thanks to his friend. He earned $7 per hour as a painter and soon paid off his friend for the *coyote* fee. Free from debt, he started his new life in Phoenix.

Like so many newcomers to Phoenix, Rodrigo felt the modern, growing, anonymous city gave him permission to reinvent himself. He didn't have to be the no-good kid his father criticized, or the closeted gay *maquiladora* worker whose alter ego was a prostitute named Erika. In America it was possible to announce you were *guey* (gay) and no one, not even other Mexican immigrants, seemed to care.

Compared to Tehuacán, Phoenix was new, huge, exciting, rich, libertine. It was also culturally segregated. Gringos and undocumented immigrants lived side by side, but they existed in different worlds defined by language and custom. Rodrigo didn't have to learn English, except for the instructions from his bosses. Hundreds of establishments catered to Phoenix's undocumented immigrants—there were stores, movies, bars, banks, car dealers, lawyers, and restaurants for Spanish speakers. Most landlords in the apartment buildings and houses Rodrigo shared with friends spoke Spanish.

Rodrigo was eager and fast and cheerful. He painted shopping malls, health clubs, and McMansions. If he worked six days a week for eight hours daily at a $7 hourly rate, he earned almost double what he made working nine hours a day at the Tehuacán jean *maquiladora*. And when an opportunity to sign on with a framing contractor opened up, he jumped on it. Soon, he was a crew boss earning $16 hourly.

He still dressed like a woman and went to the bars, but Erika didn't have to sell herself anymore; she could dress up just for the fun of it. In Phoenix, Erika had many liaisons with migrant men, who seemed more accepting of gays and less inhibited about coupling with men now that they were miles away from their wives and girlfriends. But these *mayates* rarely took Erika out for a drink, or to a store to buy her something pretty; instead, they used her sexually and she knew it. "They use us," she would tell her transvestite friends.

Erika didn't feel used, though, when her alter ego Rodrigo fell in love.

We'll call the *mayate* Chuey. He was an undocumented migrant from southern Mexico, and he worked a construction job. He was slender, handsome, with a thick head of hair, brown eyes, and a mustache. He wore cowboy hats and boots and took Erika dancing and bought her gifts, including a poster of the Golden Gate Bridge and the black floor lamp that looked like a Georgia O'Keeffe flower.

Chuey was a married man. He lived with his wife and two kids in a Phoenix apartment building. Sometimes, he invited Rodrigo to his house for dinner. The two lovers didn't think Chuey's wife knew of their affair.

Rodrigo was deeply in love with Chuey, yet willing to accept that Chuey would never leave his wife. Rodrigo and Chuey spent every minute they could with each other for five years. Just for Chuey, Rodrigo had a playboy bunny tattooed on his shoulder.

Chuey had always professed to hate gays, and in Mexico he'd actually taunted them on the streets.

"You are the first man I've had sex with; I'm not gay," Chuey told Rodrigo.

"I know you're not gay," Rodrigo answered.

Then one day in 2007, Rodrigo got a phone call. Chuey had been picked up by the police and would soon be deported to Mexico. Rodrigo could never confirm exactly who picked up Chuey, or why, but he would always assume Chuey had been stopped for a busted headlight during a raid spearheaded by Sheriff Joe Arpaio. Chuey had outstanding speeding tickets, which would have earned him a trip to jail after he'd been stopped by the cops. His status as an "illegal alien" would have been confirmed in the jail.

At first, Chuey phoned Rodrigo regularly from Mexico. He said some day he would come back to the United States, and they could be together again. After a few weeks, the phone calls weren't so regular, and finally they stopped. Sometimes, Rodrigo would bump into Chuey's wife, who was also an undocumented immigrant and struggled to support the two kids on her salary at a fast-food restaurant.

Rodrigo moved to Oregon in late 2007, in part just to get away from the heartache. He didn't like the gray sky and the rain, and yearned to be back in Arizona. But when he returned in 2008, everything was different. He couldn't get his old job back as crew boss for the framing contractor, because the Employer Sanctions Act had a chilling effect on employers who once relied on the labor of undocumented immigrants; now they were reluctant to hire them. Rodrigo became a day laborer. What's more, Sheriff Arpaio's terrifying raids were trumpeted on the evening news, and a lot of Latinos had shut themselves in their houses.

Although Rodrigo pined for Chuey, he entertained himself with a rebound relationship. But the affair ended when Rodrigo's new boyfriend got a girl pregnant and vanished.

• • •

I visited Rodrigo several times in the spring of 2009. He shared the apartment with a friend I'll call Emilio, an undocumented Mexican immigrant who had been smuggled into the United States at the age of twelve by a drug lord. Emilio had been kept in the drug lord's Chicago home and used as a sex slave. Orphaned in Mexico, Emilio didn't have a lot of options, and would never think of his years in Chicago as sexual abuse. He would instead remember them as confining. A babysitter took care of him when the pedophile drug lord was out of town, and Emilio was well fed and clothed. Mostly, he watched TV, which taught him English, played video games, and plotted his escape. He secretly communicated with another immigrant who had a relative in Phoenix, and finally the two escaped to Arizona. Emilio eventually got a job at a fast-food restaurant using a friend's Social Security card, and his English skills and work ethic soon got him promoted to manager. By this time, he was in his late twenties.

Rodrigo and Emilio both loved men, but they weren't attracted to each other. (I can attest to that, since one day at the apartment I bumped into Emilio's boyfriend, a decidedly straight-looking *mayate* who was embarrassed that I knew he was involved with a gay man.) In the one-bedroom apartment, Rodrigo slept on the living-room couch and Emilio slept in the bedroom.

A small statue of *La Santa Muerte*, or Saint Death, sat on Emilio's bed stand. The grinning skeleton saint is said to be worshipped by many involved in the drug trade. She originated in the Roman Catholic Church in Mexico, but the same church disavowed her. In 2009 President Felipe Calderón of Mexico ordered that several of her altars be destroyed as part of his professed war against drug cartels. Emilio left offerings to his Santa Muerte, mostly dollar bills and cigarettes.

Emilio paid for Rodrigo's share of the $570 monthly rent and utilities expenses. Rodrigo had pawned his jewelry to help Emilio pay the rent. Their situation was not unusual in Phoenix—undocumented immigrants like Rodrigo couldn't collect unemployment, although they'd paid plenty of taxes through their fake documents when they were working. Absent public assistance in times of dire need, undocumented immigrants took care of each other in what amounted to an underground social service network.

Rodrigo and Emilio also watched over another friend we'll call Alberto, who was "married" to an unemployed mechanic addicted to crack cocaine. Alberto had worked in a Phoenix factory but had been laid off when the Employer Sanctions Act took effect. Now he lived in a house trailer with no water and no electricity. Alberto often pushed a shopping cart through his *barrio*, collecting cans for spare cash to support himself and his *mayate*. Rodrigo and Emilio frequently checked on Alberto and brought him food whenever they could.

Rodrigo went out in search of work regularly but was turned away from fast-food houses and construction companies when he couldn't provide documents. Once, he almost signed up as a lab rat for a company that tested medicines for drug companies. The job would've paid $1,000 for the duration of the experiment, but his sister talked him out of it. Without a work routine, Rodrigo sometimes languished in his apartment. He might get up around 10:00 a.m.; clean the house, watch TV; eat his only meal, lunch, at his sister's house; watch more TV; then go to bed at 10:00 p.m. He felt trapped, but he didn't want to return to Tehuacán for a visit because he didn't think he could successfully re-enter the United States, what with ramped-up border enforcement and exorbitant fees charged by smugglers.

Like thousands of other undocumented immigrants, he hunkered down in Phoenix, waiting for an improved economy, waiting for the ouster of Sheriff Joe, waiting for comprehensive immigration reform that would bring him out of the shadows.

Frankly, I figured that sooner or later Rodrigo would get so desperate for cash, he'd turn into Erika and start turning tricks. Through the months, I would ask him over and over if he was prostituting himself to survive. He would always say he wasn't. I worried out loud that if Rodrigo unleashed Erika as a sex worker, he risked contracting HIV, the virus that causes AIDS. Since Rodrigo himself had never been tested for HIV—he told me he wanted to get tested but was too frightened to do so because he feared the results—if he was a carrier, he might unwittingly infect some married man, who might infect his wife, who might infect her baby.

Rodrigo would nod and fold his hands and look down at his feet and say one day he would get tested.

• • •

Rodrigo's attraction to declared heterosexuals with wives and girlfriends, and their attraction to him, fascinated me. I wanted to learn more about the cultural motivations for this behavior among conservative Catholic Mexicans, so I headed to the library. I learned that a lot of research confirms that migrants get HIV/AIDS during their travels and then bring it back to their wives and girlfriends.

I found a sobering 2007 article in the *American Journal of Public Health* that detailed the results of a study on a rural Mexican village that relied heavily on migrant remittances. "Marriage presents the single greatest risk for HIV infection among women in rural Mexico," the *Journal* reported.

I won't go into the whole well-researched article or all of its credible conclusions, but one particular section caught my eye. It had to do with a "compulsory heterosexuality" levied on men who had "same-sex desires." In the Mexican village, the researchers wrote, they became "acquainted with a number of feminine-appearing men who had a great number of sexual partners locally, many of them married men, some of whom paid them, some of whom they paid, and others with whom they had sexual intercourse in a context of short-lived romantic affectivity. We also observed masculine-appearing men in pursuit of these feminine-appearing men or, when drunk, in pursuit of each other." The authors discovered a "sexual geography" that defined where it was permissible to engage in extramarital sex—places like bars where wives rarely ventured.

Having sex with another man was presumed to be safe because "neither man would fall in love (supposedly), neither could get pregnant, and another man could certainly be trusted not to tell one's wife," the authors wrote.

Oddly, what the working-class Mexican men considered *socially safe* actually put their wives at *higher risk* for contracting HIV.

Practically everything Rodrigo had told me about his behaviors in Mexico and Phoenix was echoed in the *American Journal of Public Health* article. I wanted to learn just how often these culturally induced behaviors noted in the article were observed in Phoenix, so I visited Diana Diaz at the Southwest Center for HIV/AIDS in Phoenix.

Diaz, a tiny, energetic Colombian dentist who had specialized in treating people with immunodeficiency disorders, like HIV/AIDS, had fallen in love with an American engineer. She left Colombia and her career to be with her husband in the United States. She didn't yet have her license to practice dentistry in the United States, so she worked in Phoenix as a counselor to Latino clients who were either diagnosed with or were at risk for HIV/AIDS. She had seen numerous cases of what is known in street parlance as the "down-low phenomenon"—self-professed straight guys having secret sex with men. She confirmed that working-class men on the down-low who are from conservative Catholic countries like Mexico don't want to be stigmatized with an HIV diagnosis. "Some people don't want to know if they have HIV," Diaz told me. "They don't want to be identified."

And undocumented immigrants had other worries—they feared that if they got treated, they'd be deported. If they got full-blown AIDS, however, they almost always ended up visiting clinics or hospital emergency rooms, where their diagnosis would be confirmed. But once diagnosed, Diaz told me, some Latino immigrants remained in denial and weren't always compliant about taking their meds or practicing safe sex.

Undocumented immigrants at risk for HIV/AIDS often feared getting initial testing because they mistrusted government, and they associated health care with government.

The irony was that Arizona, notoriously stingy with services provided to undocumented immigrants, actually provided free health care for people diagnosed with HIV/AIDS if they met certain poverty guidelines. The money for this free health care came from a federal program named for Ryan White, a young hemophiliac who contracted HIV through a blood transfusion in the 1980s.

Although I couldn't find a separate statistical category for men on the down-low who live with HIV/AIDS, there's no doubt that HIV/AIDS was circulating in Phoenix. As this book went to print, the Southwest Center reported that about 70 percent of the thirteen thousand Arizonans with HIV/AIDS lived in the Phoenix area. The Southwest Center estimated that another 4,300 people in the state might carry have HIV and not know it because they had not been tested. Most people living with the virus were men who had sex with men. There aren't any statistics that would show how many of these cases involved undocumented immigrants.

The Latino Commission on AIDS, a New York–based nonprofit, reported in 2008 that "accurate data on Latinos diagnosed with HIV and/or AIDS is still not available."

In the 2008 report, the commission nevertheless detailed concerns about the spread of HIV/AIDS among Latino migrants, precipitated by exposure to the United States culture, a transient lifestyle, use of prostitutes and drugs, and the "loneliness and isolation that can mean that male migrants may engage in sex with male partners."

The stigma of HIV/AIDS and the fear of deportation "further complicate matters as few of those who are diagnosed in the U.S. are willing or able to seek care, and some never make it back to their countries of origin.

"Men who have sex with men but do not see themselves as gay, bisexual, or transgender are difficult to reach," the commission reported. "One of the challenges in providing treatment and prevention services in the Latino community has been the difficulty of reaching men who self-identify as heterosexual but have sex with other men."

• • •

Once, Rodrigo took me to a central Phoenix store where he had purchased Erika's clothes, back in the day when he had money to spend. The store offered one-stop shopping for Latino immigrants; the place sold everything from men's and women's clothing to flat-screen TVs to kids' bikes. The Spanish-speaking sales clerks greeted Rodrigo, and he smiled hello, flashing his big, strong teeth. He wore a macho uniform that day—a long-sleeved T-shirt, jeans, and spit-shined steel-toed black boots—but he spent all his time looking at women's clothes. He stood before the mirror for what seemed like hours, holding one sexy top and tight skirt after another against his slender body. He tried on a patent-leather high-heel women's boot. He looked at gold necklaces. He didn't look at any men's clothing that day. He reserved that shopping for the Mormon thrift store near his apartment.

I once asked Rodrigo if he ever wanted to go through a sex-change operation, and he'd said he once floated the idea of becoming a woman to his family and they didn't like it, so he'd never do it. He guessed that about 60 percent of him wanted to remain a man and 40 percent of him wanted to be a woman.

He even transformed himself into Erika one Saturday night, just so I could watch him metamorphose. To begin, he pulled out three large foldout makeup cases (one belonged to Emilio) loaded with pancake bases, eye shadows, false eyelashes, mascara, eyeliner, lipsticks,

Erika in her Phoenix apartment.
KATHY MCCRAINE

glosses, and nail polish bottles. By the time I had arrived, he'd already combed Erika's black wig, blown it dry, shined it up with baby oil, and stuck it on a candlestick. As he applied Clinique foundation to his face, neck, hands, and even his knees, he told me his biggest fear in life was contracting HIV. His greatest joy, he said, was that he'd never been seriously ill a day in his life. As he began to look more and more like a woman, our conversation morphed into a kind of girlfriend-to-girlfriend conversation, complete with tips on how to curl eyelashes with a teaspoon. Throughout all of this, some guy who worked in a car wash kept texting Rodrigo, wanting to get together.

"He's bald, dark, and ugly," Rodrigo sniffed, ignoring his belligerent cell phone. He wanted to pair up with somebody, be part of a monogamous couple, he said, but he acknowledged that his desire for married men sabotaged his dreams. Married men just didn't leave their wives.

He put on a strapless bra with falsies, stepped into the privacy of another room to pull up a girdlelike garment that confined his genitalia, then stepped into a tight, black, sleeveless dress and high-heeled sandals. He applied enough gel on his hair to make his wig stick, painted his nails, and transformed into Erika.

She walked seductively over to a cabinet and pulled out the perfumes she'd bought at Macy's during the good times. Should she use Donna Karan's Delicious, she asked me, or Just Me Paris Hilton? Erika wasn't the brassy transvestite I'd expected, just a warm, sweet woman. I wondered if her behavior would have been different with a *mayate*. She wouldn't be going to the bars that night, though. She didn't have any money. She'd only changed into a woman so I could watch.

"What will you do when you grow old; surely you won't wear the same clothes?" I asked Erika.

She got upset.

"I can't *think* about getting old," Erika said. "I will *die* rather than get old."

I was struck by Erika's predicament. It must be lonely enough being a thirty-something transvestite who knows her beauty will fade, but it must be lonelier still being an undocumented immigrant transvestite trapped in a foreign city that didn't want her.

I tried to cheer her up. I told her that she was beautiful and that her legs rocked.

"You can't see the varicose veins?" she asked.

I left Erika alone in her apartment, and she later told me she'd watched the news, changed her clothes, and gone to bed.

• • •

"I want to go to the bars with you," I told Rodrigo one April afternoon. He agreed.

When I drove to Rodrigo's house one Saturday night in April for my tour of the bars, Erika looked down at me from the balcony. Inside the apartment, a friend I'll call Amanda sat on the couch. Amanda was a stocky landscaper who emigrated from Mexico City. She always dressed in women's clothes, even when she raked the gringos' yards. Amanda was thirty-six years old, with long black hair, thick features, broad shoulders, a bit of a potbelly, and slender legs. I could smell her Diesel Fuel for Life when I shook her calloused hand. She wore a short tight black dress and Dr. Scholl's sandals, which she traded for black stiletto heels just before we got in the car.

"My boobies are real," she said once she'd settled in the backseat. She was on hormone therapy, she explained, and she yearned to become a woman, but she couldn't afford the sex-change operation. I tried to explain to Amanda that "boobies" wasn't exactly a dignified word, perhaps she should use the word "breasts."

"There aren't any people here," Erika interrupted as we pulled into the almost-empty parking lot of a central Phoenix bar.

"There used to be hundreds of cars here," Erika told me as she stepped out of the car. Evidently, Phoenix's crackdown on illegal immigrants had intimidated prospective bar clients. Erika hadn't been to the bars for months, and the change in attendance shocked her.

She and Amanda walked past a handful of straight-looking men smoking cigarettes, and they hooted, whistled, crooned at them. I'd expected Erika and Amanda to take me to a gay bar, but this was just a neighborhood watering hole that catered to Latino immigrants. A strobe light cast red and green dots on the empty round tables surrounding the dance floor. Images of pretty girls and cowboys danced across the two screens. A DJ played a blaring *narcocorrido* that glorified a drug dealer. Maybe twenty people were in the entire bar—a few couples, and some single men playing pool.

Erika wanted to check out the pool players, so she made her way to the women's restroom. "They're ugly," she told Amanda when she returned. She shook her head at a woman vendor who walked by with an armload of flowers, balloons, and teddy bears. The music stopped, and the DJ introduced a three-man *ranchero* band called Los Plebes de Sinaloa. Los Plebes played the Mexican equivalent of country-western. They wore white cowboy hats, matching shirts, jeans, and boots. A tall, mustachioed guitar player immediately got Erika's attention. Erika high-fived Amanda. "Look at how good-looking my husband is!" Erika joked.

Amanda smiled. Los Plebes didn't strike me as great musicians, but Erika was entranced. (After each song, the DJ played a round of canned applause, perhaps because no one in the bar clapped.) Erika tried to get the guitar player's eye, but he wasn't interested in her.

A straight-looking man sitting alone at a table whistled at Erika, and she walked over to him. He flirted with her. She walked away. He whistled again. She returned to his table. He whispered to her and laughed. They exchanged phone numbers.

"He's ugly," she told Amanda when she came back to the table.

Amanda wasn't getting much attention. A man asked her to dance, but she turned him down. She fingered her pearl necklace and played with her cell phone, showing me pictures of a recent trip to Las Vegas as well as ads run by men who want women on a site called Conexión Latina.

Like Amanda, Erika seemed sort of sad. I looked down at my Coke and thought about the differences between Erika and Rodrigo. Erika rarely smiled. Rodrigo grinned frequently. Erika seemed vulnerable. Rodrigo seemed stoic. Erika partied. Rodrigo worked.

"Let's go," Erika said. We'd been at the bar about an hour, and Erika's fantasies about the guitar player had died down, largely because he seemed to have no interest in Erika. She figured she'd have better luck at another neighborhood bar.

It was also practically empty. "This used to be jammed with people," Erika said once again as she stepped inside. She scanned the place, and noted that every man was unattractive. We ordered beers, and Erika moved beneath a revolving light with horses resembling Budweiser Clydesdales. Five couples circled the dance floor, cheek-to-cheek, pelvises apart, neutral expressions on their faces. A very short man in a sweatshirt decorated with a Virgin of Guadalupe guided tall Amanda out on the floor. They danced together without looking into each other's eyes. Erika sipped her beer, ignored the men who stared at her, and kept her eye on the door. I hadn't realized she'd been texting a man we both knew. When the man entered the bar, he saw me and hesitated. He was a construction worker, handsome, muscular, masculine, married.

I couldn't stay.

"How was Erika's night out?" I asked Rodrigo a few days later.

Erika had enjoyed a fabulous night out, he said. She'd danced with the married man until the bar closed, but she'd gone home with another guy. "So I guess Erika has a boyfriend again; he's very cute," Rodrigo told me. I asked again whether Rodrigo would undergo HIV testing.

He said he would, one of these days.

•••

Rodrigo and I became good friends. One day, Rodrigo told me he'd been to the doctor and had tested negative for HIV. He still pined for Chuey. He had one short-lived lukewarm affair, with a guy who worked in a tire store. And he couldn't afford to go to the clubs anymore.

In November 2009, Emilio lost his job and moved to California. Rodrigo moved in with his sister, who lived in Phoenix with her husband and children. Both Rodrigo and his brother-in-law were construction workers. Both were undocumented. There wasn't much work. In a good week, each might work two days. But it was enough to get by.

One day in December, Chuey called Rodrigo.

He was in Tijuana, he told Rodrigo, and he planned to cross the border. He'd come to Phoenix. Together the two men could go to New Mexico. Chuey had heard there was work in New Mexico, and undocumented people could get driver's licenses. They could be together again.

Rodrigo still loved Chuey. He thought about moving to Albuquerque with his lover, but then he changed his mind. Why would he want to stay with a guy who insisted he wasn't gay?

It was then that Rodrigo realized he'd changed. He was no longer willing to put up with *mayates* who couldn't come to terms with their sexuality. He'd stay in Phoenix, he decided, and live with his sister until he could afford to get his own place.

And maybe one day he'd meet a man who really loved him.

CHAPTER 6

A Day Late, a Dollar Short

Mexican immigrants patronized the dollar store.
So did crack addicts and a child molester.
Why didn't the owners call the police?

It didn't take me long to learn Inocencio was a prankster. One day in the spring of 2010, when I visited his dollar store in central Phoenix, he dared and cajoled me to eat a fried grasshopper.

He had brought a Tupperware tub full of the crisp, salted brown insects, called *chapulines*, into the store for his lunch, along with tortillas he'd made earlier in the morning. Inocencio was forty-three years old and had resided in the United States for more than two decades. He knew Anglos didn't eat grasshoppers.

Which was exactly why he wanted me to eat one.

"They are delicious," he said.

He set the Tupperware on the counter. The large fat grasshoppers, he said, were females and tasted better than the smaller males. He warned me to pull the legs off before popping the bugs in my mouth because the legs sometimes got caught in the throat, like splinters.

I was going to do this thing.

So, I selected a male grasshopper—less to eat—and put 50 cents on the counter for a cold can of Coke to wash the grasshopper down. With a grin on his face, Inocencio gave me to the count of three in Spanish: *Uno! Dos! Tres!* I must have had a funny expression on my face when I placed the weightless bug on my tongue and forced myself to chew.

Inocencio exploded into giggles. His wife, Araceli, who rarely smiled, laughed so hard she could barely take my picture with my iPhone camera.

Actually, the grasshopper wasn't bad. It tasted clean and slightly salty.

Inocencio told me his parents had brought the grasshoppers from southern Mexico during one of their visits to Arizona. The bugs were high in protein and low in fat, ideal for Inocencio, who'd been dieting and had just lost about forty pounds. His once-tight golf shirt and khakis now hung loose on his short frame, and that made him happy.

On this particular morning, Inocencio sat on a stool near the cash register. Araceli puttered in the stockroom. I stood on the other side of a glass counter that contained highly desirable merchandise that might be stolen: tall cans of spray paint (the kind used on freeway overpasses and freight trains), Hannah Montana toys, men's cologne, manicure kits, women's perfumes, CDs by the popular *norteño* group Los Tigres del Norte. Other items that might be shoplifted—phone cards, batteries, Tylenol, Alka-Seltzer Plus, prophylactics, pregnancy test kits, CD players, more Hannah Montana toys, makeup, lighters, cigarettes—were displayed behind the glass counter or on the walls above the cash register, where Inocencio could keep an eye on them.

About every ten minutes or so, Inocencio would ring up a customer's purchase—a Monster drink, a small bag of Cheetos, a couple of packs of Marlboros, a bicycle lock, a bag of white socks, a dozen eggs, a pound of rice.

One jittery man purchased a Bic lighter and a glass tube, which I figured he'd soon use as a crack pipe.

Inocencio wore an inscrutable expression on his face when he took the jittery man's money. The man hurried out of the store. I asked, but Inocencio didn't want to speculate about why customers bought the glass tubes. All he would volunteer was that he bought the tubes at Phoenix wholesale houses. "They're legal," he noted. He kept them behind the counter. They were made in China, and each held a tiny paper flower, called a "Love Rose." They are sold in convenience stores and small shops all over Phoenix.

Inocencio charged a dollar for each Love Rose tube that had cost him a quarter. That's a 300 percent markup.

Crack addicts hadn't done him any favors. Addict whores promenaded on the street in front of his store in the evenings. He'd been robbed twice, burglarized once, by people he assumed were addicts.

Once, a Spanish-speaking immigrant pointed a pistol at his chest and stole $160. The thief was never caught.

Another time, when Inocencio's kids and wife were in the store, an Anglo held a knife to Inocencio's side and robbed them of $100.

Burglars had robbed the dollar store at night, breaking in through the air-conditioning vent and stealing more than $300 worth of phone cards and Marlboros. They were never caught.

Inocencio insured the store against theft and vandalism and considered addicts part of the cost of doing business. He thanked God in heaven that the majority of his customers were not addicts, but immigrant families, oldsters, working people, and students. Inocencio and Araceli had chosen the location of their shop on this busy street because the duplexes and rental houses and apartment buildings in the neighborhoods behind the store were home to their customer base— Mexican immigrants.

Which is precisely why I'd sought out Inocencio and Araceli, as well as others you'll soon meet. I hadn't been able to ferret out any study on *undocumented* immigrants as retail consumers in either Phoenix or Arizona. Back in 2007, Judith Gans, of the University of Arizona, found that all immigrants, authorized and unauthorized, paid $3 in taxes for every $2 that the state spent on services for them. Those taxes immigrants paid included retail taxes, and that intrigued me.

Three years later, I hoped to find out on a purely anecdotal level what goods unauthorized Mexican immigrants purchased in the midst of a recession, the raids, and laws that made it difficult to find work, much less drive to the store. Did they buy Mexican products or American products? What shopping environments were comfortable for them? As consumers, how did they contribute, on a daily basis, to the recession-battered economy of a state that wants to shut them out?

If some immigrants had left Phoenix because it was just too unpleasant to live there and because there were no jobs, how did their exodus affect shopkeepers like Inocencio?

In many Latino neighborhoods in Phoenix, such as this one, American products are sold with Mexican marketing. KATHY MCCRAINE

I chose the dollar store because it is typical of stores in Phoenix that cater to first-generation immigrants. Inocencio fused American products with Mexican marketing. Newly arrived immigrants were comfortable shopping at the dollar store; it was as familiar to them as the corner stores back home, tiny places that sold a little bit of everything. Just like in Mexico, customers could walk to the dollar store from their homes. Inocencio helped them understand the American products and ordered what they needed.

If all the *indocumentados* were to leave Phoenix, Inocencio once told me, "I wouldn't have any business."

• • •

Like almost every immigrant I met who entered the United States illegally, Inocencio needed very little coaxing to tell his crossing-the-border story. It bears repeating that most undocumented Mexican immigrants in Phoenix, like Inocencio, entered the country without legitimate visas. They were too poor and often lived too far from government offices to try to get tourist visas to enter the United States (temporarily) legally. It was more practical for these immigrants to hire a smuggler and take their chances.

When they told their border-crossing tales to me, they wanted it understood that they'd struggled just to get to Phoenix. I sensed an unspoken subtext to these stories—after learning about what they'd endured to get here, surely Americans would understand that they *wanted* and *deserved* to be here.

Inocencio's story was a little different. Compared to others, he hadn't suffered. Plus, he had been lucky enough to be in the United States at the very time the Reagan-era government offered amnesty to undocumented immigrants. Inocencio became a legal permanent resident, thanks to the Republicans.

He was seventeen years old in 1984, the year he decided to travel from his village in Guerrero to the United States of America. By then, so many young men in the village had trekked north to work in the United States that Going North was viewed as a career option.

Young boys might ask each other: What will you do when you become a man?

Well, one might answer, I've thought of becoming a mechanic, like my dad, or I might Go North like my uncle and three cousins.

When Inocencio told his mother he wanted to Go North, she opposed him. Her older son had made the trip and had settled in Los Angeles, but Inocencio was too young, she believed. She knew Inocencio wouldn't listen to her. He'd always been hardheaded. She would never forgive him for dropping out of school after completing the seventh grade, even though she had begged him to continue with his studies, to make something of himself, for heaven's sake.

"I don't like school," he would tell her, smiling.

He was stubborn, that boy.

After he quit school, Inocencio helped his father for several years in the two family businesses—a butcher shop and a mill where townspeople ground their fresh corn. He first met Araceli at the mill, when she brought corn to be ground. Her family raised livestock—goats and cattle and chickens. He didn't think much of Araceli either way. She was skinny, plain, serious, and kept to herself. She was one of the smart kids in town, one of the bookworms who dreamed of doing something important with her life. She was a scholar. He was not. He knew the difference.

For teenagers like Inocencio, life in the village could be stifling. The village sat near a dry lakebed pocketed in the Sierra Madre del Sur. It was no tourist resort. Occasionally, a group of Mexican university students or Americans would visit to study the local pre-Columbian ruins, where highly sophisticated clay figurines had been discovered decades before. Those figurines were at least 2,400 years old and now sat in museums and private collections far from the village. Some villagers, including Inocencio, had facial characteristics—prominent, downturned noses and full lips—that resembled those of the figurines. The visitors were more interested in the antiquities, though. They might stop in town for a soft drink or a beer, then be on their way. Inocencio couldn't speak English, so he was unable to ask them about Going North.

The villagers were predominantly Catholic and celebrated Easter and Christmas and Day of the Dead with feasts and colorful processions that blended indigenous and Spanish traditions. Inocencio took these in stride. They were OK, but he wasn't terribly religious. He'd tried reading the Bible, but it always put him to sleep.

For fun, as well as a food staple, Inocencio would accompany his family to the outskirts of town, where they'd harvest wild grasshoppers, or *chapulines*. They'd head to nearby meadows and fields and return hours later with bags full of the insects, a local delicacy. The *chapulines* weren't just any old grasshoppers; they were delicately flavored and could be prepared a number of ways. They could be fried in hot oil, salted, then eaten alone as a crunchy snack or as a meal encased in fresh tortillas, seasoned with red chilies and lime juice. Ground-up dried *chapulines*, when mixed with raw egg, could be formed into little balls and then fried like falafel. Or the insects might add flavor and texture to a soup.

If grasshopper hunting was one of the community's main diversions, the village was in the backwater, all right. Coincidentally, one of the most cosmopolitan resort cities in the world, Acapulco, sits on Guerrero's Pacific coast, perhaps a two-hour bus ride from the village. Nevertheless, Going North seemed more attractive than Acapulco to Inocencio, who had never left the Sierra Madre del Sur. He was curious about the United States. He'd heard so much about it from migrants who had returned to the village.

When he got on the bus to join his brother-in-law in faraway Phoenix, Inocencio knew he'd miss home. He knew he'd miss his five siblings, his father, and yes, even his mother, who was still mad at him. But his homesickness was overpowered by excitement—finally, he was Going North.

The bus trip to Nogales, Sonora, was long and uneventful. During the trip, Inocencio had carefully guarded his savings—the peso equivalent of $250. He'd heard from other immigrants that this sum would pay for his border crossing; it was easy enough to walk into Nogales, Arizona, from Nogales, Sonora. You just needed to pay to borrow the visa of a Mexican citizen and walk right through.

The con man in Nogales, Sonora, took one look at Inocencio and knew he'd found his mark, an *indio* from the south, the kid in country clothes who looked so bewildered. "Give me your money, and I will go get you papers, and you will cross with no problem," the thief said.

Inocencio handed all his money to the man, and when the man didn't come back, he realized he'd been robbed.

He was penniless, and he still hadn't Gone North.

Inocencio promised the next *coyote* that his brother-in-law in Phoenix would pay the smuggling fee. The *coyote* dressed Inocencio up like a tourist, in shorts and a golf shirt, and gave him fake papers to cross at the port of entry. He handed Inocencio a beer for "courage" in case *La Migra* stopped him.

But no one stopped Inocencio at the port of entry. His brother-in-law picked him up in Nogales, Arizona, and paid the *coyote*. Then he drove Inocencio to Phoenix.

Inocencio found work almost immediately, as a dishwasher for $3.75 an hour. He felt rich. He soon found a second job at a janitorial service. He cleaned houses and offices and restaurants. He didn't care about saving money. He was a small-town boy in a big American city. He'd never felt so free. He danced at the big Latino clubs, like the Capri Lounge. He drank Budweisers until he couldn't see straight.

His big brother drove to Phoenix and took Inocencio back to Los Angeles, where he could keep an eye on him. "You're going down the wrong path," his brother said. Inocencio didn't think so. And anyway, Los Angeles had its own magic. It was as if the Virgin of Guadalupe herself had plucked Mexico and transplanted it in SoCal. In Inocencio's neighborhood Mexican immigrants were everywhere. People preferred to speak Spanish over English. The place even smelled like Mexico. Chilies. Garlic. Street food. For a while, Inocencio sold tacos from a truck. Sometimes, he worked as a cook in Mexican restaurants. Days off, he had his Budweiser and his *bailes* (dances). If he craved a taste of home, and if he looked hard enough, he might find a corner store that sold bags of fried grasshoppers imported from home.

• • •

After Inocencio got his green card in the amnesty plan passed by the Reagan-era government, he traveled freely back and forth to Guerrero. Soon, only his parents would remain in the village. Everyone else in the family had opted to Go North. In 1994, Inocencio moved back to Phoenix, where most of his siblings now lived.

He began to think about settling down. The Budweiser and the *bailes* no longer interested him. The young women in the bars bored him.

He was changing physically, he could see it. Growing a little fat. When he combed his thick black hair in front of the mirror, he'd spy one or two threads of gray. Smile lines were beginning to etch into the tawny skin on his face.

In 1999, on one of his trips south to see his parents, he ran into Araceli, the smart girl who used to bring corn to the mill. She was the same age as Inocencio, and she intrigued him. She was so different from the girls at the Phoenix *bailes*. She didn't wear a lot of makeup— some days she didn't wear any makeup at all. She had a no-nonsense, almost brusque way of talking. She wasn't much for chitchat. And sometimes, when Inocencio cracked a joke, she didn't laugh.

Araceli had gone to school for twelve years and had trained as a social worker. After she graduated, she'd gotten an excellent job offer to be a social worker in a larger town, but her mother wouldn't let her accept it. Araceli was bitterly disappointed, but she obeyed her mother. As a reward for her obedience, Araceli's family set her up with a corner store in the village. The years passed, other girls married. Araceli remained single.

When Inocencio proposed, she thought: "Why should I be single the rest of my life?"

One night in April 2000, a few days after she'd married her husband in Guerrero, Araceli prepared to cross into Arizona through the desert in sandals.

Araceli had bunions; close-toed shoes never fit. She could do this thing in sandals, she told herself. And she did, for a few hours, until the Border Patrol picked her up, along with the rest of her group.

Inocencio had been monitoring Araceli's progress and met her when she stepped off the Border Patrol bus at the Mexican border. He took her to Nogales, where a deal was struck with a different *coyote*. This time Araceli would attempt to cross using the borrowed visa of a Mexican citizen. Inocencio agreed to pay the smuggler $2,000 if his bride crossed successfully.

There were probably a lot of reasons that Araceli didn't raise the suspicion of the American officials who checked her visa. She was a small woman with shoulder-length brown hair and light skin. She must have resembled the woman whose picture was attached to the visa she borrowed. For sure, she didn't look like Inocencio or other dark-skinned indigenous-looking immigrants entering the United States from southern Mexico. Her Spanish showed she had schooling, and many immigrants who were pouring into Arizona at the time didn't have a lot of education. What's more, all those years as a shopkeeper had taught her to keep a neutral expression on her face because you can't judge the customer for what he buys. She had nerves of steel. She had confronted thieves who'd tried to steal from her store in the village. Why should she back down when border officials tried to trip her up on her story?

She crossed the border, and soon she and Inocencio were in Phoenix.

• • •

Araceli hated Phoenix.

The city was hot, noisy, crime-ridden, spread out, impersonal, lonely. Inocencio's siblings lived close to him, but Araceli's three sisters and five brothers were back in Guerrero. There was no one she could confide in. She missed her little store and the rivers and mountains and the tall cacti grabbing at the sky with their thick green arms. She couldn't speak English, so the Anglos were a mystery to her.

One day soon after she'd arrived, Araceli looked Inocencio in the eye and said: "I'm going back home."

But she didn't go back because, as arrangements were being worked out for the return journey, she found out she was pregnant. In the span of three years, she had two children, a daughter we'll call Mitzi and a son we'll call Jack. And of course, once her American citizen kids were born, she knew she'd probably never live again in Mexico.

Araceli and Inocencio now lived in a mixed-status family. She was an unauthorized immigrant; he was a legal permanent resident; the kids were citizens. In Phoenix and across the nation, such mixed-status families were becoming common. Increased border enforcement made border crossings more dangerous and smuggling fees more expensive. It was just too costly and dangerous for migrants to visit their families in Mexico, as they had done for decades. Instead, wives joined their husbands in the United States and had American kids. In 2009, the Pew Hispanic Center reported that about 73 percent of the children of undocumented immigrants were American citizens.

High-strung, temperamental, take-charge Araceli and good-natured, happy-go-lucky-yet-stubborn Inocencio built a good marriage. Inocencio worked for a janitorial company; Araceli stayed at home with the kids. When she shopped or visited the Laundromat, she took notice of nearby apartment buildings and duplexes and trailer parks where a lot of Mexican immigrants lived. There was money to be made there, she knew it.

On weekends, Araceli and Inocencio and the kids became door-to-door peddlers, selling sheets, blankets, and other bedding to people living in these high-density areas. Inocencio purchased the linens wholesale from an American distributor in Los Angeles. Araceli and Inocencio merged two cultures when they combined Mexican marketing with products they purchased in the United States. The door-to-door selling was common in villages in southern Mexico, and newly arrived immigrants felt comfortable with itinerant vendors who spoke their language and understood their customs. Interest-free credit arrangements could be made with a handshake; installment payments were agreed on. The informal credit arrangements were key to success.

• • •

You had to find just the right place to sell just the right product—that's how Araceli and Inocencio had always seen things. In 2006, Araceli and Inocencio augmented their door-to-door peddling business when they rented one hundred square feet in a local Laundromat patronized almost exclusively by newly arrived immigrants. They paid $700 a month for the space, about $7 a square foot, but the Laundromat had a lot of customers who bought Ariel laundry soap (a Mexican detergent imported by an American company), as well as sodas, snacks, stuffed animals, gifts, and, yes, linens, from Araceli and Inocencio.

Inocencio quit his day job at the janitorial service.

Business was so good, Inocencio and Araceli saved $15,000.

Inocencio leased an empty 1,800-square-foot store near the Laundromat for $1,000 a month. He started up an LLC. He got a business license. He officially became one of about thirty-five thousand licensed Hispanic business owners in Arizona that, at the time, produced statewide revenues of about $4.3 billion.

He and Araceli stocked the store with about two thousand different items, most of which were American products. Among other things, they stocked toasters and toilet seat covers and coffeemakers and milk and tortillas and eggs and potato chips and teddy bears and Mexican laundry soap and ceramic salt shakers designed to resemble strawberries. They sold phone cards and made commissions on remittances sent by immigrants to family members in Mexico. Back then, the foot traffic on the street was thick and steady at certain times, when school let out, after the workday, on weekends.

The first year, Inocencio reported a personal income of $72,000 and paid taxes on it. Araceli and Inocencio bought a house (in the same neighborhood where Inocencio's siblings lived) for $156,000. Araceli indulged herself with frequent trips to Mervyns and Ross.

Then, in late 2008, business began to decline. The Employer Sanctions Act had taken effect. Sheriff Joe stepped up his raids of Latino neighborhoods and workplaces. The recession ate away at the construction and hospitality industries that employed so many undocumented Mexican immigrants in Phoenix.

Vacancy signs began to sprout up in immigrant neighborhoods. We'll never know how many undocumented immigrants left Phoenix, because we'll never know how many were here, exactly, in the first place. What we can surmise, though, is that many lived in Maricopa County, the most populous county in Arizona.

The Department of Homeland Security's Office of Immigration Statistics estimated in 2010 that one hundred thousand undocumented immigrants left Arizona in one year—from 2008 to 2009. According to the federal agency, about 560,000 undocumented people were thought to live in Arizona in 2008. By 2009, only about 460,000 were thought to remain. That's a nearly 20 percent drop in the number of undocumented immigrants in Arizona.

Inocencio and Araceli guessed that 30 percent of undocumented immigrants left the Phoenix metro area. Sales at the dollar store dropped by 50 percent.

When I first met them, in late 2009, Inocencio and Araceli were considering closing down the store. They decided that before giving up they'd change the name of their store, which they'd previously called a gift shop, to a "dollar and more" store. The name change worked. More immigrants started wandering into the store, looking for deals.

Even so, a lot of the inventory they'd already purchased was not moving. Inocencio and Araceli climbed on ladders and rearranged the hard-to-sell merchandise—the ceramic salt-and-pepper shakers and small appliances and such—stacking it on the highest shelves. Customers had no money for such luxuries, and some said there was no point buying nice stuff, since any day Sheriff Joe could pick them up.

Inocencio's American suppliers felt the pinch too. Few immigrants wanted to buy American party goods, for instance. No one bought the paper birthday plates with matching tablecloths and napkins. No one bought gift cards or ribbons or wrapping paper. Inocencio and Araceli moved those goods into the back stockroom, leaving just a few out for view. They replaced several shelves that had contained party goods, linens, and tchotchkes with food, like cans of hominy, dry pastas, pancake mixes, and other groceries they bought at Sam's Club and Costco. After all, people still had to eat.

They still stocked the store with a few new "luxury" items that women requested—inexpensive American hair dye, mascara, eyeliner, lipstick. Women also still bought cheap plastic earrings and bracelets and hair clips made in China. Shoplifting was on the upswing, and Araceli had posted signs (black marker, white paper, and no-nonsense Spanish) that said shoplifters would be turned in to the police.

The signs were meant to terrify customers into behaving. It was unlikely that Araceli would actually call the police. But practically every undocumented immigrant with sticky fingers knew that a shop owner's calling the police was tantamount to calling *La Migra*. That's because if you got arrested for shoplifting, you went to Sheriff Joe's jail, and if you went to Sheriff Joe's jail, the deputies had an agreement with ICE that allowed them to check your immigration status.

On the days I visited the store, this is what Spanish-speaking immigrants bought: Marlboros, Monster drinks, Pepsis, Coca-Cola, cheap plastic toys made in China (cowboys, Indians, farm animals, blond dolls, guns), Cheetos, Doritos, milk, eggs, Clamato, Clorox,

Funyuns, Gatorade, Capri Sun, bicycle locks, pencils, notebook paper, pliers, socks, soap, lighters, and the Love Rose tube.

Araceli wrote out lists of products that had been sold and needed to be replaced. She wrote a different list for each warehouse Inocencio purchased from. On the first day I visited, one list read:

12 scissors
14 razors
22 boxes aluminum foil
30 trinkets or toys made in China
12 bicycle locks
5 bags clothespins

Inocencio and Araceli marked most goods up 30 to 50 percent. The Love Rose tubes, marked up 300 percent, were an exception to the rule.

They needed to clear about $36,000 a year to meet their living expenses. Rent and utilities for the store cost about $13,500 annually. By my calculations, if they marked up merchandise 30 percent, they had to gross about $350 a day to cover both the store expenses and their living expenses. The week I visited, they grossed $220 to $300 a day.

Their customers paid 8.6 percent sales tax on nonfood items, which Inocencio, in turn, paid to the state and Maricopa County, which funded Sheriff Joe Arpaio's agency. (Inocencio was no fan of Sheriff Joe; he'd once joined a march to protest the sheriff's treatment of immigrants, but the heat had made him queasy.)

Sometimes, families dropped by to send money home. The way it worked, a family member picked up a special telephone behind the counter, which connected to an operator for the company that would wire the remittance to a relative's bank account. Araceli would collect the cash and write a receipt. Later on she'd deliver the cash to a nearby bank, and the money would be wired to Mexico. Araceli and Inocencio got $5 for every remittance sent to Mexico. Araceli told me remittances were down about 40 percent since 2007. During the week I visited the store, three families sent a total of $1,000.

The decline in remittances at the dollar store mirrored a national trend that showed the interdependence of the Mexican and American economies. Migrants sent $26 billion home to Mexico in 2007, but as the American economy worsened and more migrants returned to Mexico, remittances shrank to $21 billion in 2009. The remittances are critical to Mexico's financial stability. Only two other industries, drugs and oil, infuse so much cash into the Mexican economy.

• • •

Araceli and Inocencio decided in 2009 that they would make more money if they kept the store open longer—from 7:30 a.m. to 9:00 p.m. every day but Sunday. This was hard on their two kids, nine-year-old Mitzi and seven-year-old Jack, who were confined to the store from school until bedtime. Inocencio had yanked two seats out of his van and arranged them in front of the small television in the stockroom. From behind the stockroom curtain, Jack watched TV and played video games. Sometimes, he'd sneak onto the family's Toshiba laptop and order games without his parents' permission.

Mitzi wrote an essay about the store for me.

"The store looks big, huge, large," she wrote. "It is a big place with many, many things in it. It is also a beautiful place."

A few sentences later, she noted: "I kind of like the store but not too much."

She wrote that she liked ringing up sales on the cash register and helping her parents stock shelves. She didn't like being cooped up all day after school, or on weekends, unless her cousins visited to play. Her parents were nice, she wrote, but sometimes they treated her and Jack "like little babies."

Mitzi believed her mother and father were overly protective. Every day, Araceli didn't just drop the kids off at school, she marched them into their classrooms. She was the only mom who did this, and it embarrassed Mitzi.

And at the store, Araceli frequently checked up on the kids in the stockroom.

What Mitzi didn't know was that a thirty-nine-year-old Anglo registered sex offender came to the store frequently. He lived in the neighborhood, and immigrants who'd lived in the area for a while told Inocencio that the guy was a sex offender and that some official had gone door-to-door warning people about him. I actually saw the sex offender in Inocencio's store one day, buying a treat for a little girl who looked about five or six years old.

The scene bothered me so much I looked up the man's court records. He was indeed a registered sex offender and had served time in prison for molesting his nine-year-old stepdaughter. He was categorized in the sex offender registry as a Category 3 offender, which meant he was very likely to reoffend.

He admitted on more than one occasion that he was a crack addict, according to his files in Maricopa County Superior Court. He was the father of two kids himself, and had signed them over to his mother and father, with whom he lived. He served time in an Arizona prison for robbing an old man at knifepoint. Another time, he was incarcerated for auto theft.

So, what was this self-admitted drug addict and child molester doing buying treats for a little girl in the dollar store?

I asked Inocencio why he didn't bring the matter to the attention of the police.

What he said speaks volumes about the consequences of law-enforcement officers, like Sheriff Joe, doubling as immigration enforcers. Inocencio had lost faith in the police. Araceli had no papers. What if he went to the police and they deported his wife?

Inocencio made the mistake of calling the police back when another Anglo guy had robbed him at knifepoint.

As a result, Araceli had been subpoenaed to testify for the prosecution at the upcoming trial. She didn't want to testify, because she thought she might be apprehended when she went to the courthouse.

In the undocumented underground, all police and law-enforcement agencies had been lumped in with Sheriff Joe. Distrust that began with Sheriff Joe's raids was reinforced by media reports detailing how law-enforcement officials had double-crossed immigrants. The *Los Angeles*

Times, for instance, reported in 2010 that some ICE agents reneged on promises of legal status to undocumented immigrants who had acted as valuable informants.

As far as Inocencio and Araceli were concerned, it was better to stay under the radar.

• • •

Competition for customers was fierce and unrelenting.

As many immigrants in Phoenix lost their jobs to the recession or to ramifications of the Employer Sanctions Act, unemployed immigrants took to selling whatever they could to other immigrants. Yard sales became more prevalent and frequent. *Paleteros*, those energetic Mexican vendors who sold icy treats from their handcarts, fanned out after school and sold ice cream late into the night. Spanish speakers with driver's licenses ran informal taxi and shuttle services for those who feared driving. Peddlers took orders for everything from vegetables to T-shirts and made home deliveries. Corn vendors set up impromptu storefronts in vacant parking lots.

Just down the street from Inocencio and Araceli's dollar store, a sixty-something-year-old former construction worker we'll call Samuel parked his old pickup in an empty lot every day and sold fresh corn, roasted peanuts, and citrus from the back of it. Samuel told me he netted $5 to $140 daily, depending on blind luck. His wife raised chickens (she bought the chicken feed at Costco) and sold eggs door-to-door.

I asked Samuel why a customer would buy corn from him or eggs from his wife instead of purchasing the same food at the grocery store, and he said: "We let them sample it."

He and his wife had total monthly expenses, including rent, of about $2,000. Their kids, who were grown, helped them with expenses if the egg sales and corn vending didn't pay the bills. They were undocumented and got by, he told me, just hoping President Obama would make good on his promise and bring about that elusive immigration reform.

Samuel hoped to return to construction work when the recession ended. He wouldn't go back to Mexico, not if he could help it, even if he could only make ends meet by standing around all day in an empty parking lot waiting for other immigrants to buy corn and peanuts from the back of his truck.

"My whole life is here in Phoenix," he said.

• • •

Samuel's sentiment was the sentiment of many migrant vendors at *Los Perros*, which means "The Dogs." *Los Perros* is a large Phoenix swap meet that resembles an open-air market in a big city in southern Mexico. Spanish speakers call the place *Los Perros* because the complex of storage sheds and shaded stalls sits on the parking lot of a shuttered dog-racing park in southeast Phoenix. The Anglos have another name for it: Park N Swap. It's been around for at least thirty years.

Park N Swap had once been entirely Anglo, but on the day in 2010 that I visited, the crowd was predominantly Latino. A few Anglo holdouts (mostly middle-aged men with straggly goatees and tattoos) still manned booths stocked with knives and martial arts paraphernalia. One Anglo woman sold rocks and gems and tie-dyed T-shirts. Mostly, though, Spanish speakers sold other Spanish speakers a variety of goods, including brand-new rakes, tamale steamers, overalls, gloves, sheets, towels, Malverde (the drug saint) dashboard ornaments, St. Jude medals, used cars, shoes, candles, CDs, saddles, parakeets, blankets, Chihuahua puppies, mangoes, caramels, cucumbers, plastic jewelry made in China, toilet paper. People queued up to get their computers fixed at various computer booths, and others bought curative formulas for colds and coughs from herbalists. Kids rode the Tilt-a-Whirl. Some of the wares were garage sale junk, like used toasters or old shoes, but most of the products were new, and of these, most were either made in America or imported by American companies.

What's key is that vendors used Mexican marketing to sell goods they purchased from American companies. In produce stalls, for instance, some vendors displayed fruits and vegetables on small paper plates on long tables. A plate of small tomatoes sold for a dollar. The same tomatoes could be found in bins in local grocery stores for about the same price, but newly arrived immigrants preferred the small-plate-for-a-dollar marketing. It reminded them of home.

About 15 percent of the stalls in *Los Perros* were empty, an indication that people had either left town or were too spooked by the sheriff and the laws to shop in an open marketplace.

They had reason to be spooked.

Sheriff Joe's deputies had twice raided the *Mercado*, another open-air swap meet. Once, in 2007, deputies said they were investigating underage drinking. The second time, in 2009, they said they were investigating complaints of sales of pirated videos. A few arrests were made, but the effects on this once-popular Mexican immigrant market were more than damaging.

In the early 1990s, a lumber company owner and palm-tree farmer named Herb Owens noticed that Latinos frequented a nearby swap meet. He figured that if he shaded his parking lot and added

The once-thriving Mercado *in Phoenix was raided by Sheriff Joe Arpaio's deputies.* KATHY MCCRAINE

bathrooms, he could offer a better venue to these Latino merchants and shoppers. His *El Gran Mercado* (The Great Market) was an overnight success. He expanded the space, added two dance pavilions, and booked some of the best Latino bands in the country. This way, he attracted two crowds—families in the daytime and men and women dressed to the nines for the evening concerts and dances.

Herb Owens was born in 1932 in Phoenix. His parents were local Anglo farmers who eventually branched out into construction. Like most people who grew up on farms around Phoenix, Owens learned Spanish as a child. The agricultural workers were Mexicans, and so were his schoolmates. He respected Mexican culture.

When I first wrote about Owens's *Mercado* in 1997, 1.5 million people visited it each year. The last time I talked to him, the two raids had taken their toll. Visitor attendance for 2009 had dropped to 750,000—about one-half of the pre-raids count. What's more, after Sheriff Joe's second raid, monthly attendance plummeted once again—down from ninety-five thousand visitors in March 2009 to thirty thousand visitors in September 2009. He needed sixty thousand monthly visitors to break even.

Owens viewed the last raid, in which deputies combed the *Mercado* for hours and arrested seven adults and three kids in connection with allegedly pirated videos, as "disastrous" and an "abuse of power" that had the intended effect of frightening customers and vendors from the swap meet.

The *Mercado* had been successful because first-generation Mexican immigrants felt comfortable there. They wanted to buy American goods as well as Mexican imports. But they preferred the atmosphere of the Mexican-style open-air market to American stores with fixed prices. The raids impacted not only swap meet vendors but also American wholesalers, importers, and, of course, Herb Owens.

For years, Owens had hired Sheriff Joe's off-duty deputies to act as security guards for the *Mercado*. It had been a happy arrangement, Owens told me, until several years ago, when the off-duty deputies were no longer allowed to work for him. "The sheriff withdrew them," Owens said. That happened about the same time that Sheriff Joe began his raids.

Recently, I visited the *Mercado*. The Spanish-speaking vendors were dispirited; many said they weren't making enough money to break even and they were thinking of pulling up stakes and moving to another state.

"We depend on undocumented people," said Angela, a vendor who sold religious amulets, paintings, statues. Some weekends, Angela didn't sell enough to cover her $173 rental fee for the stall, and her booth was one of the most popular, because, Angela said, "desperate people pray."

Jesus icons and rosaries still sold well, she told me. The best-selling saint was the *Virgen de Guadalupe*, the Madonna of Mexico, but St. Jude, the patron saint of lost causes, came in a close second. After that, other saints competed for the dollars of those "desperate people" who pray.

• • •

One morning, Inocencio let me accompany him on a buying trip to his suppliers—warehouses owned by American companies. Our first stop was at a large Mexican import warehouse in south-central Phoenix. The warehouse was owned by an American company and carried American products too.

Inocencio took his sweet time, wandering up and down the aisles looking at cases of prayer candles. Araceli had been after him to buy a case of those thick candles encased in glass stamped with images of religious icons, like the Virgin of Guadalupe. Araceli knew that in hard times these prayer candles sold well. She'd seen them fly off the shelves of *yerberías*, the Mexican herbal remedy stores patronized by many newly arrived immigrants.

The warehouse carried the largest variety of candles Inocencio had ever seen. There were cases of Shut Up candles (you lit the candle, and by the time it burned out a few days later, the person who'd bad-mouthed you would shut up) and cases of Come Back to Me candles (for jilted lovers), to name a few.

Inocencio purchased a case of Virgin of Guadalupe prayer candles, a case of Mexican Coke in bottles, and a case of Fanta sodas. Soon we were driving down Indian School Road in his old van, listening to *cumbias*.

The second warehouse was stocked with goods ranging from Love Rose tubes to baby diapers to manicure chairs. Inocencio hoped to sell a lot of Mylar balloons on Valentine's Day (he would rent a helium tank and fill the balloons at the dollar store), but he seemed stumped by one balloon that said: *When I said I liked you I was Lion! I love you!*

I translated.

He didn't say anything.

Inocencio chose instead a dozen bright-pink balloons with the words *You are my best friend and I love you!* along with *It's a Girl!* balloons and *It's a Boy!* balloons, a large case of Soft and Silky bathroom tissue, and a big carton of bleach.

Back in the van, Inocencio got lost, so we had a long time to talk. He told me Americans tended to have tidier yards than Mexicans. He told me the economy failed in part because immigrants had returned to Mexico. And he told me some immigrants cheated on their taxes, claiming more children than they had just so they'd get refunds. This infuriated Inocencio, who paid his taxes and wanted Americans to have good impressions of Mexican immigrants. "These cheats," he said, "don't make it easy for the rest of us."

We drove around an industrial park, trying to find the small warehouse owned by the American who'd stopped by the dollar store just to get Inocencio's business. The American worked with a lot of Mexican corner store owners, and unlike other wholesalers Inocencio patronized, the American delivered the goods to his customers in his delivery truck.

We finally found the warehouse. The American wasn't around, but a Latina clerk greeted us. Inocencio spent almost an hour in the showroom, sniffing aftershave, puzzling over boxes of cake mixes—he almost bought a case of spice cake mix, mistaking it for vanilla—pricing candies and soap. He purchased cases of Mentos, cases of cleaning products, several bags of Mexican candies, laundry soap, and a few boxes of cake mix.

The total bill for all three warehouses came to $391.21, and Inocencio had paid once with cash and twice with his credit card from Wells Fargo Bank. He owed about $3,000 on the credit card, most of these expenses related to the store.

When we returned to the dollar store, Araceli helped him unload the soda and candles, the bleach and Mylar balloons.

I thought back to what she'd told me when we first met. Mexican consumers, she said, were impulse buyers who liked to enjoy themselves when they had the money to do it.

"They like to eat and they like to buy, eat and buy, eat and buy," she'd said.

Inocencio and Araceli figured that if Sheriff Joe had a change of heart and the recession let up and immigration reform passed, they'd once again have a robust clientele who would eat and buy, eat and buy. They would hold out at the dollar store as long as they could, regardless of the personal sacrifices, because, honestly, they'd never been happier.

CHAPTER 7

Don't Stop the Music

Mexican music fed their souls,
and the radio station helped them survive.

I couldn't help it. From the minute I met Ivan Bojorquez at a Dunkin'
Donuts in west Phoenix, I liked the guy. And it wasn't just because he
insisted on buying my coffee or because he was one of the few Mexican immigrant musicians who returned my telephone calls. What I
liked about Ivan was his enviable work ethic and his cheerful, unfet-
tered optimism in the face of tough odds.

When I met Ivan in 2010, he was nineteen years old. You wouldn't
have been able to pick him out of a crowd of college students. He was
tall, thin, with short dark-brown hair and an easy smile. He spoke perfect English and dressed like many Americans his age—tennis shoes,
jeans, hoodies.

Ivan immigrated to Phoenix from his hometown of Sinaloa de
Leyva, in the state of Sinaloa, in northwestern Mexico, when he was
ten years old. His dad, a migrant laborer, had obtained legal residency
through a 1986 law passed by the Reagan-era government that gave
amnesty to undocumented immigrants who were residing in the
United States at the time.

In 2001, after years of waiting, Ivan's father obtained legal residency for his wife and two sons. After Ivan moved to Phoenix with his
mom and brother, he mixed easily with Anglos. He picked up English
from his Anglo friends and spoke English almost exclusively outside
his home.

But when he attended Alhambra High School, he switched to
Spanish. In high school, it was only cool to speak Spanish. It was also
cool to listen to Mexican music.

Ivan had always loved the music of the Mexican countryside, in
part because he'd heard it all his life. His uncle was a musician, and

Ivan had learned to play guitar in Mexico. After he graduated from high school with honors, he put off going to college so he could work in Phoenix for his uncle, mixing playlists of Mexican music for radio stations in the United States and Mexico.

The music that Ivan mixed is known in the United States as "Mexican regional." It is the music most listened to by Mexican immigrants, and they consume it with such enthusiasm that in 2009 Mexican regional music sales made up 60 percent of Latin music sales in the United States, according to *Billboard* magazine. That's because the music speaks to the Mexican immigrant. It's music from home, and it honors the immigrant's struggles.

Having lived in Arizona most of my life, I grew up hearing this music, and I love it, but I knew next to nothing about it until I called an expert—*San Antonio Current* music writer Enrique Lopetegui—to get a better understanding of the different types of Mexican regional music.

Enrique said if I wanted to listen to *ranchero* music, I should buy a record by singer Vicente Fernández. His songs are often accompanied by *mariachis*, and older ladies love his style. According to press reports, in 2006, the aging crooner packed a bigger crowd at the Cow Palace than the Rolling Stones. *Norteño* music is accordion based, with only four or five members in a group. *Banda* groups are a bit larger and include a tuba or tambora. And of course in all these groups, you'll hear guitars and singers. The tuba and accordion reflect the influence of Germans who immigrated to Mexico in the nineteenth century.

One of the top-selling Latin bands in America has long been the California-based *norteño* group Los Tigres del Norte (The Tigers of the North), whose music is infused with all sorts of double entendres, code words, metaphors, and similes that resonate with the undocumented immigrant in the United States. In 2009, for instance, Los Tigres came out with a hit song called "La Granja" (The Farm), accompanied with a video of Orwellian-like farm animals. While the group remains mum on the meaning of the song, it has been widely interpreted as a jab at the players in the drug wars that have gripped Mexico.

As I write these words, I'm listening to my iPod. I downloaded a Los Tigres album, *Pacto de Sangre*, and just about every song is about the immigrant experience. As I type, they're singing "El Santo de los Mojados," which means "The Saint of the Wetbacks." In the song, a migrant prays to St. Peter, "the patron saint of the undocumented." The migrant prays because he's about to make the perilous journey across the desert because the Mexican government has turned his homeland into "hell." The song ends with a plea for immigration reform—to St. Peter, of course.

Like Los Tigres, who are Mexican immigrants, Ivan Bojorquez knew how to tap into the immigrant experience. In 2008, he joined a *norteño* band called Los Herederos de La Sierra, which means "Heirs of the Mountains." When I met up with Ivan in the Dunkin' Donuts, the group had just won a $5,000 prize for winning a battle of the bands sponsored by Budweiser, which, incidentally, sells a lot of its product to Mexican immigrants.

The Herederos consisted of an accordionist named Luis, two guitar players, and a singer. The Herederos started out playing at backyard barbecues, and performed for free at radio-station promotions, then graduated to clubs and concerts in Phoenix. Like a lot of Mexican regional groups, Herederos got a MySpace page and recorded a CD themselves.

Ivan was the only group member with a steady job; the three others were construction workers whose work had mostly dried up. The group performed at least once every weekend, sometimes three times. The gigs brought in a monthly total of about $2,400, or $600 for each musician.

Money was tight. One month's income did not even cover the $800 the Herederos each paid for their matching cowboy outfits. White hats. Red shirts. White belts. Jeans. Western-style jackets. White boots.

They wore those outfits, without the jackets, on the Saturday night in 2010 I saw them perform at a west Phoenix club. Like so many venues that had once attracted healthy crowds of undocumented immigrants, this facility could easily accommodate three hundred people.

It became clear that despite the wild popularity of Mexican regional music in the United States, the musicians and clubs that catered to undocumented immigrants in Phoenix were struggling.

On this night, despite the reasonable $10 cover charge, the club was almost empty. A couple of men sat at the bar, staring at a Virgin of Guadalupe painting, drinking beer. There were perhaps forty-five round tables with chairs, and most of these were vacant.

A man at a table near mine drank cold beers he pulled from an ice bucket set in front of him. Two women in their twenties sat with him. One woman smiled. The other woman stared at her drink or the crowd. The two women wore tight skirts and blouses and high heels. The man wore a cowboy hat, jeans, and boots, just like most of the other men in the room.

The Herederos played enthusiastically, but I couldn't really enjoy the music. Too many eardrum-shattering squeaks and screeches from the less-than-perfect sound system. Almost everyone danced, but the dance floor seemed empty. A waiter told me the place would fill up, just wait and see. But the place didn't fill up, even though the Herederos played their hearts out.

Later, the promoter for this unattended event, a man named Ernesto Ruelas, told me that about half of the Phoenix clubs had gone out of business—and 75 percent of the clients had disappeared from the clubs.

Ernesto's income had dipped precipitously because club owners couldn't afford to pay much for the groups he represented. He was grateful his wife had a job at Burger King.

"Everyone tells me the same thing," Ernesto said. "They tell me that as soon as Arpaio retires they'll go to the clubs again. Until then, they'll stay at home. They're scared to go out."

• • •

A few weeks later, the Herederos played at Herb Owens's *Mercado*. "It wasn't nearly as full as it used to be," Ivan told me over the phone.

"People tell me they're afraid of Arpaio," he continued, echoing Ernesto. "That's the main reason they don't come. It's not the money. People can afford us." He said clubs usually charged $5 to $10 covers. So it couldn't be the economy that kept them away. It was fear of Sheriff Joe, he just knew it.

I checked on YouTube and found that a couple of uncomplimentary *corridos*, or Mexican ballads, about Sheriff Joe were circulating. Sheriff Joe was a current event, and *corridos* were like musical newspapers.

In 2010, northern Mexico was consumed with the cultivation, manufacture, transportation, and sale of drugs; the smuggling of drugs and humans; and the ongoing inchoate "drug war" launched by President Calderón in 2006. This explains the popularity in Phoenix of *narcocorridos*, or ballads about drug wars, drug lords, and drug smugglers. Mexican regional music referencing *narcotraficantes* was becoming increasingly popular. It reflected the outrage of the common people over what they viewed as senseless violence. After all, *narcotraficantes* had been around for decades. So, Mexicans not involved with the drug trade just looked the other way. Why had the government stirred up so much trouble by going after some of the drug cartels?

This popularity of music that referenced *narcotraficantes* helped me understand Ivan's new marketing strategy. The last time I talked to Ivan, in the early spring of 2010, he told me the band had changed its name to Los Herederos de Culiacán.

Culiacán is the capital of Sinaloa, which in turn is the home base of Joaquín *El Chapo* Guzmán Loera, head of the Sinaloa drug cartel. In 2009, *Forbes* listed El Chapo as number 701 among the world's richest men. He was reportedly worth $1 billion. The drug lord is a folk hero to some Mexicans, who think of him as a major employer in a country with few decent-paying jobs. Drug lingo is laced through a lot of Mexican regional music. Every now and then the Herederos will throw in a narco song too.

Adding Culiacán to the band name made sense because all the Herederos had been born in Sinaloa, and two of them actually grew up in Culiacán. The name carried more cred and narco cachet.

"Right now," Ivan explained, "there are a lot of narco references in Mexican music because the people like it. That's what they want to hear."

• • •

Even if they weren't going out as much at night, undocumented immigrants still enjoyed their music. They downloaded Mexican regional music onto their cell phones, paying with their phone cards. When they hung out at home on weekends, making *carne asada* or burgers, they listened to the music. And during their work commutes, many turned their radio dials to 88.3-FM, KNAI, Radio Campesina.

Consider the stresses of those commutes. In sprawled-out metro Phoenix, round-trip commutes could take more than an hour. Undocumented immigrants had no Arizona driver's licenses. They could be stopped on a whim, many believed, just because they looked Mexican. Then they'd face deportation. Radio Campesina not only played hits by Los Tigres del Norte and Vicente Fernández, but it also warned of where, exactly, the sheriff might be patrolling that day. What's more, it routinely offered airtime to immigration lawyers who detailed what to do in case you did get picked up by the sheriff or any other authority. The attorneys were trolling for clients, no doubt, and gave out their phone numbers, but their general advice was nevertheless worthwhile to listeners.

Radio Campesina in Phoenix was founded in 1990. It is a public radio station like NPR, but that's where the comparison ends.

The radio station is run by a foundation controlled by the descendants of César Chávez, the Chicano hero who organized farm workers into the United Farm Workers of America in the 1960s. Chávez understood the importance of music to the Mexican soul, and he figured that if a station played the music people loved, they would also listen to his public service announcements, like organizing updates and campaigns to register voters. The first Campesina (farmworker) station was started in California in 1983, and the Phoenix station followed.

Chávez was an American. He was born in Arizona in 1927 and died in Arizona in 1993. In those days, many farmworkers were Americans who traveled to different harvests around the country. Many of these people were Mexican-Americans, like Chávez himself. He was proud of his roots, yet he opposed illegal immigration.

There are stories of Chávez telling undocumented people to go home and of Chávez opposing a guest worker program for Mexican agricultural workers.

The reason: American growers hired undocumented Mexican immigrants during strikes organized by the United Farm Workers of America.

"He was not against undocumented immigrants; he was against scabs. They broke the strike lines," Alejandro Chávez, the hero's grandson and a political consultant in Phoenix, told me one day when we spoke on the phone.

Things had changed since the 1960s.

"Campesina is an advocate for educating and informing all people, including the undocumented," Alejandro said. "Campesina doesn't look at citizenship. It looks at people."

By 2010, César Chávez's famous rallying cry—*Sí se puede* (It can be done)—had become the rallying cry of undocumented immigrants and their advocates and was chanted over and over at Phoenix marches.

Some pro-migrant activists criticized Radio Campesina as being too "commercial" because it played popular songs and had too many lawyers and chiropractors as "sponsors," but in 2010 it was widely viewed in the undocumented underground as one of the few institutional advocates for the undocumented in Phoenix. When unauthorized immigrants had no place else to turn, they sometimes showed up at the front desk of the radio station headquarters on West Thomas Road. Sometimes, people made inquiries about family members lost in the desert. Other times, they had immigration problems. Or they had to raise money to ship a loved one's remains back to Mexico and sought radio publicity for a car wash fund-raiser. Or they had just been evicted. Or their bosses hadn't paid them. The Campesina personnel weren't social workers, but they could at least point people to churches, private charities, nonprofits, and medical clinics that helped undocumented people. What's more, Campesina still had excellent results with labor disputes and had branched into low-income housing and education programs. It obtained pharmacy discount cards for undocumented people who had to buy medicines.

Undocumented people also undoubtedly made up a big chunk of the approximately ninety thousand people who listened to Radio Campesina each hour it was on the air. (Campesina broadcast from 4:30 a.m. to 7:30 p.m. daily. A fundamentalist English-language Christian station took over the dial at night.)

In 2010, one of the most popular Spanish-language hosts in Phoenix was a Campesina personality who hosted the late-afternoon/early-evening slot.

He was known as *El Parientito*, which means, more or less, "Little Homey." One evening I visited *Parientito* in his sound booth at the Campesina office. The sound booth was small, spare, encased in glass. *Parientito* sat at a desk in front of a mic, wearing earphones. He was twenty-eight years old, slightly built, with short, gelled dark hair and a wide, easy smile.

For the most part, the music for his show had been preselected and programmed by Alejandro Chávez's cousin, which was good in a way because it gave *El Parientito* the time to create his own alter egos. His imaginary sidekick was named *El Marciano* (The Martian), and he sounded a lot like a Mexican ET, except that unlike ET, this Mexican extraterrestrial laughed maniacally with callers. *JA JA JA JA JA*, *El Marciano* would chortle, and then the caller would chortle right back: *JA JA JA JA JA*. Then there would be more programmed music, a break for blaring "sponsorships" for clubs and attorneys and mortgage adjusters that sounded a lot like ads, and then *El Parientito* would take another call.

When he was off the air, *El Parientito* told me his real name was Octavio Bailon, and he was a former plumber. He'd come to Phoenix legally, at the same age and for the same reasons as Ivan Bojorquez, but his experience as an immigrant was entirely different. As a child, he cried every day, he told me, pining for his native Chihuahua. He felt cooped up and lonely in Phoenix. Then, one day a Catholic priest gave his mother an old rickety church organ. Octavio taught himself how to play it.

He dropped out of school when, at the age of seventeen, he fathered his first child and married. He worked at McDonald's, and the marriage lasted six months. After McDonald's he became a salesman for a company that sold wholesale beef. Then he became a plumber, where he listened to Univision Spanish-language radio as he worked. He admired one particular host, *El Gatillero*. One evening at a concert, Octavio bought *El Gatillero* a beer. The older host could see that Octavio had talent. For several years, Octavio served as *El Gatillero*'s on-the-air sidekick and straight man. Then the two parted ways, and he landed at Campesina.

He told me that he earned about $40,000 annually and that he could "make more money plumbing." What he liked about the station was its public-service aspect, the fact that his creativity was not stifled, and the closeness of the station to the undocumented community. He would never forget his own immigrant experience.

"I'm someone they can identify with," he told me. "They can forget about their troubles for a while."

Undocumented immigrants, he told me, were hanging low, sure the anti-immigrant atmosphere in Phoenix would pass because gringos could not live without Mexicans, who did the dirty work.

"Mexicans like to overcome hurdles," he told me. "We will do whatever it takes to feed our families. If we don't find one job, we'll come up with something else."

Just hang low, hunker down, listen to *Parientito* on Campesina. Things will get better.

"If we go to McDonald's and only have money for a hamburger, that's fine," he said. "If you're an American, you don't want just the hamburger. You want the hamburger and the fries and the Coke."

Octavio owned a home-based recording studio and had started a group called El Parientito y su Crazy Mafia, which had signed with Sony Records. His music, he told me, targeted young second- and third-generation bilingual Latinos. It fused reggae with Mexican regional. I checked the MySpace page for El Parientito y su Crazy

Mafia and watched the slick videos. In one, a foxy schoolgirl tantalized the crooning *El Parientito*, who wore baggy clothes and dark glasses and grabbed at his crotch a la hip-hop. In the other video, he sang about a girl with a sexy tongue.

Compared to the Herederos, the Crazy Mafia seemed more American than Mexican.

And compared to Ivan, Octavio seemed more Americanized.

I once asked Octavio where he saw himself in ten years, and he envisioned himself living in Beverly Hills, having won his fourth Grammy.

What could be more American than that?

• • •

But there you had it. The Americanized Octavio had created the entirely Mexican *El Parientito* and was a hit with newly arrived immi-

El Parientito *(l) and Michael Nowakowski in La Campesina Studio in Phoenix.* KATHY MCCRAINE

grants. If it weren't for *El Parientito* and other Spanish-speaking Campesina personalities who played Mexican regional music, immigrants probably wouldn't tune in to Campesina. And if they didn't tune in to Campesina, they would have one less place to turn to in times of crisis. Undocumented immigrants weren't eligible for publicly funded social services.

If there was no place else to turn to, at least there was Campesina.

"When people need help, they come to us," Phoenix City Councilman Michael Nowakowski, the Latino general manager of Campesina, told me one day as we wandered through the radio station's office, a warren of small rooms decorated in the bright red and yellow farmworker colors. On the walls, likenesses of Chávez and Barack Obama competed with posters of famous *norteño* singers.

Nowakowski, who had majored in religious studies in college and had once served as a Hispanic outreach minister for the Catholic diocese in Phoenix, looked at me and shook his head. He didn't know how much longer these people could hold out.

"We talk about helping Third World countries," he said, "but we need to look at the people in our own country first."

CHAPTER 8

Joaquín's American Dream

Joaquín had to choose whether to die
slowly in the United States or return to
Mexico and take his chances.

After his father died in 1999, thirteen-year-old Joaquín dropped out of
school and started hanging out on the streets of Mexico City. To earn
a few cents, he cleaned taxis and recruited passengers for the drivers.
He wasn't into drugs yet, but he was heading toward trouble. All of
this worried Joaquín's mother and his extended family, which explains
why one day Joaquín's Uncle Domingo suggested that Joaquín come
with him to Phoenix, Arizona. "Do you want a better life for yourself?"
Uncle Domingo asked.

Joaquín guessed he did. A few days later, he and Uncle Domingo
crossed into Texas and drove to Phoenix. Joaquín was in culture
shock—Phoenix was so impersonal, so dry, so hot. He went to school
(even though at first he didn't understand a word of English), then
came home every afternoon without hanging out on the streets. His
uncle worked late, and Joaquín was often alone. He pined for his family. His loneliness peaked during the holidays, when he yearned for
the large family celebrations on Christmas Eve. There weren't many
presents back in Mexico City, but people took the time to laugh, eat,
and enjoy each other. In Phoenix, Joaquín thought, the holidays were
sterile—no Christmas Eve celebrations, just fifteen minutes opening
cheap presents on Christmas Day.

Five years later, eighteen-year-old Joaquín still lived with his
uncle at an apartment complex in central Phoenix. By then, he spoke
enough English to get by and was closing in on his high school graduation, after which he aspired to be a computer technician. It would
be a sign of weakness to show his loneliness, so Joaquín hid behind a
clownish persona. He cracked jokes. He teased.

His life changed when he helped a blue-eyed girl named Tanya move a couch. Tanya was sixteen, an American citizen, the daughter of an unemployed truck driver and a stay-at-home mom. Tanya was every bit as lonely as Joaquín and was, at the time, living with her grandmother in the same apartment complex where Joaquín lived. She had thick strawberry-blond hair, a sturdy build, and a seriousness that offset Joaquín's buffoonery.

Six months after they met, Tanya and Joaquín married at the courthouse. They didn't have a cake. They didn't have a party. They didn't need to prove Joaquín was a legal resident.

And of course, since Joaquín had entered the United States illegally, the marriage didn't change his status—he was still an unauthorized immigrant.

For their wedding portrait, Tanya wore a white sleeveless dress and Joaquín wore a white baseball cap turned backward, a gold chain, and a black T-shirt and jeans. In the portrait, which now sits on my desk for reasons I'll explain later, Tanya looks reserved and older than her sixteen years, and Joaquín smiles broadly. The newlyweds are both pudgy. The word *LOVE* stands out in fancy cursive on the white mat bordering the photograph.

After the two married, they both graduated from high school. (Tanya was the first in her family to get a high school diploma.) Gradually, Joaquín let go of his dream to become a computer technician and supported Tanya through a series of low-paying jobs. He painted stove fans. He assisted carpenters. He flipped burgers. Sometimes, he used Tanya's Social Security number. Other times, he used his fake documents, which cost him $75. Eventually, he landed a job as a painter. He worked with a crew that painted publicly funded projects like sections of Phoenix's Sky Harbor airport, fire stations, and police stations. The crew also painted hospitals, a casino on an Indian reservation, homeless shelters, condos, multimillion-dollar homes. Something was changing, though. His back ached when he used the paint sprayer. He lost weight. He felt queasy. He worked slower.

Muévete, get moving, his Mexican coworkers yelled.

"You're lazy," his boss said.

Joaquín quit, hired on at a different painting crew. His new boss didn't make him use the sprayer because he could see Joaquín wasn't strong enough. Instead, Joaquín caulked and puttied and masked windows and painted with a roller brush. By then, it was late 2007, his son Mike had been born, and Tanya was pregnant again.

Joaquín and Tanya were living out their version of the American Dream. They owned a two-story Phoenix condo and a $32,000 Nissan Titan pickup truck. They couldn't afford the payments for either on Joaquín's salary of about $2,000 a month. Joaquín attributed his sleeplessness, backache, nausea, and fatigue to financial stresses. He never thought of going to the doctor. With the debt they'd racked up, he couldn't afford it. And state law prevented him from signing on for non-emergency services from the Arizona Health Care Cost Containment System (AHCCCS), Arizona's Medicaid program for poor people.

In February 2008, Joaquín became so nauseated he couldn't keep anything down for days. Tanya took him to the emergency room, thinking he had the flu. The doctors didn't think so. His blood pressure was 210 over 150. (Normal blood pressure is about 120 over 80.) After a series of tests, Joaquín was diagnosed with end-stage renal disease.

He grinned when he received the diagnosis. He didn't understand what the doctors were talking about because he didn't know what the English word "kidneys" meant.

The doctors figured that years of undiagnosed high blood pressure probably caused the renal failure, but no one knew for sure.

A social worker explained that because hemodialysis (commonly known as dialysis) was an emergency treatment that Joaquín needed to stay alive, Joaquín qualified for emergency assistance through AHCCCS.

In early 2010, AHCCCS was an $8.5 billion program and served 1.2 million clients. About 75 percent of AHCCCS funds came from the federal government; the remaining 25 percent came from the state of Arizona.

State and federal law barred undocumented immigrants from receiving publicly funded health services. Only life-saving emergency services were covered.

As anti-migrant fervor swept the state, Arizona had tried to bar undocumented immigrants from getting dialysis through AHCCCS. The state maintained that dialysis wasn't a life-saving emergency service. Not everyone agreed. The state was sued in U.S. district court in Tucson by the Arizona Center for Disability Law and the William E. Morris Institute for Justice. In 2007, the year before Joaquín's kidneys failed, the federal court forced Arizona to pay for dialysis as an emergency medical service. This meant that despite his undocumented status, Joaquín could get free dialysis indefinitely. His treatments would cost about $36,000 per year.

• • •

After Joaquín told me about his medical problems, I wanted to understand exactly what kind of burden undocumented immigrants put on the nation's health-care budget.

What I learned surprised me, given all the inflammatory rhetoric on talk radio about immigrants running up the national debt with health-care costs.

In general, immigrants, documented and undocumented, use fewer health-care services than U.S. citizens because they are healthier. This is particularly true of Mexicans.

Health statisticians call it the "Hispanic Paradox."

Even though Mexican immigrants are poorer than most citizens, they don't get as sick, Jim Stimpson, a professor of social and behavioral sciences at the University of North Texas Health Science Center in Fort Worth, told me over the telephone in early 2010.

Stimpson was the lead author of a 2010 study in *Health Affairs* that indicated that health-care spending was much higher for citizens than noncitizens.

He also told me that, contrary to public opinion, undocumented immigrants *don't* tend to use hospital emergency rooms for regular health care. Instead, they tend to visit the ER when they give birth, when they receive workplace injuries, and when they suffer a catastrophic onset of an end-stage disease, like kidney failure.

"All of the well-done independent studies have shown clearly that immigrants, documented and undocumented, are not the driving force behind the health-care problem," he said.

It's impossible to figure how many undocumented immigrants have private health insurance, but those without insurance remain excluded from 2010 health-care reform measures. Some emergency health care is still available to the undocumented, but for the most part they are prevented from accessing any publicly funded health care.

Migrants still have the right to visit hospital emergency rooms, but in Arizona, at least, many fear deportation if they show up at the hospital.

Sometimes, Arizona hospitals stabilize undocumented immigrants, then send them back to Mexico for expensive treatments. The most notorious case of ambulance deportation occurred in 2007, when the Catholic nuns running St. Joseph's Hospital sent eighteen-year-old Joe Arvizu, an undocumented immigrant with leukemia who longed to serve in the United States Army, back to Mexico in an ambulance. American doctors told the boy's mother that Joe had an 85 percent cure rate, according to the *Arizona Republic*. The nuns had determined that Joe was stabilized, and that meant he didn't qualify for emergency treatment.

He died in Mexico a few weeks later.

• • •

Compared to Joe Arvizu, Joaquín was lucky. He could get free medicine and dialysis indefinitely. For two and a half weeks after his initial diagnosis, Joaquín stayed in the hospital. His doctors created an arteriovenous fistula by surgically connecting an artery and a vein in his forearm. The procedure produced a super-vessel for the dialysis machine, which did the work the kidneys could no longer do by removing Joaquín's blood, cleansing it, and returning it to his body. Tanya understood the doctors to say that Joaquín could survive on dialysis for about five years, but then he'd need a kidney transplant to stay alive.

Of course, there was a hitch—the state would not pay for a kidney transplant for undocumented immigrants. Transplants were not considered life-saving emergency procedures in federal and state healthcare regulations.

Joaquín now realized the gravity of his illness. The high blood pressure problem ran in his family; his father had died young, and his brother had just died of complications from high blood pressure. His mother, too, had high blood pressure. Since Joaquín was uninsured, he'd never gone to a doctor for a checkup, and the high blood pressure went undetected for years. If he'd had regular medical care, his health catastrophe might have been prevented.

Nothing was easy now.

Joaquín's eyesight was starting to fail. His weight dropped from 250 to 200 pounds. At five feet ten inches, he still looked strong, but he wasn't. His three-day-a-week dialysis sessions prevented him from working as long or as hard as before.

With less income, his financial problems mounted. Joaquín and Tanya lost the truck. They lost the condo. They moved back into the very apartment complex where they'd met several years before. After their second son, Tom, was born, Tanya began working weekends at a nursing home.

Still, the collection agencies called almost every day.

Tanya and Joaquín had already asked an immigration lawyer about obtaining a green card for Joaquín. After all, Tanya was an American citizen. But, like thousands of other couples, Joaquín and Tanya learned that since Joaquín had entered the United States illegally, his chances of obtaining a green card were slim under current immigration laws.

• • •

I first visited Joaquín and Tanya in late March 2009. Their central Phoenix apartment complex was a grimy sand-colored cluster of two-story rectangular buildings opening onto littered parking lots. Hibachis, mops, brooms, bikes, plastic chairs, and toys cluttered the small dirt patches in front of the apartments. The sounds of Mexican music and traffic from nearby Indian School Road fused into an incessant background noise.

Tanya had just quit her weekend job as an assistant at a nursing home, a job she'd held only for a few months. It paid about $2,000 monthly. Largely because of her salary, she and Joaquín had squirreled away about $5,000 in savings. Although bill collectors were after them, Joaquín and Tanya wouldn't touch this money.

They had other plans for it.

When I arrived at the apartment, Joaquín had just come home from work. He wore painter's pants and a gray long-sleeved T-shirt. There was white paint on his face, white paint on his fingernails, white paint on his hand, white paint on his swollen purple-blue dialysis fistula.

"When they put the needles in, they have to pick the scab off, and because the fistula has been infected twice, it hurts and is sometimes very sore during treatment," he said. "If I move too much during the dialysis, the needle will hurt even more."

Tanya, Joaquín, and the boys in Phoenix, before the Mexico City trip.
TERRY GREENE STERLING

Mike, who was almost three, climbed in his father's lap and babbled in half-English-half-Spanish. Nine-month-old Tom sat on the carpet pounding a toy against a plastic baby walker. Joaquín feared the two boys had inherited his genes and that they, too, might develop deadly high blood pressure and kidney failure. Joaquín patted Mike's back.

"Our condo had a lot more room," he said.

Joaquín and Tanya sat on one of two beige entertainment-center-style couches, the kind with cup holders in the arms, which took up most of the room. A coffee table held a blue plastic cup, the wedding portrait with the cursive *LOVE* insignia, and a remote control. The movie *Transformers* played on the flat-screen TV, the booming sounds competing with the whir of a portable fan running at full speed because the air-conditioning didn't work. A calendar hung on the wall, the page turned to February, even though it was late March.

Tanya communicated with her kids in fluent Spanish; she'd learned the language after hooking up with Joaquín. Her English sounded more like Joaquín's now; she spoke with a Mexican accent, pronouncing "kids" as "keeds," for instance.

She seemed embarrassed about the cluttered apartment. "I have to clean all the time," she said. "Make sure you warn me before you come again so I can clean again." She told me she couldn't get rid of the roaches. She sprayed and sprayed, but the roaches kept coming. There were roaches in the tiny kitchen, roaches in the bedroom that Tanya and Joaquín shared with the boys, roaches in the hall closet.

During my visit, *Transformers* ended and *Wheel of Fortune* came on. Vendors knocked on the door twice. First, a woman hawked fresh oranges she pushed through the apartment complex in a grocery cart. Another woman peddled tamales. Joaquín bought me a dozen pork tamales, fresh from the steamer, for $10. I felt guilty, suspecting he had very little cash, but I knew if I refused I'd hurt his feelings. Joaquín earned about $1,600 a month. His family's monthly expenses included $650 for rent, $500 for food, $50 for the phone, $25 for the TV, and $200 for miscellaneous expenses. That left less than $200 a month to pay the bill collectors.

He'd lost control of his life.

Of course, in hindsight he knew it was unrealistic to think his painter's salary would have paid for a fancy truck and condo, but he had become an American dreamer—he had envisioned himself grilling burgers by the pool in the backyard for his wife and kids. And back in 2006 and 2007, lenders of subprime loans were eager to front him the money to fulfill his fantasies of success. Joaquín had fallen into an equal-opportunity subprime-lending trap that ensnared millions of Americans—native, documented, and undocumented.

Now his American dream had evaporated. No condo. No truck. No kidney transplant. No health insurance. No documents.

"I work and work and work and work," he said, "and I don't get nothing done. I don't advance. Now that I'm sick, it's worse."

He and Tanya had few adults they could rely on for advice. They muddled through life on their own.

"I'm sick and tired of dialysis," Joaquín said one time.

And another time: "I'm not having a life right now, you can say that."

Joaquín hadn't seen his mother in ten years, but he talked to her regularly on the phone. She said things were better in Mexico City. Joaquín's sister had done some research and told Joaquín that dialysis and kidney transplants were free in Mexico.

Everything seemed better in Mexico City than in Phoenix, Arizona, where you didn't have health insurance and couldn't get a transplant, where you woke up in the morning and wondered if you'd be deported that day, where you looked in the rearview mirror because you never knew where Sheriff Joe's deputies were hanging out.

For all these reasons, Joaquín and Tanya decided to move their family to Mexico.

Their plan: Take their $5,000 in savings, build a house, buy a car, and become itinerant peddlers selling items purchased in Mexico City big-box stores to country people.

Joaquín figured he'd get a kidney transplant in Mexico City—perhaps his mother could be a donor—and the family would survive. Eventually, they figured, they'd have enough money to get Joaquín's papers in order. Then they'd return to Phoenix.

"I do want to come back," Joaquín said. "I like this country. I have found a lot of good people here. I found my wife. I have a lot of friends that are white, and they are very good. My boss is white, he's American, and he's been very good with me even though I'm sick. He always helps me with hours, gives me jobs, asks how I feel, and says, 'Just chill and do what you can if you feel sick.'"

I asked: Are you sure about this?

I asked: Why give up free dialysis?

"Mexico couldn't be any worse than here," Tanya said. "Here you work all the time just to survive. There you work all the time just to survive."

She used the word "survive" a lot. He was twenty-three and suffering renal failure. She was twenty-one and facing possible widowhood. They didn't appear to have much extended-family support. They made their decision to escape to Mexico on their own.

By the time I visited with them, they'd already bought their plane tickets.

• • •

On the day before Joaquín and his family were scheduled to leave for Mexico City, Joaquín had a dialysis treatment. He knew he would die if he went longer than a few days without dialysis, but he had no firm plan on where, exactly, he would get dialysis in Mexico City. He planned on having yet another treatment in the morning, before he got on the plane.

I caught up with Joaquín at the central Phoenix dialysis clinic, where he was receiving the first of the two planned treatments. The clinic was a small odorless room with half a dozen gray upholstered reclining chairs, where patients lay while tethered to the machines. Each chair had a little television above it, but most patients were too sick to watch TV. Miniblinds blocked out the hot desert sun. The room was decorated with a poster illustrating the step-by-step surgical fashioning of a fistula. Close to that poster was another, more colorful illustration of a winding road leading into green hills and a setting sun.

Several dialysis nurses bustled about the room, tending to Joaquín and two other men hooked up to the machines. Martín was an undocumented immigrant in his thirties who laid tile floors for a living. His eye teared constantly; he'd injured it with a splinter of tile. Like Joaquín, his kidneys had failed due to untreated high blood pressure. Like Joaquín, he was an undocumented immigrant married to an American citizen.

Next to Martín was Fernando, a legal resident who suffered from chronic kidney disease. He was in his early twenties and had already undergone one kidney transplant, which went sour when he failed to take his medicines. Now he was hoping for a second transplant. Joaquín was exhausted that day.

He and Tanya had partied the night before, gone dancing and stayed out all night. They figured that since they had a babysitter they'd do it up big, celebrate their adventure in Mexico City.

Joaquín closed his eyes and lay against the gray plastic. The machine sounded like a small windmill rhythmically pumping water out of the earth. It sucked Joaquín's blood out from the fistula in his left arm through clear tubes and cleansed it, dumping the excess toxins and liquid and returning the clean blood through a plastic tube and reinserting it into his body. A computer monitored Joaquín's vital signs. His heart was beating one hundred times a minute, and his blood pressure was 154 over 72.

"My mother's going to see if she can give me a kidney," Joaquín told his dialysis friends.

"We've got an appointment with a doctor."

Orale, Martín said. Cool. Go for it.

"In Mexico City, they give you home dialysis through your stomach. It's much better than this," Joaquín said.

"You can always come back," Martín said. "I know a smuggler who will cross you for $1,500. But he doesn't cross people in the summer, it's too hot."

• • •

On April 4, 2009, Joaquín and Tanya sat on the floor of their living room, waiting for Joaquín's uncle to arrive and take them to the airport. Joaquín had just returned from an early-morning dialysis treatment. His pulse was 115, and he felt lightheaded. He tried to eat breakfast at Jack-in-the-Box but couldn't touch his food. His mouth was dry, yet he didn't want to drink, because he didn't know when he'd get his next dialysis treatment in Mexico City and he feared his body would store too much liquid if he drank anything.

Mike, dressed in a striped T-shirt, jeans, and athletic shoes with twinkling red lights, climbed over the twelve brand-new black suitcases Tanya had packed the night before. They'd packed their iPod, Tanya's C-Pap machine for her sleep apnea, meds for Joaquín, clothes, a few toys.

Joaquín had sold their couches, the TV, and a few other prize possessions. The new owner of the TV hadn't picked it up yet, and Tom watched *Cars* as he drank his bottle. The family would leave behind hundreds of belongings—CDs, toys, sheets, a bed, mattress pads, a baby crib, blankets, a vacuum cleaner, a scale, a coffeemaker, toothbrushes, two large bottles of shampoo, dishes, pots and pans, the fan, textbooks from high school, photo negatives. The discarded belongings were strewn about the apartment. I asked Tanya what would happen to all the stuff left behind, and she said the landlord would have to take care of it.

There were certain things Tanya loved but couldn't fit in the suitcase. She wanted to give them to me. She handed me a bilingual Bible, the Good News Translation, because it would be bad luck to just abandon it in the apartment. A ribbon marked a page with a psalm, which said, in part, that God will protect the faithful from "all deadly disease."

Tanya handed me her framed wedding portrait, bottles of TRE-Semmé antibreakage shampoo and conditioner, and a "Tales of Taverna" ceramic plate decorated with jumping dolphins. I told Tanya I'd store the items for her and return them when she got back to Phoenix.

She hadn't slept the night before. She worried that her in-laws in Mexico wouldn't accept her. She worried the plane would crash. She worried their plan would fall apart. She worried Joaquín would die.

"I'm just very, very scared," she said.

"Don't think about it," Joaquín said. "What do you do? You try to stay alive. You try to survive."

He was decked out in his finest—a Giants baseball cap, a black-and-white-striped shirt, jeans, new white tennis shoes. Of course, he had his own acculturation fears. He hadn't been back to Mexico City for ten years. Would he fit in with his family? Would accessing health care be as easy as his mother and sister told him it would be?

I asked Tanya where she saw herself in ten years. "I can't tell you what will happen in ten years," she said. "I could be happily married, but then again I could be a widow, I don't know. So that's one thing I want to start thinking about now. Anything could happen between now and then, and right now it's too early to tell."

Like Joaquín, she was dressed in new clothes: A bright yellow shirt, brown pants, white tennis shoes. She was determined to make the Mexico City dream work. She would just grit her teeth and go forward, she told me. She had no choice.

Then Joaquín's uncle arrived. Joaquín and Tanya loaded the luggage in the back of his truck. They climbed with the kids into the double-cab, and their uncle drove them to the airport that Joaquín had once painted.

It was a hot day, and their uncle parked in a distant parking space instead of dropping them off at the passenger curb. Joaquín and Tanya had to make several trips, lugging kids and the twelve pieces of luggage. After checking in, they had pepperoni pizza and coffee, boarded the plane, and flew off to their new life.

• • •

I called Joaquín two weeks after he'd arrived in Mexico City. He was living with his mother. Nothing was as he'd expected. Because he'd never worked in Mexico, he could not apply for publicly funded medical assistance. He had to pay for dialysis—it cost about $80 per treatment—so he dropped his treatments down to twice a week. The dialysis machines were old. He had to pay for his medicines, which cost several hundred dollars each month. Their savings had dwindled from $5,000 to $4,000.

He had no transplant donors. Blood tests showed his mother was not a match. Tanya was too fat, the doctor said. Joaquín figured that if things didn't get better, he'd come back to the United States. "I'm doing OK," he told me. "Hopefully, I'll be able to see you again."

Their plans were collapsing. He didn't have enough money to build a house, buy a car, or purchase inventory at a big-box store.

He wondered if he had enough money to stay alive.

Two weeks later, I called Joaquín again. (I was lucky to reach him; he happened to be at his mother's house even though he and Tanya and the boys had moved in with his grandmother, who didn't have a phone.) The $5,000 stash had now dwindled to about $2,000.

"Things are starting to get tough," he said.

Swine flu had hit Mexico City, but Joaquín and his family escaped it. Now they wanted to escape Mexico City. Joaquín asked me to give him the phone number for a nurse at the dialysis clinic. I told him I'd race down to the clinic and call him back. When I called from the clinic, his phone line was busy. I called several times.

The next day, I visited the clinic again and dialed up Joaquín. He talked to his dialysis buddies, told them the medicine was expensive and the dialysis was expensive and he was running out of money. Then, the line went dead.

Ten days later, Joaquín called me. He'd misdialed. He'd meant to reach his father-in-law, to make arrangements to be picked up at the border.

In early June, Joaquín once again rang my cell phone. Did I have the number for the dialysis nurse? He was set to cross the border. Before I could answer, the line went dead. A week later, he called again. Tanya and the kids crossed the Texas border, but "they deported my ass."

He was back in Mexico City. He felt like a fool. Why hadn't he stayed in Phoenix?

We arranged to talk by phone at his mother's house the following day. When I phoned at the appointed time, he wasn't there. His mother told me that Joaquín was sort of OK and that I should call again. I called several times, and left voice-mail messages. No reply.

A year after Joaquín and Tanya had left Phoenix for Mexico City, the Tales of Taverna plate still sat on a shelf in my office, next to their wedding picture.

I called again. Joaquín's sister answered the phone this time. Joaquín was alive, still getting dialysis. Tanya was still in the United States with the kids, but Joaquín's sister didn't know where and she didn't have Tanya's phone number.

Joaquín's sister gave me a cell phone number for Joaquín. I dialed, left voice messages, texted.

I never got a reply.

CHAPTER 9

Child of the *Posada*

Viri was an honor student at Arizona State University.
And she lived a double life.

Eight-year-old Viri hadn't seen her father in two years. He was an auto mechanic, and he lived in faraway Phoenix, Arizona. A lot of the dads in the village had traveled north to the United States, and it seemed like more were going every year. Viri lived with her mother, Alicia, and sister, Guadalupe, in a small house in the village of El Obligado, in the Mexican state of Zacatecas.

With no husband to help her make decisions and raise their two daughters, Alicia made do. She missed her husband, but she kept herself busy. She sold clothes she purchased from Mexico City wholesalers to village women who trusted her taste and sense of fashion. Sometimes, Alicia took her two daughters on buying trips to the big city. She never let the girls wander out of sight.

Every December, Alicia and the girls visited Alicia's mother in the neighboring state of Guanajuato. There, they participated in *posadas*, evening religious processions meant to recall the travails of biblical characters Mary and Joseph, who emigrated to Egypt to escape Herod, the Hebrew child killer. The *posadas* reenacted Joseph's "no room at the inn" search for shelter when he was on the road with his pregnant wife. Alicia and her daughters walked the dark streets with dozens of other celebrants, holding sparklers or candles, singing, praying. After the *posada* ended, children cracked open piñatas filled with oranges and peanuts and sugarcane.

Alicia was devoted to the Virgin of Guadalupe. She said Rosaries and prayed to be reunited with her husband, Federico. For Alicia, the remittances from Arizona didn't compensate for the long separations. She knew something was wrong. Federico had sometimes promised to come home for holidays but had failed to show up. Village gossipers said he'd fallen in love with another woman in Arizona. When Alicia confronted Federico on the phone, he wept and denied it.

One summer day in 1998, Alicia told her daughters: "We're going to Phoenix to live with your father." The girls cried and protested, sensing that nothing would be the same once they left their beloved El Obligado. But Viri and Guadalupe knew that when their mother made up her mind, there was no changing it. Alicia packed food, money, a few clothes. She and her daughters boarded a bus that took them to the border town of Agua Prieta, Sonora. There, she negotiated with a *coyote*.

She was about to take her daughters on a very different kind of *posada*.

Alicia and the girls crossed the desert into Arizona and climbed into the *coyote*'s truck. They smelled the alcohol on the *coyote*'s breath. He careened through the rocky borderlands like a madman. The truck left a contrail of cocoa-brown dust in its wake and soon caught the attention of the Border Patrol. The *coyote* spotted *La Migra* in his rearview mirror. He stopped the truck. He jumped out. He yelled *¡Corrale!* (Run!). He disappeared into the desert. Alicia and her bewildered daughters got out of the truck, stunned. They were transported to a Border Patrol station, fingerprinted, and returned to Agua Prieta.

The second *coyote* was cautious and avoided detection by hiking at night through gullies, veering up into mountain passes in the moonlight. At one point, he let Alicia and the girls rest. Alicia lay on her back on the rocky desert floor. She put one arm around Viri and one arm around Guadalupe and asked the *Virgencita* to intercede with God on her behalf. *If a snake or a spider or an animal bites one of us, may it bite all three of us so we all die together,* she prayed.

Three days later, Alicia and the girls arrived at a Phoenix drop house. It was Viri's ninth birthday. The intense heat in the drop house caused her to vomit. Federico didn't show up until late afternoon. By then, every one else had been picked up.

Alicia had come all the way to Phoenix from El Obligado to see for herself that the village gossipers had been correct—Federico had fallen in love with another woman.

Federico refused to live with Alicia, although he arranged for an apartment for her and the girls. Alone in a strange city in a foreign country with no blood relatives but her own daughters and a husband who didn't love her, Alicia relied on her common sense and the *Virgencita* for survival. A little tree grew outside the apartment, and Alicia often sat beneath it and prayed. Two weeks after she arrived in Phoenix, Alicia found a job selling women's clothing for a merchant at Herb Owens's *Gran Mercado*. At night she sorted packages for the U.S. Post Office.

Every night during her break, Alicia phoned her little daughters, who stayed alone in the locked apartment.

"If someone knocks on the door, don't answer. Hide in the bedroom," she told them.

Shortly after she arrived in Phoenix, Alicia asked Federico to pose for a photograph with her and the girls. In the picture, no one looked happy. Nevertheless, Alicia sent a copy of the portrait to her mother, just so she wouldn't worry.

• • •

Viri didn't understand English on the first day she walked into school in Phoenix. Soon after she sat down at her desk, though, she found a language she recognized—the language of numbers—math. It turned out that the little girl from El Obligado had the best math skills in the class.

Like many immigrant children, Viri wanted to learn English quickly so other students wouldn't tease her for mispronouncing or not understanding a word. But Spanish speakers in Viri's school didn't get much help learning English—once a week, an aide took Viri and the other Spanish speakers aside for an hour of English instruction. Viri listened carefully when the instructor said things like: "The plural of *sheep* is *sheep*, not *sheeps*."

In a matter of months, Viri had learned English. She began to understand that undocumented families struggled in ways that other families did not.

Alicia gave Federico two years to come back to her. He did not. Then, she started dating Martín, who was also an undocumented immigrant. (The couple would have one child, a boy.) Alicia allowed Martín to move into her apartment on one condition: He could not lay a hand on or discipline her daughters.

In 2003, Alicia bought a small two-bedroom townhome. The bank was happy to loan her the money, given her credit rating and steady work history. The little unit she purchased sat right in the middle of a crime-ridden neighborhood, but she transformed it into a warm cocoon for her family. She painted the walls a peach color, tiled the floors, and built a large shrine to the *Virgencita* in her living room.

She knew she'd lose the house if she was ever deported, but she wouldn't allow herself to think of it. Instead, she reasoned, it was better to pay for a house than to pay rent. Stay positive.

Through all of this, she urged the girls to study so they would not have to struggle as she had.

"If you study hard," she said, "in this great country there is no limit to what you can accomplish."

• • •

Portate bien.

Behave.

That's what Alicia told Viri in 2003 on her first day at Carl Hayden High School in Phoenix. Almost all of the two thousand or so students who attended the inner-city school were Latinos, and many were undocumented. It wasn't unusual for Viri to hear Spanish as she bolted across the concrete courtyards. She was a small girl with large brown eyes, glasses, and long hair. She often toted an enormous backpack filled with textbooks. She joined Junior ROTC, enrolled in honors classes, and continued to astonish her teachers with her superior math skills. In the summers, she took college-level classes at a community college. In her spare time, she volunteered in soup kitchens and nursing homes.

When Viri was fifteen years old, her mother threw a *quinceañera* birthday party for her, just as she had thrown one for Guadalupe. Five hundred people came to the gala. They brought food and gifts and money and love. Viri danced with her dad, and that made her happy. She still hadn't forgiven him for what she viewed as abandonment, though.

Federico, for his part, felt terrible about the psychological damage that the divorce had caused. He was so proud of his daughters, if only Viri could understand that.

Viri did all she could to ease her mother's burden—she cooked, cleaned, babysat her little brother. Each year, she tried to say the Rosary with Alicia during the Rosary season, which lasted from late October until December 12, the feast day of the *Virgen de Guadalupe*.

On the first day of the season, Alicia always held the Rosary ceremony in her house. She filled the living room with folding chairs. She made big pots of rice and chicken. She placed flowers and fresh candles at the feet of the statue of the brown *Virgencita*. In the evening, fifty or so guests would arrive—mostly women and children. The smaller kids would be restless, scampering between chairs and playing tag outside. But when Alicia led the Rosary, they climbed into their mother's laps and fell asleep to the chant of Hail Marys.

Between each decade of the Rosary, the women sang *La Guadalupana*, which commemorated the appearance of the *Virgencita* to the Mexican Indian Juan Diego. After the Rosary ended, everyone ate Alicia's spicy chicken, along with tortillas, rice, a hot fruit punch, and a version of *atole* called *champurrado*, a thick hot chocolate-cinnamon drink. The Virgin of Guadalupe statue was carried to a different house each night, and the ritual was repeated. On December 12, the statue would return to Alicia's home accompanied by *matachines*.

This was especially meaningful in a neighborhood infested with gangs and crime.

Viri shut that world out when she walked into her house, and she did the same thing when she went to school. Carl Hayden High School was an intellectual oasis for kids who had the *ganas*, or desire, to stay out of trouble and make something of themselves. No one believed in the students more than Fredi Lajvardi, Viri's cross-country coach and the driving force behind Carl Hayden's famous robotics team. In 2004, the team beat out MIT in the Marine Advanced Technology Education Competition for Underwater Remotely Operated Vehicles. In 2008, the team won the Chairman's Award in the National FIRST (For Inspiration and Recognition of Science and Technology) Competition. Dozens of other awards were displayed in the robotics lab.

Viri helped design and build robots for national and international competitions. Her engineering and math skills were key to the robotics team, and "Coach Fredi" mentored her and pushed her. He helped her overcome paralyzing shyness.

Coach Fredi didn't know it, but Viri viewed him as a substitute father.

She believed Coach Fredi and all the other teachers who recognized her math and science talent and told her that if she worked hard, she'd succeed.

Viri studied because she loved numbers and because she loved science. She studied for her mother, her teachers, and herself. And she studied because a part of her wanted to show her father that she could succeed without him.

• • •

In high school, Viri had been granted a merit-based scholarship for college. She thought she was set to go to Arizona State University in Tempe, Arizona, a suburb of Phoenix.

Then suddenly the scholarship was taken away.

Arizona voters made it almost impossible for undocumented kids to go to college.

In 2006, voters passed Proposition 300, which took effect in 2007, Viri's senior year in high school. The new law denied undocumented students state-funded scholarships and in-state tuition breaks at Arizona's public universities.

A few days before Viri donned her cap and gown, the Arizona Legislature invited the Carl Hayden robotics team to the state capitol to honor the students. Legislators gave the team a standing ovation for its math and science achievements. Next, the students were ushered into a hearing room, so they could see Arizona government in action. In the hearing room, legislators discussed the implementation of Prop 300.

Why, Viri wondered, had the voters made such a decision? She hadn't deprived American citizens of *their* scholarships; she had instead competed for scholarships based on academic achievement. She didn't seek an advantage just because she had brown skin or came from a poor family. She had competed academically—and won.

These voters—if they had a chance to know her, would they change their minds about her?

• • •

By the time I got to know Viri, she had—without state assistance—completed two years at Arizona State University and was a straight-A student in the College of Engineering. Local Latino leaders had pooled enough private funds to pay her way through those first two years. Proposition 300 not only prevented her from getting any publicly funded financial assistance, but it also forced her to pay out-of-state tuition, which ran about $18,000 per year. (In-state tuition, by comparison, cost about $6,000 per year.) Living expenses added another $5,000 to the annual bill. State laws prevented Viri from working so she could not legally help pay her own way through school.

When I met Viri in the summer of 2009, her tuition and expenses had been paid through the fall semester. But she had heard rumors that the scholarship fund was almost gone. She had registered for twenty credit hours for just that semester, trying to get as much coursework accomplished as possible in case the scholarship funds dried up.

My first impression of Viri was that she was very smart, very sweet, and very stressed. For years, she'd told herself not to worry about her undocumented status, because surely by the time she finished college, immigration reform would be passed and she'd become a legal resident of the United States.

Now she had only two more years left to go. She hung her hopes on newly elected President Barack Obama, who'd promised immigration reform and a "pathway to citizenship."

I'd gotten in touch with Viri because I'd become interested in the Dream Act, proposed federal legislation that would grant a six-year temporary legal status for undocumented high school grads who'd grown up in the United States, had no criminal records, and wanted to attend college or join the military. The most recent data indicates that about sixty-five thousand undocumented students graduated from high school each year.

The Dream Act would give these special high school grads, known as "Dreamers," a chance to complete two years of college or military service, after which they would be eligible to apply for legal residency in the United States. It would allow hundreds of undocumented students like Viri, many of whom excel in math or science, to qualify for in-state tuition, get scholarships, and/or work their way through college and grad school.

At the end of the first decade of the twenty-first century, the United States was behind twenty-one other nations in graduating students with engineering degrees. Viri knew that if the Dream Act passed, she could help fill a critical engineering shortage and give back to the country she loved. She wanted to help fix America. She wanted to pay taxes. She wanted to hold her head high.

The Dream Act made sense.

Yet Congress had failed to pass it every single year since 2001. About the time I met Viri in the summer of 2009, the Hispanic Caucus in the House and Senate had sidelined the Dream Act in order to focus on health-care reform. Latino leaders vowed to wrap the Dream Act into comprehensive immigration reform legislation in 2010.

Another year's wait was hard on Viri. She fought off conflicting feelings of anger, fear, despair, and hope. Keep studying, her mother told her. Something good will come from all this. It always does.

Viri vowed to finish college, no matter what.

The Latino leaders who'd gathered private scholarship funds for undocumented college students in the wake of Prop 300 were ruthless in meting out dollars. There were too many promising undocumented college students in Arizona. The out-of-state tuition was exorbitant. Only the best of the best got the precious scholarships.

• • •

Alicia's housing complex resembled an urban battlefield. Gangs had tagged walls. Bullet holes had shattered the windows of the recreation room. The swimming pool had been filled with dirt. The homeowners association had stopped watering the common areas some years before. Neighborhood children kicked soccer balls over glass-flecked dirt where lawns had once grown. The tall skeletons of shade trees that had died of thirst could not protect the children from the fierce sun.

Within the complex, Alicia's home was a refuge. The air was perfumed with the scent of candles and garlic and chilies simmering on the stove. The walls were covered with photographs of Viri and Guadalupe dressed like princesses in long dresses at different stages of their lives—First Communions, confirmations, *quinceañeras*, proms, and graduations. A large statue of the brown Virgin of Guadalupe stood prominently in the room, surrounded by bright pink, red, and orange flowers as well as tall votive candles. Several large rosaries dangled from the neck of the *Virgencita*.

Alicia, a short, solid woman with tightly cropped black hair, lively dark eyes, and a smile made all the more engaging by a silver-lined front tooth, told me the *Virgencita* would give her the strength to overcome anything, including the racism that had swept over this desert city.

She told me she still worked two jobs, thanks be to God. Early in the morning, she left home to prepare items for shipping for a big-box store. Eight hours later, she sold clothes door-to-door from large plastic tubs in her car. She sold everything from bras to sportswear to clients in their homes. She knew their sizes. She knew their needs. And she worked out informal credit arrangements for financially stressed immigrants.

Alicia said she'd sacrificed herself for her girls, and if things didn't turn around soon, if laws weren't changed and if her children were not allowed to prosper despite their hard-earned academic accolades, she would feel as if her entire life had been a waste.

Guadalupe listened to her mother talk as she sat on the floor. Her long black hair was gathered in a ponytail. She wore a uniform from the fast-food restaurant where she worked. She was twenty-one years old, married, the mother of a baby. She attended college like her sister—on a similar privately funded scholarship. She hoped one day to earn a doctorate in psychology and open a behavioral health clinic for troubled Latino kids.

I figured Guadalupe for the fiery sister, the one with the gumption. Once, Guadalupe told me, "No one will ever make me leave this country."

Viri, on the other hand, internalized her stress and anger and fear. Sometimes, she seemed on the edge of tears.

Who could blame her?

She hadn't chosen to come to the United States, but she had chosen to work hard in school and excel academically. Now, this hard-working straight-A engineering student faced graduation in 2011, and she feared she'd be thrust right back into the undocumented underground, working at a McDonald's.

• • •

No one in Phoenix has been more of an advocate for the Dream Act, and the kids who struggle without it, than Carmen Cornejo.

One day in 2009, we sat in her living room in a Phoenix suburb, watching a shaft of sunlight play on a coffee table laden with atlases, histories, and novels. Carmen and her husband, Marcos, are both Mexican immigrants who have become American citizens. They became interested in the Dream Act after Marcos, who works for Intel and speaks six languages, began mentoring the Carl Hayden robotics kids several years ago. When I met Carmen, she mothered the few undocumented students, like Viri, who still stuck it out at Arizona

State. She helped students obtain dwindling scholarship funds. She lobbied Congress. She organized events. She stood up against Minutemen at rallies.

Oddly, all of this distanced her from some Mexican-Americans.

"They think the way to integrate into the American life is to be anti-immigrant," she said. "Some Mexican-Americans don't talk to me anymore. Some of my dearest friends and supporters of the Dream Act are Anglo, for God's sake."

In fact, the undocumented kids were more American than Mexican. "They aren't Mexicans anymore, they are Americans," Carmen told me.

"Their expectations and sense of possibility are purely American."

Unless the Dream Act is passed, she told me, "These kids have no future. As it stands now, even if they finish engineering school with honors, they will wash dishes."

• • •

While most engineering students spent their summer in prestigious internships that Viri could not apply for because of her undocumented status, Viri went home to Alicia's town house and babysat her brother and little niece. She didn't have Internet access, so she kept in touch with her friends by texting on her phone. Sometimes, she and her brother went to a nearby park and kicked the soccer ball around. Viri cleaned the house and cooked but felt guilty that she wasn't contributing enough to the family.

She'd never really had employment. Not working and going to school made her feel helpless and selfish. And yet, Viri knew on some level that her mother's struggles would only be validated if she succeeded academically.

She felt caged.

At Arizona State, she didn't dare tell other students she was undocumented. She was social but not social. She begged off going to Mexico for spring break. She said she had to study when other students asked her to attend an R-rated movie or go clubbing, because all of these required an ID. When it came time to apply for internships, she always told the other students she was going to summer school instead.

I watched her live that double life on the day she picked up her dorm key for the first semester of her junior year. She was excited and happy to start school again. But she was also guarded. I could see it in her face as she passed tall bouquets of helium-filled green balloons and walked into the stadium. Happy, upbeat music blared from speakers.

Viri stood in line, a tiny girl with a full, black ponytail. She wore a pink-and-black T-shirt, jeans rolled up to midcalf, and black flats. She carried a large white purse with blue and pink flowers. She filled out a form on a clipboard, and after she'd gotten her key, we wandered through a tented area where local merchants had set up booths and were giving away free samples—cookies, bottled water, shopping bags, flashlights, key chains, pencils. Viri spotted an IKEA booth that offered a free shopping spree to a lucky student to be picked in an upcoming drawing.

She began filling out a card until she came to a section that said the winner must be a legal resident of the United States.

Viri's dorm room was almost as big as Alicia's house. She didn't have much—a yoga mat, her printer, her Dell laptop, and a comforter. She cleaned the bathroom with Lysol and paper towels, then wiped off the plastic covering of the bed. After the Lysol dried, she sat on it and looked around at the emptiness. This was so different from her mother's house, with the *Virgen* and the votive candles and the peach-colored walls with flower prints.

"I really like this room," she said. "But I feel kinda lonely."

She missed her mother, even though her mother lived only about a half-hour's drive from the dorm. A cultural divide separated them when Viri attended college. Viri spent every weekend at home and then threw herself into her studies during the week.

• • •

The policeman stopped Viri as she drove her mother's car to a meeting of church volunteers. When the cop stopped Viri and asked for her license, she giggled and handed him her college ID. Of course, Viri knew, the policeman could arrest her for being undocumented. She chatted him up. She talked too much.

Fortunately, this policeman had a kind heart. "You should not be driving without a license," he said.

After he drove off, her entire body trembled.

How much longer could she hide her secret?

A few months later, a policeman stopped Alicia too. The cop impounded her car but let Alicia go free. It would cost $1,000 to get the car out of impound. Alicia thought about going home and crying. Instead, she hitched a ride to work. She would not be defeated. Later, she drew from her savings account and had a friend get the car out of impound.

• • •

Viri studying at Arizona State University in Tempe. KATHY MCCRAINE

The last time I talked to Viri in March 2010, she said both she and Guadalupe were awarded private scholarships to attend Arizona State for the spring semester. Viri had been in touch with her father, who was still a mechanic in Phoenix.

"He's very proud of me," she said.

Like most undocumented college students, she was increasingly angry, sad, scared, and worried about the future. President Barack Obama had devoted only thirty-eight words to immigration reform in his State of the Union Address, and undocumented immigrants widely viewed this as a sign that, despite all the assurances, immigration reform might not be passed in 2010.

Advocates for the Dream Act, like Carmen Cornejo, continued hoping for its passage, regardless of the future of comprehensive immigration reform.

Why would Congress not pass a law that gave temporary legal status to hardworking college students who excelled academically, could fill critical professional shortages, and would shore up America's shrinking middle class?

Viri couldn't let herself think too much about it.

Just as her mother focused on work instead of fear, Viri focused on her studies. If she had an exam, she would not allow herself to sleep until she knew all the material inside and out. Often she studied for eight hours.

If you saw her walking across the Arizona State campus, you'd see a small girl weighted down with a backpack full of books, a yoga mat, a bagged lunch, and high heels for a salsa class.

You'd see a young college student rushing to class.

You wouldn't guess her heart was full of rage, fear, and hope.

CHAPTER 10

Dairy People

Eduardo could cure milk cows.
But he had no cure for the problems
that afflicted his family.

"When I was a little kid, I thought a lot about going to college, but I learned in high school you can't go to college unless you're legal," Eddie told me one evening as he and I sat outside his family's mobile home tucked in a corner of a large dairy farm on the eastern edge of Phoenix. "So I kind of forgot about college and my grades were real average. I played soccer a lot, and partied. I guess you could say I had a lot of partying distractions."

Unlike Viri, who tried hard not to give up hope in the American Dream, Eddie had abandoned it in high school.

It was a breezeless October evening, and the salmon-hued sunset radiated heat. A covered plywood porch extended along the western edge of the trailer that twenty-year-old Eddie shared with his parents and three siblings. The porch was furnished with a few plastic chairs and stools, and in the far corner, a washing machine connected to a hose that drained soapy water onto the lawn.

Eddie sat on a stool, absently holding his BlackBerry. He wore a sleeveless green shirt with BOSTON written across the front, baggy rayon shorts, and basketball shoes. He'd been kicking a soccer ball on the lawn when I arrived. He still played in an adult soccer league. Even so, he yearned for the camaraderie of his high school team, and he missed his high school friends whom he rarely saw even though some "live, like five minutes away."

He seemed lonely and said he wanted to marry soon. He hadn't met the girl yet, but in his dreams his wife was Mexican or of Mexican descent. She would keep a clean house and cook tasty *sopes*, cornmeal cakes topped with combinations of fresh salsa, beans, shrimp, meats, or vegetables, just like the ones that his mother made. The woman Eddie hoped to marry would be the opposite of the American girl who had just dumped him. The American girl had gotten pregnant and couldn't make up her mind if the baby's father was Eddie or the man she chose over Eddie.

Eddie was brought to Arizona when he was seven years old. He spoke easy, fluent English. Although he'd never felt the sting of one-on-one racism, he lived in a state with laws he considered racist. "I'm kind of used to it," he told me. "They don't want us here. OK. That's fine. I'm over it. I set it aside." What made it easier for Eddie to cope with living in Arizona was that he told himself he was *just visiting*. So, even though he had lived most of his life in Maricopa County, and even though he worried about how well he'd adjust to Mexico if he were deported, he told himself that in his heart and soul he was a Mexican.

Sometimes.

But other times, he didn't know who he was.

Or where he belonged.

And this angered him.

• • •

I first met Eddie and his family one Sunday morning in 2009 when I accompanied my friend, a journalist named Valeria Fernández, through the outskirts of Phoenix. We were searching for undocumented immigrants who worked in local dairies. Local dairies supplied Phoenix with all its fresh milk, yet few people realized dairies in Arizona and across the nation had grown increasingly reliant on the labor of undocumented immigrants.

Our guide on that Sunday was Gregorio, an immigrant from the Mexican state of Oaxaca, and he knew about the dairies through his job as a Phoenix truck driver. Gregorio guided us to a clump of dairies on the eastern flank of the Phoenix suburbs. Farms had once surrounded the dairies, but now the farms were being slowly cannibalized by housing developments, gas stations, and convenience stores. The first dairy property we visited was fronted by an average-size 1970s-era home with a lawn and shade trees—Gregorio told us only dairy owners and managers lived in such houses. We passed corrals enclosing scores of black-and-white dairy cows standing in mud and sand and their own waste. We passed silage pits, tractors, trucks, a milking barn, and a milk-loading area until we reached an enclave of trailers and shacks where the immigrants lived. We knocked on doors and called "*Hola*" and "*Buenos días*," but no one answered. For all the people inside knew, we were agents for *La Migra*.

Gregorio guided us to the next dairy and suggested we put people at ease by engaging in small talk and asking where we could buy *queso fresco*, fresh cheese. He told us some immigrant dairy workers made the cheese by hand and sold it as a side business. There was a big market for the crumbly white cheese, which was often sprinkled on Mexican dishes. We pulled into the second dairy, followed a little dirt road past the owner's house, past white goats in a pen, past a red-brown horse locked in a corral, past dairy cows craning their necks through fence slats to compete with chickens for scraps of feed. Rounding a curve in the road, we found ourselves face to face with Eddie atop a tractor.

"You go," Gregorio told me. "Get out of the car. Tell him you want to buy *queso fresco*."

This was the first time I'd laid eyes on Eddie, and I figured him for an American, with his goatee and his crew cut and his facile, accent-free English. He told me he and his father worked on this particular dairy farm. The entire family lived on the farm and, yes, his mother made and sold *queso fresco*. Then his BlackBerry chimed, and he became distracted by a text message.

After thanking Eddie, I eased the car around thickets of barbed wire, discarded fans that had once cooled cow barns, rickety farm equipment, a mountain of used tires, and the skeletons of old vehicles. We passed a silvery pond filled with wastewater generated by the daily hosing down of cows and milking barns. A ladder leaned against a giant prickly pear cactus. Someone had climbed the ladder and harvested a few of the tender new cactus buds, or *nopales*, which are a food staple in many parts of Mexico. Beyond the cactus, barbells and other exercise equipment lay on a yard of dirt and grass, which led to the mobile home where Eddie lived with his family.

An old man sat on the porch watching over a baby sleeping in an infant seat. Pink baby clothes dangled from a clothesline strung along the eave of the porch. The old man's name was Diego, and he was from Zacatecas. The baby was his grandchild, Mirabel. Diego and his wife, Maria, were visiting their daughter Juana, who came to the door dressed in a T-shirt and jeweled jeans. Her long brown hair was pulled into a ponytail. We introduced ourselves and expressed an interest in buying a round of *queso fresco* (at $5 per round), and we also explained we were journalists. Would the family agree to interviews?

They agreed. In the months that followed, we would visit and interview the family several times and would witness their reaction to an unforeseen crisis.

This is their story.

An Arizona dairy farm. TERRY GREENE STERLING

• • •

Maria and Diego had five daughters and eight sons, and believed each child was a gift from God. The couple lived in La Tazajera, a village of fewer than three hundred people in a desert valley surrounded by high mountains. (Locals spell the name with a z—La Tazajera—but on maps it is La Tasajera.) Maria and Diego farmed and owned milk cows, and Maria and her daughters made and sold *queso fresco* to bring in a few extra pesos.

Although Maria and Diego were devout Catholics who treasured their large family, they understood that their children could not survive in a poor village with few jobs. In time, seven of their children moved to the United States and six stayed home. The wrenching family demographics mirrored the immigration pattern of Zacatecas itself. According to the Mexican state's Web site, 50 percent of the population of Zacatecas is now thought to live in the United States.

In 1995, Maria's daughter Juana and her husband, Eduardo, decided to move with their two young sons to Arizona. In Mexico, Eduardo had supported Juana and the boys by helping tend his family's goats. When Eduardo's eight siblings decided to liquidate the goats, he knew he'd have to migrate to feed his young family. He learned from his friends and relatives that dairies in the Phoenix area were hiring Zacatecan immigrants. Eduardo knew he could succeed at a dairy. How different could a cow be from a goat?

He left Juana and the boys in La Tazajera and got a job at the dairy near Phoenix where he still worked in 2009. He saved his money and soon sent for Juana, six-year-old Eddie, and the baby Guillermo. After crossing the desert (it took a few tries; she was robbed, abandoned by a *coyote*, and picked up by Border Patrol agents), Juana and the two boys settled with Eduardo in an apartment in an immigrant enclave in Chandler, an eastern suburb of Phoenix. Eduardo commuted to his dairy job. A few months after she arrived, Chandler police and federal agents conducted a controversial raid, arresting hundreds of immigrants for being in the United States illegally. Juana was a country girl. The raid terrified her. She locked herself and the children in the apartment. She was afraid to take out the garbage. Every morning when she kissed Eduardo good-bye, she worried that she would not see him again.

A few months later, Eduardo had good news. The dairy owner offered him a trailer right on the dairy property. The young couple from La Tazajera moved to the closest thing to the country that the Phoenix metro area had to offer.

Juana told Eduardo: "I can breathe again."

The used trailer had three closet-sized bedrooms, a bathroom, and a kitchen with a window facing south. Juana scrubbed her new home and painted it. By then she was pregnant with her third child, Graciela. She decided this would be her last child, and wondered how her mother could raise thirteen kids with such apparent ease.

Juana enrolled little Eddie in a nearby public school, where he thrived and learned English. She herself signed up for English classes. Life on the dairy was good. Juana and Eduardo had married when she was only sixteen and he was twenty-one. She had fallen in love with him because he was the best-looking man in La Tazajera. He had been drawn to her slender figure, light skin, long brown hair, and pretty face. As they matured and had children, they grew to love each other more deeply. When Eduardo became seriously ill five years after they arrived, he and Juana decided that the entire family should return to La Tazajera. That way, if Eduardo should take a turn for the worse, Juana would be with her parents. After a few months in La Tazajera, Eduardo healed. The problem, doctors told him, had to do with esophageal and gastric reflux disease.

On the return trip to Arizona, Juana and Eduardo crossed the desert together, along with Eddie, Guillermo, and Graciela. They'd paid a *coyote* $2,400 to smuggle them across the desert. (The smuggling fee included $300 for baby Graciela, even though she was an American citizen.) It was a traumatic crossing. Eddie saw a man dying on the desert floor. The traveler had apparently collapsed of fatigue and dehydration and had been abandoned by his group. Of course, Eddie's group also left the man, and Eddie was powerless to help him. He would carry this memory of death in the desert into adulthood.

Juana walked close to Eddie and prayed that the Border Patrol would come upon the dying person and save his life. *I will never cross this awful desert again,* Juana told herself silently.

She wanted nothing more than to return with her family to her trailer at the hidden dairy, where she could raise her children in peace. She wanted her children to prosper. She wanted Eddie to graduate from high school and attend college so that he would have a better life than his parents and never, ever have to be in the position of crossing this desert like an animal.

As time passed, it was hard for Juana to see Eddie working in the dairy, just like his dad. Juana had hoped the Dream Act would be passed, but she now had her doubts and understood her dreams for her son had withered.

Eduardo had climbed as high as he could in the dairy. He was the de facto veterinarian, a prestigious position. He understood the science behind dairy cow diets, how to proportion maize, cotton seed, silage, barley, millet, DDE, alfalfa, green almond leaves, grapefruit, oranges, and cantaloupe. Eduardo was also in charge of the cow infirmary, a lean-to near the corrals with a refrigerator full of medicines and carefully kept logs with Spanish headings in uneven handwriting.

Este mes vender. Sell this month.

Este mes muerto. Dead this month.

Tienes que escribirlo. Tienes tu pluma y libretto? You have to write it down. Do you have your pen and notebook?

Next to the dairy infirmary was a chute where Eduardo treated the sick cattle. Eduardo knew when a cow was taking ill. She became *triste,* or sad. Her behavior would change. She would stand apart from other cows. She wouldn't eat. Eduardo would check her for diarrhea, constipation, fever. He would figure out the proper remedy—fever reducer, penicillin, Terramycin, doses of mineral oil. Sometimes, cows would collapse after giving birth and would be unable to get up. He would give these animals calcium and Dexamethasone, and soon they would improve. Occasionally, a cow might act crazy, biting and licking the air. Such animals might have given up so much milk that their internal blood sugar was unbalanced, and Eduardo knew the exact doses of dextrose that would heal the cows in five days. He could also perform surgery. Say a cow had an infected hoof. Eduardo would load the cow in the chute, secure her with belts so she couldn't move, administer an anesthetic, and then cut her cloven hoof with a lathelike tool. He'd dig out the infected parts, sand the hoof, then pack the clean wound with antibiotics. Sometimes, a cow would get "blue bag," a staph infection that ate away at a cow's tender udder. He would doctor the suffering animals with antibiotics, and took pride when they survived.

He had a special compassion for *las pobrecitas vacas*, the poor cows. "These cows don't have a very good life," he once told me. He knew the cows would live only a few years before they could not give sufficient milk and would be slaughtered, just as he knew the young calves that were taken from their sides were regularly butchered for veal. This was the way life was, and there was nothing he could do about it. It was his job to keep the cows healthy when they were alive. For this, he earned an annual salary of about $24,000, plus the free trailer.

• • •

Maria and Diego had tourist visas, and they visited Arizona about once a year. Several of their children lived in the Phoenix metro area, and the couple visited each child's house. At first, their children were happy. But as anti-immigrant sentiment intensified in Phoenix, Maria saw changes in her children's faces. Sometimes, the children living in Phoenix acted as if they lived in a prison. At least at the dairy, one felt more hidden and secure, and life had a manageable and predictable pace. Every morning at five, Eduardo and Eddie left for work. Each afternoon, they returned, leaving their manure-caked boots outside, entering the trailer in their stocking feet. At this point, they would have worked for almost eight hours. They ate a large meal, then resumed working until nightfall.

Juana purchased two flower-print velour sofa beds for her parents, so that they would be comfortable in the trailer living room with its warm brown walls and the flat-screen television in the entertainment center with its framed portraits of twelve-year-old Graciela grinning, fourteen-year-old Guillermo with his gelled hair, and handsome, proud Eddie on the night of his high school graduation. When Maria lay down on the sofa bed at night, she could see a poster of Jesus in the heavens blessing La Tazajera, nestled in the desert valley in Zacatecas.

Maria and Diego loved their newest grandchild, Mirabel. Juana and Eduardo had been surprised by the pregnancy, but felt blessed by it. Eddie, especially, viewed her birth as one of the happiest moments in his life, just as his parents and siblings did.

Despite all the happiness, the family had its own tensions. Guillermo and Eddie shared a room, a bed, and a computer, but lived worlds apart. Guillermo's Spanish had an American twang, and the family chided him for it. Guillermo was a Mexican citizen, but he preferred pizza to his mother's *sopes*. He communicated with sexy-looking fourteen-year-old girls on MySpace. He spiked and gelled his hair. He wore baggy jeans and trendy T-shirts. When he grew up, he wanted to retool junky cars just like in the show, *Pimp My Ride*. He loved hip-hop. His favorite celebrity was Michael Jordan because he was a good basketball player and he wore cool shoes. He watched a lot of MTV and played multiplayer games on the Internet. He forgot to sign up for soccer at school. His favorite class was P.E., and his least favorite was science because there was too much to learn.

How would such a child survive in La Tazajera?

The thought worried Juana and Eduardo at night.

Guillermo sometimes helped out at the dairy, moving cows from one corral to another, feeding the herd, working on the machines. Still, Eddie didn't think Guillermo worked hard enough. The way Eddie saw it, Guillermo was a lazy American through and through.

Unlike Guillermo, Graciela moved easily between two cultures. She was a pretty twelve-year-old, slender and soft-spoken. She helped her mother cook, took care of the baby Mirabel. She spoke Spanish and English. Sometimes, she sneaked into Guillermo's room to see what craziness he had pulled up on the computer. Other times, she practiced the violin. She watched *iCarly* on Nickelodeon with her school friends, but she didn't complain when her mother would never let her participate in that strange American custom—the sleepover.

The subtle culture clashes within the family were layered with other uncertainties. Eduardo and Juana hunkered down, not knowing what to do. Should they stay at the dairy or return to Mexico? And if they returned to Mexico, what would become of the children? On the one hand, they liked the dairy, but on the other hand, life in Arizona was precarious for undocumented people. One never knew if one would get caught, and deported. Eduardo and Juana had hung their hopes on Barack Obama's campaign promise of immigration reform, but as each day in 2009 faded, so did a little of their hope. Eduardo and Juana believed that if they could not become legal soon, they might eventually return to La Tazajera. Sometimes, Juana thought, it would be better to be poor in Mexico where people loved you than to be comfortable in Arizona, where Mexicans were no longer welcome. Other times, she wanted to stay in Arizona.

• • •

One day in May, Eduardo's boss, the dairy owner, pulled him aside. The recession had deepened, and the dairy could not go on. Within a few days, he would sell the dairy herd for slaughter. He was going out of business. He hoped to lease his farm to another dairyman, and if the new boss liked Eduardo, maybe he would hire him.

Eduardo was caught in the clutches of a national dairy crisis. In the heady boom times of the early 2000s, dairymen began exporting milk to a voracious global market. They expanded their herds. They borrowed money. Then, when the world economy plunged into recession, the global market for dairy products collapsed. American dairymen had too many cows and too much milk on their hands. Milk prices plummeted by nearly one-half from 2008 to 2009.

"There's too much milk in the United States," Eduardo said when we visited him in early June.

By then, all of the cattle except for the pregnant cows and a few cows with baby calves had been shipped to slaughter. Eduardo hadn't much to do, so he fixed and filled the swimming pool for the kids. It was a large pool, the kind that has a ladder on the side. "It's a good one," he said. "I've taken care of it and patched it and it has lasted a long time." Just then, a flock of doves flew into the sky, their wings whistling. They'd been eating grain meant for cows that were no longer there.

Eduardo and Juana had made a contingency plan should they be asked to leave the dairy. They would move the family to a dairy on the eastern edge of Texas, where a relative worked and could get Eduardo a job. Sometimes they talked of moving back to Zacatecas. They had saved $20,000 and maybe that would be enough to get a business going. They weren't sure what kind of business, exactly. Maybe a little store. Maybe a tortilla shop.

All of this talk made Guillermo uneasy. His family told him he couldn't speak Spanish well, and yet it seemed they might move to Mexico permanently. He might never return to the United States. What would he do?

As it turned out, the new boss, or *patrón*, hired both Eduardo and Eddie. Like a lot of dairymen, he relied on Mexican immigrants because no one could do it as well and as cheaply.

"We don't take Americans' jobs," Eddie told me. "We take all the dirty jobs they don't want. We don't steal their secretary jobs or whatever they do. Even out here in the dairies, you don't see Americans applying for work. American people only apply for work at the mall. They'd rather not work here, because these jobs require a lot of effort."

I asked him what the word "American" meant to him.

"They're lazy people," he said. "Like my brother. My brother makes me really mad. He's lazy, and he complains a lot."

• • •

On our last visit to the dairy, Valeria and I sat at the kitchen table with Juana and Eduardo. Juana served fresh grapes, chips, homemade salsa. By then, Mirabel was walking. She was a healthy, happy child, and everyone, including Guillermo, delighted in her. But a cloud of uncertainty was hanging over this family, and every time we visited the dairy, they seemed less decisive about their future.

Eduardo once considered investing their $20,000 savings in a house in Arizona, since the recession had created good deals in housing. But if they bought a house, Eduardo wondered aloud, who's to say they wouldn't be kicked out of the country and then what would become of their investment?

They'd lose everything.

Perhaps they should stay in Arizona another five years or so, let the kids graduate from high school. Or maybe Juana and the girls should accompany Eduardo to Zacatecas and Eddie could stay in Arizona with Guillermo until the younger boy turned eighteen and could make up his own mind about where he wanted to be. Or maybe they should all return to Zacatecas and Eduardo would buy a tortilla shop. But maybe that wasn't such a good idea, because Eduardo would have to get up at four in the morning to make the tortillas.

"You get up early in the morning now," Juana pointed out.

Juana had heard disturbing stories about life in Mexico. One distant relative was kidnapped for ransom; another was tortured and murdered in the border state of Chihuahua, where thousands had been slaughtered in 2009 alone. Things weren't much better in Zacatecas. The bloodthirsty *Zetas*, thought to be responsible for many brutal killings in Mexico, were now extracting "taxes" from businesses in the La Tazajera area.

While their parents mulled over the possibilities, Eddie and Guillermo and Graciela huddled near their laptop in a bedroom, listening to Valeria's public radio piece about immigrant dairy workers in Arizona. As they listened, Mirabel played on the bed.

I could hear the anger in Eddie's voice as he talked on the radio about how immigrants did all the dirty work, and I sensed that anger had not diminished as he listened to himself on the radio.

His young life was on hold. He lived an increasingly anxious existence, but for now, at least, he had a home, a job, and his family. He told himself it could be a lot worse. And he wondered how he'd fare in Mexico. Some cousins who once lived in Phoenix had returned to Zacatecas and were working twelve to fifteen hours each day for a weekly salary of about $100. "I don't want to go back to Mexico like that," he told me. "I want to stay here until I can save a decent amount of money so I can open a business. Otherwise, I'd be poor."

When he returned to Mexico, he was going to be middle class and solid, not a near-starving laborer. If he returned and became poor, all the family's risks and sacrifices in the United States would have been for nothing.

I asked him what would happen if he were offered legal status in the United States. Would he still return to Mexico permanently? His face softened, just for a second. If that were the case, he'd only return to Zacatecas for visits.

Mirabel looked up at him and smiled.

Chapter 11

La Pastora

Magdalena believed God had led
her to the Promised Land.
An immigration judge didn't agree.

Thousands of Latino immigrants live in enclaves in Mesa, Arizona. But even if you walked from one end of Mesa to the other, you'd have a hard time spotting the undocumented underground. It is lost in the sprawl.

Mesa is an eastern suburb of Phoenix that was founded in the late nineteenth century by Mormon pioneers. It grew from a farming community into a city of roughly a half-million residents. It's a destination for "snowbirds," mostly retirees from the icy American heartland who winter in Mesa RV parks that offer affordable postage-stamp-sized parcels of sunny Arizona. The town is also a bedroom community for commuters who work in other parts of the Phoenix metro area. These commuters include Latino immigrants, who are camouflaged in Mesa's unpretentious geography.

Take, for instance, Lindsay Main Plaza, a Mesa strip mall I visited one day in January 2010. In one corner, the Donut Hole catered to snowbirds from the Mesa Spirit RV Resort across the street. Other tenants of the little shopping center included Century 21 Realtors, Lee Chiropractic, Danceworks, Décor Unique, and JR's, a purveyor of dolls, gifts, and home accents. If it hadn't been for the white oilcloth sign DISCÍPULOS DEL REINO: METODISTA LIBRE (DISCIPLES OF THE KING-DOM—FREE METHODIST) dangling from one of the storefronts, I would have missed Pastor Magdalena Schwartz's church completely.

The storefront church consisted of a gray-carpeted room that looked as if it had once been an insurance office. A banner of flags from Latin American countries, as well as the American flag, was tacked on the back wall.

In the front of the room, electrical cords dangled from the ceiling, connected to the sound system—a few amps and a microphone. Handmade curtains the color of golden poppies covered the windows and complemented the rows of navy blue chairs, the sort of seating you'd see at hotel conventions.

About fifty men, women, and children stood singing praise music in Spanish. Magdalena Schwartz, known to her flock as *La Pastora* (the pastor), pranced, walked, and danced in the front of the room. She sang. She praised Jesus. She strummed her acoustic guitar. She rattled her tambourine. She clapped. She belted out enthusiastic hallelujahs.

The church service was a family affair. Mark Schwartz, the *pastora*'s husband, sat in the front row. Magdalena's twenty-nine-year-old son, Carlos Salas, stood near her, playing his guitar. Her thirty-two-year-old daughter, Ester Salas, sang in the background, cupping the microphone in her hands like a professional singer, eyes closed. Fifteen-year-old Josh Schwartz operated a laptop that projected the Spanish lyrics to the praise songs karaoke-style onto a screen in the front of the room.

Looking around the church, I was struck by how it differed from Roman Catholic churches attended by many Phoenix-area immigrants. Catholic churches that cater to Spanish speakers often have mini-altars to saints. Statues of the saints are sometimes surrounded by clusters of votive candles, photographs of loved ones, hair cuttings, and little scraps of paper that say things like: *Dear Saint Anthony, If you give me this one miracle and guide my wife and children safely through the desert, I promise I will attend Mass every day of my life.*

The Catholic icons were conspicuously absent in Magdalena's church, which was associated with the Free Methodist Church of North America. Instead of saints, snapshots of church members attending a fiesta were tacked up on the wall. And the centerpiece of the Roman Catholic altar, the crucifix, the dying Christ on the cross, was absent. Instead, a wooden cross, about four feet tall, without Christ and draped with crimson fabric, was propped up against the wall, almost like an afterthought. "Jesus isn't on the cross," *La Pastora* often told the flock, "he's moved to heaven."

The praise singing went on for almost an hour. Magdalena Schwartz sang in the passionate belt-it-out style of legendary South American *cantoras* like Soledad Bravo.

This wasn't the kind of born-again church where people fell into trances or spoke in tongues. Many in the congregation were former Catholics, and they took cues to clap, sit, stand, and pray from *La Pastora* in much the same way as Catholics take cues from a priest at Mass.

After the music ended, children were taken into an adjoining room for playtime. A man prayed aloud for immigration reform as ushers passed church collection baskets. I settled into my pew for the sermon. Unexpectedly, Magdalena asked me to address the congregation in Spanish.

"You won't believe it, but this *white woman speaks Spanish!*" she exclaimed as I walked up the aisle. I took the microphone from Magdalena. I'd come to the church, I said, because I was interested in learning and writing about faith in the Latino community in Phoenix. They applauded, and after I sat down, Magdalena announced once again how rare it was for a *blanca* (a white woman) to *speak Spanish* and take any interest at all in the undocumented community. I wondered if she was sending a message to the congregation that I was trustworthy.

After all, I was the only blond, blue-eyed person in the room with the exception of Mark Schwartz, Magdalena's fifty-eight-year-old American citizen husband.

Mark understood Spanish, so he could follow along as his wife preached. The topic of her hour-long sermon was the power of prayer as it related to the plight of the undocumented immigrant toughing it out in Phoenix, Arizona. As she preached, she frequently quoted chapter and verse from the Bible, and congregation members followed along in their Bibles and scribbled on notebooks in their laps.

"How many of us have prayed for an end to the injustice in Arizona?" she asked.

Virtually everyone in the room put down their pens and pencils and raised their hands.

"We have enemies in Arizona who don't love us," Magdalena said. "But we don't have to fight them. God will fight them for us. All *we* have to do is love God. He brought us here, and he doesn't want us to go back. He promised us the Promised Land, and he brought us to this great nation. ..."

"They say we immigrants rob and steal. We know that is not true. We are Christians. We are children of God. We have come to worship God in a way many of our enemies have rejected." As she said this, she bounded across the front of the room with such enthusiasm that her short, thick, frosted-brown hair bounced up and down.

"God has power over *everyone's* circumstances," she yelled.

"God cares about immigrants!"

"Raise your hand if you have no green card," *La Pastora* ordered her congregation.

Most people in the room raised their hands. *La Pastora* smiled. "In God's eyes, you are legal," she said. "We already have our green cards to go to heaven."

"In Arizona, soon, we will know justice," she went on. "This year, 2010, is the Year of the Immigrant. In 2010, we will have immigration reform!"

As I sat in *La Pastora's* church, I remembered Alfredo Gutierrez's observation during Sheriff Joe's raid of Guadalupe two years before, when he'd said Phoenix was to present-day Latinos what Selma and Birmingham had been to African Americans during the civil-rights era. How different, I wondered, was *La Pastora* from the African American pastors in the South who assured their congregations that God was on their side, who preached peaceful resistance, and who organized political movements from their pulpits in the 1960s?

• • •

I had sought out Magdalena Schwartz and her church not only because she was a prominent local pro-migrant activist, but also because her church was part of a growing religious trend among Latinos in Phoenix and the rest of America. The dominant church of Hispanics in the United States, the Roman Catholic Church, is losing members to Protestant Evangelical sects. In part, that's because worshippers want a different and more direct relationship with God than the one Catholicism offers. Catholics might pray to a favorite saint or the *Virgencita* to intercede on their behalf with God, but Evangelicals chat directly with God every day, with charismatic gusto.

According to a 2006 study by the Pew Hispanic Center, about 15 percent of Latinos in the United States were Evangelicals and 68 percent were Roman Catholics. The rest of the Latino population were mainline Protestants, Jews, Mormons, or "seculars," which meant they didn't worship at any organized church.

Some of those "seculars" probably included an unknown number who belonged to outlaw religious cults associated with narcotics trafficking. They bought their spiritual paraphernalia (candles, amulets, effigies, statues, prayer cards, framed portraits of their "saints") at swap meets instead of church stores.

The biggest drug saint of all is Jesús Malverde, reportedly an early-twentieth-century Robin Hood–like bandit who performed miracles in the state of Sinaloa in northwest Mexico. Mexican law-enforcement officials supposedly executed Malverde. He soon became a folk saint. Not a Catholic saint, mind you, but a saint of the poor people of Sinaloa, who believed Malverde could intercede with God in matters of health, prosperity, and luck. Now that Sinaloa is one of the drug-trafficking centers of the hemisphere, Malverde the folk saint has morphed into Malverde the narco saint. In paintings and posters sold at Phoenix swap meets, he's portrayed as a wide-eyed fellow with bushy black eyebrows and a thick black mustache, and he's viewed as a supernatural power who will keep you safe when you're hauling a load of pot through the desert.

Most undocumented immigrants I met still belonged to the Roman Catholic Church. Many, like Marco and Lucy, who were arrested in the car wash raid, identified with the "charismatic Catholic" movement, in which worshippers had direct revelations from and conversations with God, just like Evangelicals. This is not unusual among Mexican Catholics influenced by the burgeoning Evangelical movement. Many Roman Catholic priests in Phoenix-area parishes have fused some of that Evangelical style into their Masses.

After attending a Discípulos del Reino service, though, I knew few priests could compete with a dynamo like *La Pastora*.

Magdalena thought it was her Christian duty to advocate for the undocumented. She gave frequent interviews to English- and Spanish-language media. Much of what she did went unnoticed by the Anglo community, despite her high-profile activist status in the Latino world.

At Christmas, for instance, her church hosted a party for kids who had lost parents to deportation. She promoted and participated in legal clinics so that undocumented people could learn their constitutional rights. And as the anti-immigrant laws in Arizona intensified, so did her efforts on behalf of undocumented immigrants.

And there was a reason for all of this.

She had been an undocumented immigrant herself.

And, although she was a temporary legal resident, her struggle to stay in the United States was ongoing. For eighteen years, she'd been battling the same immigration judge who wanted to deport her. Their dispute had picked up in the last five years, after two earlier convictions for crimes she said she didn't commit. By 2010, she'd exhausted her appeals in immigration court and faced a final deportation hearing that August.

● ● ●

Magdalena Schwartz was born in a small town in central Chile. Her father was a guitar-playing Pentecostal pastor and her mother was a housewife. Magdalena grew up, married a man named Carlos, and by the time their two kids were born, lived with her family in the picturesque Chilean port city of Valdivia. Magdalena and Carlos were grindingly poor, and this led to marital problems.

To feed her two young kids, she'd worked out a complicated bartering business. She had purchased life-size stuffed animals (Donald Duck, Mickey Mouse, etc.) at a Valdivia market. From there, she boarded a bus to the richest neighborhood in town and traded the giant stuffed animals for the used clothing of rich people. Then she'd board the bus again, head out to the country, and swap the cast-off clothes of the wealthy for fresh milk, eggs, and meat. Sometimes she brought live chickens home, and once she even carried a lamb on the bus. In Valdivia, she would save some beans, rice, eggs, and milk for her family, then sell the surplus. With the profit, she'd buy another stuffed animal and repeat the process.

Magdalena and her family rarely ate animal protein, but once she cooked a chicken as a special feast for her twin sister, Elizabeth, who had married a minister and moved to Phoenix and had returned to Chile for a visit. Elizabeth, noticing how Carlos and Ester hungrily eyed the chicken, ate only a bite of the precious protein.

"We eat chicken every night in Phoenix," Elizabeth later told Magdalena. She handed her sister Christian self-help books.

"You need to get out of here, come to Phoenix," Elizabeth told her sister.

It wasn't so easy. Magdalena failed three times to get tourist visas from the Chilean government for herself, Ester, and Carlos. She wouldn't give up, though. Riding the bus to the immigration office to try for the fourth time to obtain visas, she closed her eyes and envisioned the documents in her hand. This time, the visas were granted.

Magdalena and her two children landed on the hot tarmac of Phoenix Sky Harbor International Airport in the spring of 1988. (Their airline tickets had been purchased by a friend of Elizabeth's.) Compared to Valdivia, Phoenix was a sprawling, treeless, waterless place. But to Magdalena Salas, it was the Promised Land. And in her mind, this journey was no longer just a visit. Six months later, when their visas were set to expire, Magdalena asked seven-year-old Carlos and nine-year-old Ester if they wanted to return to Chile.

"No way," the kids said in English.

The three became undocumented immigrants.

• • •

Magdalena began volunteering for Christian churches almost as soon as she arrived in Phoenix. She played her guitar, sang, and ministered to drug addicts and alcoholics at a rehab center. By 1989, she was a bilingual assistant at a Christian chiropractor's office. She loved the job, except for the Puerto Rican coworker who asked her several times to go out with him.

"I don't want a man," she told him. She was, after all, a busy single mom with two kids and a full life. She would soon divorce her Chilean husband.

"Magdalena," the Puerto Rican told her, "I know your visa has expired. If you don't go out with me, I will call *La Migra*."

Federal immigration authorities raided the chiropractor's office a few days later. "We know all about you," the authorities told her. "You came from Chile on a visa. That visa has expired. You're in the United States illegally."

The Puerto Rican had made good on his word.

The authorities ushered Magdalena into their car. She prayed all the way to the building where immigrants were processed. Magdalena remembered that her father had often warned her never to sign anything she didn't understand. She refused to sign papers the immigration authorities had asked her to sign. If she had, she likely would have been deported.

Instead, she was released. She was ordered to appear in immigration court in Phoenix on June 2, 1992. At this hearing, she would have a chance to tell an immigration judge why she should not be deported. She had originally entered the United States legally, with a visa—not illegally, on foot, like most undocumented immigrants in Arizona. Because immigration regulations favored those who entered the country with visas, even if they allowed their visas to expire, she had a shot at persuading the judge not to deport her.

Magdalena received notice of her June immigration court date, but she didn't show up. Instead, she appeared in court the next day. She told the clerk she'd gotten her dates mixed up because she'd had emergency gall bladder surgery and her pain medicine had confused her. But the clerk told her she'd missed her day in court and a judge had already signed her deportation orders. Thirteen days after she missed her court date, Magdalena formally appealed the deportation orders.

• • •

One day, Magdalena suggested we have lunch at California Pizza Kitchen, an establishment she believed only Anglos frequented. She selected the restaurant because she wanted to talk to me privately, in a place where fellow Hispanics wouldn't recognize her.

The narrative you're about to read is pieced together from our three-hour lunch interview, as well as court records. Mark Schwartz declined to be interviewed. I could not interview John Richardson, the Phoenix immigration judge, because Magdalena's case was ongoing. "Immigration judges cannot comment on ongoing cases. The reason for this is it would violate the Privacy Act," Charles Miller, a spokesman for the Executive Office for Immigration Review, wrote me in a February 2010 e-mail.

After Magdalena was apprehended by *La Migra* in 1989, she lost her job at the chiropractor's office. To earn money, she cleaned houses. On weekends, Magdalena and the kids made beef *empanadas*—a mixture of beef, eggs, avocados, onions, and olives encased in bread dough and baked golden brown. She sold batches of a dozen for $12. She volunteered at a Latino Evangelical church and found herself empathizing with unauthorized immigrants ensnared in a legal system they didn't understand.

In 1992, she met Mark Schwartz when she took Carlos and Ester to a Mesa park to play basketball. Mark was a recovering drug addict and alcoholic who'd once been a pharmacist. The two married in 1994, and she often joked that God brought her all the way to Arizona from Chile so she could find her true love on a city park basketball court. Their only child, Joshua, was born about a year after they married.

In 1996, Mark and Magdalena began offering clinics for immigrants who wanted to become citizens. They opened ten schools and served approximately nine thousand clients. The clinics were approved by the federal government, which had started a program to encourage immigrants to become citizens by taking their citizenship tests in community-based clinics.

Magdalena continued advocating for immigrants tangled up in a system they didn't understand, and local media took notice. She used her increasingly public persona to help raise money for homeless, sick, or imprisoned immigrants.

She would always say that her public advocacy for immigrants made her a target for prosecution in racist Arizona.

In 1998, a federal grand jury indicted Magdalena and Mark on charges stemming from allegedly giving away the answers to the citizenship test. They were accused in U.S. district court in Phoenix of several serious felonies, including conspiracy, procurement of naturalization unlawfully, and pretending to be employees of the United States. If convicted of all the felonies, Mark and Magdalena could spend years in federal prison.

Even though federal prosecutors alleged Mark and Magdalena had gotten rich abusing immigrants at the citizenship clinics, the couple had no money to pay a lawyer. They each were assigned a public defender. Their public defenders advised them to take a plea deal offered by the government—if they each pleaded guilty to one felony, they would avoid a trial, stay out of prison, and the other felony charges would be dropped.

Mark pleaded guilty to one felony: impersonating a government official. He was sentenced to three years' probation and ordered to pay a $1,000 fine.

Magdalena wanted to fight the charges. Her public defender insisted that she'd lose her case if she went to trial—a brown-skinned immigrant had little chance of acquittal from a jury in Phoenix. If she lost her case, she could go to prison for years, and she would be deported to Chile after she served her sentence. She'd never see her kids again.

Magdalena's immigration case had been put on hold pending the outcomes of her case in federal court. Magdalena worried that if she took the plea, her ongoing immigration case in Judge Richardson's court would be damaged. Roger Strand, the judge overseeing her criminal case, gave Magdalena extra time to determine if admitting guilt would affect her immigration prospects.

Magdalena told me she sought the advice of an immigration attorney, Ronald Flater. She told me that at a meeting she attended with the public defender, Flater said that pleading guilty to the felony would *not* hurt Magdalena's chances in immigration court.

In 2000, Magdalena pleaded guilty to one felony: making and using a false document. She was placed on probation for three years. She was ordered to pay the court $2,100 in fines. According to records, she paid the court $795 in restitution to the victims. Only four of the nine thousand clients had asked for their money back.

Now, Magdalena thought, she could concentrate on her immigration case. She thought that her case would progress rapidly, and soon she'd have legal residency. She didn't know that pleading guilty to an aggravated felony was the worst thing she could have done for her immigration case. Immigrants convicted of such crimes are usually deported.

• • •

Ronald Flater, the guy who'd allegedly told Magdalena's criminal attorney she could plead to a felony and it wouldn't hurt her immigration case, had been admitted to the Utah State Bar in 1994. With his Utah license, he could legally practice immigration law in federal immigration court in Phoenix. This explains why Magdalena found his name on a list at the immigration court. A year later, Flater resigned from the Utah Bar "pending discipline" for allegedly mishandling immigration cases. A few months later, the Arizona Supreme Court censured him for allegedly mishandling cases in Arizona.

I found Ronald Flater on Facebook.

I wrote him an e-mail via Facebook on January 23, 2010: *hi, if you live in phoenix area and worked on the law case of Magdalena Schwartz, please email me back. thanks. terry greene sterling.*

The same day, he replied: *I was of counsel, meaning advising another attorney, years ago. I now work for the government. Both because of confidentiality & because of my present employment, I wouldn't have anything to say about her.*

I shot off an answer: *can you talk about her case at all? can you talk about your case with the utah bar and the az bar?*

He didn't reply.

• • •

By 1999, Mark and Magdalena were no longer running the citizenship clinics, but they had launched Latino Community Services, a document-preparation company that assisted immigrants with immigration and tax forms. Latino Community Services also sold international driver's licenses for a Texas corporation. Magdalena was in the midst of her criminal case over the citizenship clinics when she read in the newspaper that the Arizona Attorney General's Office had clamped down on one company that sold international driver's licenses.

Fearful of getting into more trouble with the law, she and Mark sought the attorney general's opinion about whether they should continue selling the licenses. They met with an assistant attorney general for two hours. The letter from the Attorney General's Office, acknowledging their 1999 meeting, still sits in court files. The assistant attorney general who met with Mark and Magdalena said she'd get back to them about whether they could sell the licenses.

They didn't hear from her for a few weeks. So they phoned her. Could they sell the international driver's licenses? Yes? No? She seemed vague. They figured that since she did not tell them to *stop* selling the licenses, they had a green light. They continued selling the licenses. They made a serious mistake.

Three years after they met with the assistant attorney general, they were indicted for selling the very international licenses they'd asked about.

Magdalena and Mark were each charged with two felonies in Maricopa County Superior Court. According to prosecutors, Magdalena told immigrants the licenses were "official" and they could use them to drive. Mark and Magdalena denied it, saying they told immigrants the licenses were only good for IDs.

Once again, Magdalena was torn between the desire to clear her name and the risk of prison and subsequent deportation if she lost her case before a jury in Maricopa County, the same county that had elected Sheriff Joe Arpaio. She and Mark decided once again to plead guilty to reduced charges. This time, they each pleaded guilty to a misdemeanor and agreed to pay the state $5,000 for its investigation of them. Latino faith leaders were outraged. In dozens of letters on file at the court, they documented Magdalena's good deeds, ranging from her long-term care of a man with no legs to helping hurricane victims.

In 2004, a Maricopa County judge dismissed their case and vacated the judgments of guilt.

The misdemeanor was erased from their records.

It was as if it had never happened.

I asked Magdalena why, given her federal criminal case, she risked selling the international driver's licenses in the first place. She told me she thought the Attorney General's Office had given her the go-ahead, and she felt good helping immigrants have a valid form of ID in Arizona.

Judge Richardson didn't agree. The driver's license conviction, along with the citizenship-clinic felony, showed a pattern of moral turpitude, Richardson said. The judge wrote this about Magdalena, in part: "The respondent has been convicted of very serious offenses that go to the very heart of our system of government. Yet, she seemingly has no remorse, at least none that this court can detect. She denies any wrongdoing. She accepts no responsibility or blame. … She claims she just wants to help the Hispanic community. She did so by actively helping them circumvent the laws of the United States and Arizona, which she deems unfair. Yet she did so by profit—a very lucrative profit."

Magdalena wrote the Executive Office for Immigration Review, seeking a new judge for her case. She noted that the misdemeanor conviction had been expunged from her record.

Magdalena's request for a new judge was denied.

She took her citizenship-clinic case all the way to the U.S. Court of Appeals for the Ninth Circuit, which ruled in 2007 that the felony stemming from the citizenship-clinic case was not a deportable offense.

Finally, Magdalena thought, her troubles were behind her. The misdemeanor had been expunged, and the Ninth Circuit had ruled that her citizenship-clinic felony did not warrant deportation.

Magdalena thought that the case was closed, that she'd finally gotten around Judge Richardson, and that she was finally going to become a legal permanent resident of the United States.

She was wrong.

The United States Attorney's Office represents the Department of Homeland Security, the umbrella agency for ICE and the Border Patrol, in immigration courts. After Magdalena's Ninth Circuit victory, the federal lawyers argued successfully in Judge Richardson's court that Magdalena was *still deportable* under a different legal theory. Basically, the federal lawyers argued that taken together, the driver's-license misdemeanor and the citizenship-clinic felony showed a clear pattern of moral turpitude, which, again, was a deportable offense. Judge Richardson agreed.

According to court records, Judge Richardson noted that Magdalena's two convictions revealed "her involvement in lucrative fraudulent money-making schemes that defrauded and deceived aliens, a very vulnerable group of people." The judge gave Magdalena one more chance to present new evidence that would help her case and scheduled the final court date for August 2010. (The hearing will occur after this book goes to press.)

When Magdalena told me about this court date at the California Pizza Kitchen, the reality that she might finally be deported seemed to sink in. Maybe she'd come to the end of the road. For the first time, I saw a different side of the fiery *pastora*. She was, just for a few minutes, a vulnerable, bewildered immigrant.

• • •

Once, I visited Magdalena at the house she shares with Mark and Josh. On this day, Josh, a tall kid who physically resembles his Anglo father, was in school. Josh had a 4.0 grade-point average. He wanted to be an engineer and had his eye on Cal Berkeley or Stanford.

I sat at Magdalena's oak table in the breakfast area adjoining the kitchen. A plaque of the Last Supper hung from the wall. The room smelled faintly of the pomegranate-red candle centerpiece. The adjoining family room was furnished with a large couch, an old television, and bookshelves. Carlos, who, along with his sister, Ester, had become a legal resident of the United States in 2001, had just been laid off from his job at an employment agency. He'd brought his toddler son, Magdalena's only grandchild, for a visit. The child played on the flowered carpet with Ester. She'd just been in a minor traffic accident and had taken the day off from her job as an accountant for an auto auction company.

As we all talked, Magdalena's BlackBerry frequently jingled in its purple case. Every single caller was a Mexican immigrant seeking her help.

Mostly, the callers sought advice for pending immigration problems. She couldn't give legal advice, she said, but she had a list of lawyers she trusted and she'd be back in touch. I asked her if the lawyers to whom she referred immigrants paid her any sort of fee for the referrals. She said the lawyers didn't pay her a cent.

She told me that she and Mark earned around $35,000 a year from their document-preparation business. If she and Mark had made hundreds of thousands of dollars fleecing immigrants with citizenship classes, as the federal government alleged, I couldn't see any evidence of it in the small tract home where they'd lived for years. Their furniture was shabby. Their cars were old. And on the day I visited, their water had been shut off.

• • •

I wanted to see Magdalena in one more setting, so I asked to join her at a pro-migrant march on a Saturday morning in January. She agreed. I met her early that morning at the Discípulos del Reino church. Magdalena had decided that her flock would need a good breakfast before marching three miles in downtown Phoenix. There was no real kitchen in the storefront church, but she and several volunteers sautéed chopped tomatoes, onions, peppers, ground beef, and eggs in electric frying pans. They made pancakes, brewed coffee, sliced oranges, and boiled oatmeal. When the oatmeal was cooked, Magdalena poured it into a blender to make energizing *atole de avena*— a steamy hot milk-based drink thickened with oatmeal. The bottom of the blender wasn't screwed in tightly. Boiling oatmeal spilled onto Magdalena's right hand.

She leaned over the sink, let cold water run over her hand, prayed fiercely to Jesus in Spanish. Volunteers scrambled to wipe the oatmeal off the walls, the curtains, the counter, the floor. One man suggested Magdalena put chopped tomatoes on the burn. Someone else suggested a salve of butter.

After breakfast, we all crowded into an old gray church van. The driver was a Mexican immigrant we'll call Hector. Magdalena sat in front, opposite Hector. Her guitar rested between her knees; a large plastic bag of orange slices took up most of the space between the driver seat and the passenger seat. She held her burned hand out the window; the cold air soothed it.

Hector had been the boss of a construction crew and had earned more than $20 an hour. But the construction industry in Phoenix had atrophied. He was laid off. Still, he told me he was grateful God had found him a new job as the supervisor of a janitorial crew. He earned one-third as much as he'd earned before, but he thanked Jesus anyway.

As we pulled off the freeway toward Falcon Park, where the march was scheduled to begin, trucks and cars filled with Latinos clogged the streets. The sight of the turnout delighted Magdalena.

Phoenix might be the worst place in the nation for an undocumented immigrant to live, but that very fact had turned the city into a hotbed of pro-migrant, pro-human rights, anti–Sheriff Joe activism. I doubted if any city had as much activism per capita. I'd visited pro-migrant prayer vigils, fasts, fund-raisers, student demonstrations, speaker forums. I'd attended at least a dozen press conferences held by politicians who had something to say about illegal immigration. I'd covered the Reverend Al Sharpton when he came to Phoenix to spar with Sheriff Joe Arpaio. I'd covered a forum in which the Southern Poverty Law Center had come to town to talk about hate groups. And this was the third pro-migrant march I'd reported on in a year.

With each march, the number of pro-migrant participants grew as the pro–Sheriff Joe supporters shrank and then disappeared altogether. I couldn't be sure how many marchers gathered at Falcon Park that morning; estimates varied from ten thousand (Phoenix police) to fifteen thousand (Latino organizers). The marchers were of all colors and all ages, but most were Latinos.

Falcon Park sits right across the street from Carl Hayden High School, Viri's alma mater, home of the world-champion robotics team that included undocumented students. As always, there was an element of Mexican religion to the march. *Matachines*, Virgin of Guadalupe banners. A shaman said a prayer. The air smelled of sage smoke.

Hundreds of immigrant families—grandparents, teenagers, parents, young children in strollers—crowded into the park. Many carried signs reminding President Barack Obama of his campaign promise to enact immigration reform, which in their minds meant a pathway to legalization. OBAMA: ¿DÓNDE ESTÁ LA REFORMA? (WHERE IS THE REFORM, OBAMA?) These people knew the political climate in America was changing. Democrats seemed to be losing their power and will to enact immigration reform in an election year, and many placards waving in the air indicated that Latinos in Phoenix, Arizona, were not going to let immigration reform fall through the cracks.

Not if they could help it.

Magdalena guided her church members through the crowd to a picnic table. Nearby, a few marchers slathered their faces, hands, and arms with green, purple, or blue theater greasepaint. "We're illegal *aliens*, get it," one said.

The marchers from Discípulos del Reino Metodista Libre Church began making poster-board signs with markers. They crafted messages like: CHILDREN CRY FOR THEIR PARENTS, PARENTS CRY FOR THEIR CHILDREN, AND GOD CRIES FOR HIS CHILDREN. And: WE ARE CHILDREN OF IMMIGRANTS AND CHILDREN OF GOD.

A large Penske rental truck with a rear lift hoist was parked in the middle of Falcon Park. A sound system had been set up on the truck bed, with large speakers on either side of the truck near some trees, where march organizers passed out water bottles. The lift hoisted up singer Linda Ronstadt, who had called for immigration reform. Then it hoisted up Dolores Huerta, who had worked by the side of United Farm Workers of America founder César Chávez. She urged everyone to keep up the struggle.

Then it was Magdalena's turn to be hoisted onto the truck. Magdalena wore a golf-style church T-shirt over her navy blue turtleneck. She wore jeans and hiking boots. She carried her guitar. She didn't look like a rock star, but the crowd treated her like one.

Thousands of people roared as Magdalena strummed her guitar and began belting out a song called *Muévete*, which means something like "Move Over!" or "Get Out of the Way!" Roughly translated, the song says that if you have pure faith, you can tell a mountain to move, and the mountain will move. Magdalena sang and sang, and the crowd sang and sang with her. Her voice was strong. Her spirit seemed unbroken.

"Let's march!" she exclaimed after she was hoisted back down to the ground. Hector had brought a portable sound system, which consisted of a speaker he held in the air and a microphone he held close to Magdalena's face as she made her way through the crowd, strumming the guitar, belting out *¡Muévete! ¡Muévete!* The church members followed, carrying posters, singing along. The scene reminded me of videos I'd seen of civil-rights marches in the 1960s in the South. Peaceful, with guitars and religious songs. People holding hands. Determined faces. The line of marchers must have extended for at least a half-mile.

Most of the neighborhoods we passed seemed to be Latino neighborhoods. A few families were having *segundas*, or yard sales. From their front yards, other immigrants stared out at the marchers. Their faces were expressionless.

I stayed close to *La Pastora*, listening to the crowd sing along with her. When she tired of playing (the hand scalded by oatmeal, incidentally, no longer hurt and Magdalena considered it a small miracle), she exclaimed to the marchers:

Guitar-strumming Magdalena Schwartz in a Phoenix pro-migrant march.
KATHY MCCRAINE

¡Aquí estamos! (Here we are!)

¡NO NOS VAMOS! the crowd yelled back. (WE WON'T LEAVE!)

Y si nos echan..., Magdalena hollered. (And if they throw us out...)

¡REGRESAMOS! the crowd yelled back. (WE'LL COME BACK!)

She sang and walked for about an hour and a half. Through all of it, Hector held the microphone in one hand and the speaker in the other. We passed Payday Loan stores, grocery stores, Mexican boot shops, fried-chicken establishments, beat-up houses, nice houses, banks, drug stores, even a Jewish cemetery. Several *paleteros* worked the crowd, selling icy Popsicles. The sound of their jingling carts mixed with the sounds of Magdalena's guitar, the beat of a steel drum down the line, and an occasional police siren. An old Mayan woman marched next to Magdalena for a while, but she was slow and dropped behind. A Dreamer played *Muévete* with Magdalena, then moved ahead.

I felt as though I'd been transported into the living soul of the undocumented underground.

Toward the end of the march, a clown dressed up like Sheriff Joe beat people with an air-filled toy bat. A few marchers stood around, waiting to confront him. It was street theater, and Mexicans loved street theater. "You're a jerk!" one man might yell at the clown. And the clown would pretend-beat the man with the toy bat.

Overhead, a black Maricopa County Sheriff's Office helicopter hovered above the crowd. "That's my tax money at work," Magdalena hollered, pointing up at the helicopter. We passed uniformed sheriff's deputies. We passed the road leading into Tent City. So many times at press conferences after these demonstrations, Sheriff Joe would say he had a "surprise" for the activists. Generally that would be taken as a veiled threat for another raid.

Look, we're still here, the immigrants seemed to be saying as they marched past the sheriff's complex. The sheriff was going down, people said. The Department of Justice was investigating him, his office was part of a grand jury inquiry, and his poll numbers were slipping. And much of this was because the undocumented underground had risen up against him.

They felt he had miscalculated their strength.

After the march broke up on a side street near Tent City, Hector raced off to get the van. As they waited for Hector to return, a few church members passed out cards Magdalena had printed.

To Whom it May Concern:
From: The Fifth Amendment to the United States Constitution.
Please be informed that I am choosing to exercise my right to remain silent and the right to refuse to answer your questions. If I am detained, I request to contact an attorney immediately. I am also exercising my right to refuse to sign anything until I consult with my attorney.
Thank You.
When an alien lives with you in your land, do not mistreat him.
Leviticus 19: 33.

People took the cards, tucked them in their wallets.

Hector soon returned with the van. We climbed in. Magdalena passed around the orange slices. She was exultant. The march, the singing, the closeness to thousands of people who struggled as she struggled, all of this had energized her. She had felt a renewed strength. She would fight for undocumented immigrants ensnared in a system they didn't understand. She would fight for human rights in Phoenix.

And she would fight just as fiercely for herself in Judge Richardson's court. Her eighteen-year immigration battle was drawing to a close. She'd appealed and appealed, and now the appeals were over. But she had the Lord on her side, and she wouldn't give up.

¡Muévete! ¡Muévete!

Get out of the way, mountains!

She would fight to live in her Promised Land.

EPILOGUE

No one knows whether the recession or the anti-migrant climate or a combination of both prompted about one-fifth of the state's undocumented immigrants to leave Arizona in one year, from 2008 to 2009.

The half-million or so unauthorized immigrants who remain in Arizona, like Araceli the shopkeeper or Viri the straight-A engineering student, are likely to stay. This is their country, too, they say, and they love it.

They're not leaving.

What happens to Viri and Araceli and other undocumented people who make up about 3.5 percent of the population of the United States is more than just a moral question.

It's a practical question.

Would it make more sense for Viri to become a professional engineer who helps shore up the American middle class, or should Viri be relegated to the undocumented underground, working in a fast-food restaurant?

Would it make more sense for Araceli to have a green card and cooperate with the police, or should she look the other way when a child molester with a kid in tow walks into her store?

These are the questions policymakers must ask themselves as they decide whether to enact immigration reform that would bring unauthorized immigrants out of the shadows and into the American Dream.

I don't doubt the nation's leaders will look to Arizona for answers as they wrestle with the fates of 10.8 million undocumented immigrants. After all, Arizona is ground zero for the immigration debate.

And what they'll learn is this: The real losers of Arizona's immigration battle are not the persecuted immigrants, who have faced their troubles, for the most part, with courage, hope, and humor.

The real losers are the persecutors themselves.

NOTES

PREFACE

For estimates on undocumented populations in Arizona and the United States, as well as Border Patrol statistics, I relied on the Department of Homeland Security Web site (www.dhs.gov). Other sources for this chapter include Jeff Faux, "How NAFTA Failed Mexico," *American Prospect,* June 30, 2003; Joe Stiglitz, "Best Laid Plans, the North American Free Trade Agreement Was Intended, Among Other Things, to Improve Mexico's Economy (and Thus Reduce Illegal Immigration). In Fact, It Worked to the Detriment of Mexico," *Banker,* January 1, 2007; John Judis, "Trade Secrets: The Real Problem with NAFTA," *New Republic,* April 9, 2008; Francisco Alba, "Mexico: A Crucial Crossroads," Migration Policy Institute, February 2010, www.migrationinformation.org; "Arizona: Population and Labor Force Characteristics, 2000–2006," Pew Hispanic Center, www.pewhispanic .org; Wayne Cornelius, "Reforming the Management of Migration Flows from Latin America to the United States," Center for Comparative Immigration Studies at the University of California, San Diego and The Brookings Institution, December 2008; www.ccis-ucsd.org/ PUBLICATIONS/WP%20170.pdf; Jeffrey Passel and D'Vera Cohn, "Recession Slows—But Does Not Reverse—Mexican Immigration," July 22, 2009, Pew Research Center, http://pewresearch.org.

The widely reported contention that President Calderón's war focuses on some, but not all, drug cartels comes from "Outsmarted by Sinaloa," *Economist,* January 7, 2010, and from "FCH: Falsa acusación de que protejo a El Chapo," *El Universal,* February 25, 2010, www .eluniversal.com.mx; Jason Lange, "From Spas to Banks, Mexico Economy Rides on Drugs," www.reuters.com, January 22, 2010. President Ford's remarks come from "Remarks by President Clinton, President Bush, President Carter, President Ford and Vice-President Gore in signing of NAFTA side agreements," Office of the Press Secretary, the White House, September 14, 1993.

CHAPTER 1: BY THE TIME THEY GET TO PHOENIX

I traveled through the Arizona-Sonora borderlands several times and interviewed the subjects in this chapter. I relied on several studies by Wayne Cornelius of the Center for Comparative Immigration Studies at University of California, San Diego, http://ccis.ucsd.edu; also on "Drug Violence in Mexico Data and Analysis from 2001–2009," the Trans Border Institute at the University of San Diego, Joan B. Kroc School of Peace Studies, www.sandiego.edu/peacestudies/tbi/.

The Wackenhut contract was reported on the company's Web site, www.g4s.us/en-US. The history of Mexicans in Arizona comes from the *State of Latino Arizona*, a collaborative report by Arizona State University and the Arizona Latino Research Enterprise, 2009. Other sources include Mary Jo Pitzl, "Patrols, Crossers Trash Border's Pristine Desert," *Arizona Republic*, March 25, 2005; Valerie Richardson, "De-Greening Immigration; Ecologists Duck Issue of Illegals," *Washington Times*, October 1, 2006; Associated Press, "Illegal Immigrants Burying Border in Garbage," *Arizona Republic*, June 3, 2007; Brady McCombs, "Northern Sonora Quiet Again After Armed Thugs' Invasion of Cananea," *Arizona Daily Star*, May 31, 2007; Brady McCombs, "2 Die in Shootout in Cananea," *Arizona Daily Star*, August 16, 2007; Brady McCombs, "Wet Winter Is Deadly for Border Crossers," *Arizona Daily Star*, February 13, 2010; U.S. Customs and Border Protection, "Agents Investigate New Tunnel Found in Nogales," December 30, 2009, www.cbp.gov; Lourdes Medrano, "Tunneling under Nogales: Arizona Border Town Flush with Drug Tunnels," http://abcnews.go.com, August 23, 2009; Adam Klawonn and Terry Greene Sterling, "Tales from the Border," *PHOENIX Magazine*, August 15, 2008; Kim Smith, "Three Indicted in Border Deaths" *Arizona Daily Star*, June 24, 2009; Arthur Rotstein, "Survivor Tied Suspect to Home Invasion," *Arizona Republic*, June 25, 2009; KTAR Radio, "Napolitano: Fence Will Not Stop Illegal Immigration," July 9, 2008, http://ktar.com; U.S. Government Accountability Office, "Secure Border Initiative," February 27, 2007; U.S. Government Accountability Office, "Technology Deployment Delays Persist and the Impact of Border Fencing Has Not Been Assessed," September 2009; Ben Bain, "Napolitano

Explains Why Less (Money) Is More for SBInet," *Federal Computer Week*, February 25, 2010.

CHAPTER 2: *COYOTE* TALES

The story of Selestino and Rosario's kidnapping was taken from testimony at Vic's trial at U.S. district court in Phoenix, which I attended in the summer of 2009. I interviewed Marie in her home. The data on Phoenix and kidnapping came from my interview with Phoenix Police Sgt. Tommy Thompson on May 7, 2009, and from a subsequent e-mail. Phoenix Police Chief Jack Harris's remarks came from his testimony before the U.S. Senate Committee on Homeland Security and Governmental Affairs on April 20, 2009. The story of Juan Barragan-Sierra's arrest by Maricopa County sheriff's deputies, and the Maricopa County attorney's legal position on people conspiring to smuggle themselves through Arizona, was detailed in the Court of Appeals, State of Arizona opinion filed on July 17, 2008. Details on Andrew Thomas's background, the *Illegal Immigration Crime Report*, and the *Illegal Immigration Journal* were taken from his Web site: www .maricopacountyattorney.org. My summary of his position came from court cases, his Web site, and comments from his press releases. I reported on the Employer Sanctions Act for *Newsweek.com.*

The Western Union settlement agreement was detailed in an Arizona Attorney General's Office communiqué on February 11, 2010, as well as Sean Holstege, "Western Union to Allow States to Track Cartel Payments," *Arizona Republic*, February 12, 2010. The Southern Poverty Law Center's 2007 Intelligence Report lists United for a Sovereign America as a nativist extremist group.

The failure of E-Verify is detailed in a Westat Report to the Department of Homeland Security in December 2009. Marc Rosenblum, a senior policy analyst with the Migration Policy Institute, a nonpartisan think tank, gave me excellent information on E-Verify during an interview in the summer of 2009. I also relied on his April 30, 2009, paper: "The Basics of E-Verify, the U.S. Employer Verification System."

I interviewed Russell Pearce for stories I wrote for *Newsweek.com* in 2008. I attended Pearce's press conference regarding the trespassing law in late 2009. The information on Sean Pearce's affiliation with Minutemen came from Sean's statement at his father's hearing.

Drug-war sources included: Tracy Wilkinson, "Juarez Massacre May Mark a Turning Point for Mexico," *Los Angeles Times*, February 20, 2010; Reuters, "Key Events in Mexico's Drug War," December 17, 2009; Phil Caputo, "The Fall of Mexico," *Atlantic*, December 2009; Yvonne Wingett, "County Fueds, Public Pays," *Arizona Republic*, March 21, 2010.

CHAPTER 3: ARRESTED

I interviewed Marco and Lucy, their daughter, and members of their extended family for many hours over the span of five months. Details of the investigation of the Lindstrom Family Auto Wash come from interviews with Marco and Lucy and from the Maricopa County Sheriff's Office report on the investigation.

The relationship between the 1986 Immigration Reform and Control Act and the need for immigrants to present fake documents to prospective employers has been widely reported. The most recent data on the Earnings Suspense File comes from a 2009 audit report from the Office of the Inspector General of the Social Security Administration; from February 2006 testimony of James B. Lockhart III, deputy commissioner of the Social Security Administration, before the House Ways and Means Subcommittee on Social Security.

Eduardo Porter, "Illegal Immigrants Are Bolstering Social Security with Millions," *New York Times*, April 5, 2005. Jillian Kong-Sivert, an immigration attorney in Phoenix, helped me understand the morass of immigration laws that deal with marriage to a U.S. citizen, the long delay in Phoenix immigration court, the issuance of Social Security cards and work permits while waiting for immigration hearings, and general information on immigration law.

CHAPTER 4: AMERICA'S TOUGHEST SHERIFF

I interviewed Sheriff Joe Arpaio twice in 2009 and attended his rally. I attended three anti-Arpaio marches in Phoenix. I visited Tent City twice. Two Arizona newspapers, *Phoenix New Times* and the *Arizona Republic*, write about the battles between Sheriff Joe and Maricopa County officials almost every day. Reportage by Ray Stern, Sarah Fenske, The Bird, Sean Holstage, JJ Hensley, Michael Kiefer, Yvonne Wingett, and Daniel González informed these pages. From these articles, I ferreted out original sourcing material such as court records and depositions. The *East Valley Tribune* series "Reasonable Doubt" ran in July 2008. The Goldwater Institute published *Mission Unaccomplished: the Misplaced Priorities of the Maricopa County Sheriff's Office* on December 2, 2008. Figures on the county's settlement over deaths in the jails were reported by Michael Manning, a Phoenix attorney who has represented inmates in personal injury cases, on April 23, 2009, in a letter to Michael B. Mukasey, then attorney general of the United States. Numbers on immigrants apprehended were reported on the sheriff's office Web site www.mcso.org.

I interviewed Phil Jordan in 2009. The poll "Sheriff Arpaio's Popularity Collapses" was issued by the Behavior Research Center in January 2010, www.brcpolls.com. Laura Trujillo, "Ava Arpaio Talks about Life with Her Famous Husband," the *Arizona Republic*, April 30, 2009.

CHAPTER 5: THE BORDER CROSSER

I interviewed Rodrigo (and sometimes Erika) for many hours over the span of three months. I also interviewed Rodrigo's friends. The information on Latinos in construction came from my interview with David Jones of the Arizona Contractors Association in 2008.

Other sources included: Jennifer Hirsch, Sergio Meneses, Brenda Thompson, Mirka Negroni, Blanca Pelcastre, and Carlos del Rio, "The Inevitability of Infidelity: Sexual Reputation, Social Geographies, and Marital HIV Risk in Rural Mexico," *American Journal of Public Health*, June 2007; *The Crisis of HIV/AIDS Among Latinos/Hispanics in the United States, Puerto Rico, and U.S. Virgin Islands*, Latino Commission on AIDS, 2008; William Booth, "Devotion to Saint Death," *Washington Post*, December 6, 2009; Marc Lacey, "Back from the U.S. and Spreading HIV in Mexico," *International Harold Tribune*, July 16, 2007; Marc Lacey, "A Lifestyle Distinct: The Muxe of Mexico," *New York Times*, December 6, 2008; Joseph Laycock, "Mexico's War on Saint Death," www.religiondispatches.org, May 6, 2009.

CHAPTER 6: A DAY LATE, A DOLLAR SHORT

I interviewed Inocencio and Araceli for many hours over the span of six weeks. I visited the swap meets several times and interviewed merchants there. I interviewed street vendors, taxi drivers, and *paleteros*. I interviewed Judith Gans, leading author of *Immigrants in Arizona: Fiscal and Economic Impacts*, Udall Center for Studies in Public Policy, University of Arizona, October 2007.

Information on Hispanic businesses in Arizona comes from the *State of Latino Arizona*, 2009. Andrew Becker, "Informants Can Greatly Aid U.S. Authorities but Still Face Deportation," *Los Angeles Times*, February 12, 2010. Sex offender records: www.azdps.gov/offender; Maricopa County Superior Court; Denver County Court; and Denver District Court.

CHAPTER 7: DON'T STOP THE MUSIC

I interviewed Ivan Bojorquez and his fellow band members. I visited Radio Campesina several times and interviewed *El Parientito* and Councilman Nowakowski at the radio station. The popularity of Los Tigres del Norte is widely reported; for more information on the group, visit www.lostigresdelnorte.com/english. Leila Cobo, "Fernández Breaks Attendance Records," May 15, 2008, www.billboard.biz. History of Radio Campesina at www.campesina.net; Radio Campesina listener data comes from Chávez interview; other sources include: the Recording Industry Association of America, www.riaa.com; Leila Cobo, "Off the Rails," *Billboard*, December 19, 2009; Leila Cobo, "Against the Odds," *Billboard*, June 28, 2008; Leila Cobo, "Reaching the Summit," *Billboard*, November 18, 2006; Josh Kun, "Mexican Bands Hear Success Calling," *New York Times*, April 3, 2009.

CHAPTER 8: JOAQUÍN'S AMERICAN DREAM

I interviewed Joaqúin and Tanya for many hours in the month before they left Phoenix for Mexico City. Data on Arizona Health Care Cost Containment System (AHCCCS) funds/clients came from the Web site www.azahccs.gov and a June 2009 interview with Monica Coury, AHCCCS Office of Governmental Affairs.

U.S. District Court of Arizona Consent Decree, CV02-176 TUC-FRZ, Arizona Center for Disability Law and William E. Morris Institute for Justice; Michelle Andrews, "Spending for Immigrants," *New York Times*, February 13, 2010; "Emergency Medicaid for Immigrants Goes to Childbirth," *Medical News Today*, March 19, 2007; Gretchen Livingston, "Hispanics, Health Insurance and Health Care Access," Pew Hispanic Center Report, September 25, 2009; Jim Stimpson, Fernando Wilson, Karl Eshbach, "Trends in Healthcare Spending for Immigrants in the United States," *Health Affairs*, February 2010; Laurie Roberts, "Cause of Death: Poverty," *Arizona Republic*, December 15, 2007; Jennifer Ludden, "Health Care Overhaul Ignores Illegal Immigrants," www.npr.org, July 12, 2009.

CHAPTER 9: CHILD OF THE *POSADA*

I interviewed Viri for many hours during a two-month span. I also interviewed her mother, sister, father, and adviser Carmen Cornejo. I observed two Carl Hayden High robotics team events. I found a lot of good material at http://dreamact.info and www.dreamactivist.org.

The numbers of undocumented students cited comes from a 2007 report from the UCLA Center for Labor Research and Education. The details of the Dream Act, and its sponsors, come from the Web site of the National Immigration Law Center, www.nilc.org.

Daniel González, "Immigrant College Grads in Legal Limbo Can't Get Jobs," *Arizona Republic*, February 27, 2009; Ben Meyerson, "College Board Wants to Help Some Illegal Students Find Path to Citizenship," *Chicago Tribune*, April 22, 2009; "Pass the Dream Act," *New York Times*, September 20, 2007.

CHAPTER 10: DAIRY PEOPLE

I interviewed Juana, Eduardo, their kids, and their extended family for several hours over the span of four months. Information on Zacatecan migration to the United States comes from the state of Zacatecas Web site, http://migrantes.zacatecas.gob.mx/portal/idms.asp.

Other sources: Andrea Borgerding, "Taking the Heat in Arizona," *Dairy Star*, October 23, 2009; Jill Harrison, Sarah Lloyd, and

Trish O'Kane, "Overview of Immigrant Workers on Wisconsin Dairy Farms," Program on Agricultural Technology Studies, University of Wisconsin, February 2009; Miriam Jordan, "Immigration: Got Workers? Dairy Farms Run Low on Labor—Even in Recession, U.S. Job Candidates Are Scarce; Milk Producers Relying on Immigrants Worry About a Crackdown," *Wall Street Journal,* July 30, 2009; Alia Beard Rau, Angelique Soenarie, and Edythe Jensen, "A Soured Outlook for Arizona Dairy Industry," *Arizona Republic,* August 3, 2009; Valeria Fernández and Rene Gutel, "A Tale of Two Dairy Farms," September 2009. NPR's Latino USA, http://vimeo.com/6642046.

CHAPTER 11: *LA PASTORA*

I interviewed Magdalena Schwartz for many hours over the span of two months. *Changing Faiths: Latinos and the Transformation of American Religion,* Pew Hispanic Center and Pew Forum on Religion and Public Life, 2007. Sam Quinones, "Jesus Malverde," www.pbs.org/wgbh/pages/frontline/shows/drugs/business/malverde.html; Robert Botsch, "Jesus Malverde's Significance to Mexican Drug Traffickers," *FBI Law Enforcement Bulletin,* August, 2008.

Magdalena Schwartz's court battles are chronicled in several cases. Her immigration fight is documented in her immigration court case at the Executive Office for Immigration Review, In the Matter of: Schwartz, Magdalena Salas-Mendoza. I perused Magdalena's citizenship-clinic case in U.S. District Court in Phoenix.

I read the file for Magdalena's international driver's license case, including the expunging of the misdemeanor, at Maricopa County Superior Court. The information about Ronald Flater was harvested from records at the Utah State Bar and the Arizona Supreme Court.

ACKNOWLEDGMENTS

This book would not have been possible without the cooperation, time, and trust of the undocumented immigrants whose stories appear on these pages. I am a better person for knowing them, and won't forget what it means to *echarle ganas*.

Valeria Fernández assisted with research and accompanied me on several journeys into the undocumented underground. Kathy McCraine took the excellent photographs for this book. Amy Silverman brought me cupcakes and helped me sketch out this book as we sat at my dining room table. Leslie-Jean Thornton took time out of her life for early copy editing and months of hand-holding. *Muchas gracias* to Charles Bowden, Tony Ortega, Rick Rodriguez, Carlos Vélez-Ibáñez, Kristin Gilger, Amy Silverman, Paul Perry, Ashlea Deahl, and Walt Harrington for last-minute reads.

Chris Callahan provided smart feedback, and gave me a place to write.

Jillian Kong-Sivert, Chig Lewis, and Matthew Kolken sacrificed billable hours to help me understand the befuddling maze of immigration regulations. Carmen Cornejo opened my eyes to the plight of Dreamers like Viri and provided endless encouragement. John Ochoa is the best Sonora guide ever. Robert Boos helped White Woman in the Barrio get wired. Every single person on the rockin' third-floor faculty suite at the Walter Cronkite School of Journalism and Mass Communication at Arizona State University contributed encouragement and friendship. Thanks so much to pals Sarah Wallace, Kathy Montgomery, Florence McCutcheon, and Kim McEachern, for encouragement. And thanks to @dedangelo and @marlitah and all my Twitter and Facebook friends who pushed me to write when I wanted to watch reality television shows.

Michael Lacey gave me my first journalism job, and his early mentoring influenced these pages.

Nat Sobel, my agent, represented me through thick and thin. Robert Stieve got this whole project rolling with a recommendation to Globe Pequot Press. Keith Wallman, Kristen Mellitt, and Steven Talbot at GPP provided insightful and wise editing. Thanks, guys. You rock!

My husband, Walter, put up with more than any husband should ever put up with. This book would not have been possible without his patience and love.

Big hugs to my daughters, Sara and Tina, their husbands, Hugh and Erich, my stepson, Bard, and stepdaughter, Brooke, and my grandsons, Michael and Jack.

INDEX

reasons for, x–xi
risks of, 9, 18
statistics on, 22
Sycamore Canyon, 8–9
trespassing law, 51–52
Immigration and Customs
Enforcement (ICE), 38

J
Janos Highway, 27

K
Krentz, Robert, 27–28, 53, 54

L
Lacey, Mike, 53–54
Lajvardi, Fredi, 179
Larkin, Jim, 53–54
Latino Community Services, 212
Legal Arizona Workers Act, 50
Lindsay Main Plaza, 201
Lindstrom Family Auto Wash,
65–68
Loera, Joaquín Guzmán, 45, 152
Los Herederos de La Sierra,
150–53
Los Perros, 142–45
Los Tigres del Norte, 149–50
Los Zetas, 11

M
Mabry, Johnny, 39–40
Malpai Borderlands Group, 27
Maricopa County, 41
marijuana, xii

marriage, citizenship and, 62–65
Mexican regional music, 149–50
Mexican Revolution of 1910, 13
Mesa, Arizona, 201
Migrant Resource Center, 31
Minutemen, 24, 51
Minutemen American Defense,
25–26
music
Los Herederos de Culiacán,
152–53
Los Herederos de La Sierra,
150–52
Los Tigres del Norte, 149–50
Mexican regional, 149
narcocorridos, 152–53
Radio Campesina, 153–58
types of, 149

N
NAFTA (North American Free
Trade Agreement), x–xi
Napolitano, Janet, xiii, 23, 87–88
narcocorridos, 152–53
Newell, William, 45–46
No More Deaths, 18
Nogales
border wall and, 6
current description of, 6–8
drug war violence, 6
past as tourist destination, 5–6
smuggling activity, 5
North American Free Trade
Agreement (NAFTA), x–xi
Nowakowski, Michael, 158

ABOUT THE AUTHOR

Terry Greene Sterling grew up on a northern Arizona cattle ranch and has lived in Phoenix most of her life. For over twenty-five years she has reported from Arizona for a variety of publications. She was a staff writer for *Phoenix New Times* for fourteen years and then set out on her own. Her work has appeared in the *Daily Beast*, the *Washington Post, Newsweek, Newsweek.com, salon.com*, the *Nieman Narrative Digest, Preservation Maga-*

zine, *Arizona Highways*, PHOENIX *Magazine*, the *Arizona Republic*, and *High Country News*, among other publications.

Sterling is a three-time winner of Arizona's highest journalism honor, the Virg Hill Journalist of the Year Award, and has received forty-six additional national and regional journalism awards. She is Writer-in-Residence at the Walter Cronkite School of Journalism and Mass Communication at Arizona State University, where she teaches magazine writing. This is her first book. She tweets @tgsterling and blogs at www.terrygreenesterling.com.

PHOTO BY KATHY MCCRAINE